LOWITJA

LOWITJA

The authorised biography of
Lowitja O'Donoghue

STUART RINTOUL

ALLEN&UNWIN
SYDNEY·MELBOURNE·AUCKLAND·LONDON

Allen & Unwin
83 Alexander Street
Crows Nest NSW 2065
Australia
Phone: (61 2) 8425 0100
Email: info@allenandunwin.com
Web: www.allenandunwin.com

 A catalogue record for this book is available from the National Library of Australia

NATIONAL
LIBRARY
OF AUSTRALIA

ISBN 978 1 76087 560 2

Set in 12/17 pt Minion LT by Midland Typesetters, Australia
Printed and bound in Australia by Griffin Press, part of Ovato

10 9 8 7 6 5 4 3 2 1

MIX
Paper from
responsible sources
FSC
www.fsc.org
FSC® C009448

The paper in this book is FSC® certified. FSC® promotes environmentally responsible, socially beneficial and economically viable management of the world's forests.

Aboriginal and Torres Strait Islander people are advised that this biography contains the names and images of individuals who have passed away and that historical language may offend.

Pour your pitcher of wine into the wide river
And where is your wine? There is only the river . . .

Oodgeroo Noonuccal

Contents

Book One

Land of fierce lights

I

October 1979

Lowitja O'Donoghue is standing in sandhills outside Oodnadatta, in the remote backblocks of South Australia. It is hard, dry country, unforgiving, desolate. A small group of people stand huddled in the wind, staring down into a hole.

Not a hole, a grave. Her mother's grave. Lily. The mother she barely knew.

The grave has been dug, but the wind is blowing and the sand is pouring back down into it. The men are trying to dig it out, sweat soaking their shirts, the sand pouring back down.

Lowitja's head aches.

Oodnadatta is where she was brought at the age of two, when her father, a white man by the name of Tom O'Donoghue, gave her to missionaries to raise, along with her sisters and brother—first two of them and then three more, brought in by camel and cart. Their mother is silent, invisible in his world. She was Anangu, a Yankuny-tjatjara and Pitjantjatjara woman, whose people have lived in the desert and granite ranges of Central Australia for tens of thousands

3

of years. He was first generation Australian, Irish Catholic, a stranger who stayed for a while and then went away.

When he was gone, Oodnadatta is where Lily lived, in a scrap-iron shanty on the edge of the town. It's where they were reunited, Lily and Lowitja, mother and daughter, after more than thirty years apart. They stood mute in front of one another, not able to speak the same language, Lowitja's mind full of questions that would never be asked because she could see the pain sweep across her mother's face, and decided there and then to cause her no more suffering.

Oodnadatta is not where they had intended to bury her. They'd wanted to take her north, back to her country, the Anangu Pitjantjatjara Yankunytjatjara lands where her story began; but time defeated them, so they are burying her here, in the sandhills, where they will not find her again.

Lowitja stands watching the digging, sand pouring back into the grave, sweat soaking their backs. She looks at her sister, Eileen, and laughs and then they are all laughing, while the casket sits waiting to be buried.

None of it makes any sense.

II

July 1876

A young Irishman, Timothy O'Donoghue, pushes his way along the throbbing docks of Plymouth, England, 'that excellent harbour' as the writer Daniel Defoe described it. It's loud with the sounds of cargo being loaded; men, women and children scramble to find their way; ropes strain against the tide.

O'Donoghue is twenty-one years old, the youngest son of a large, poor Catholic family from Killorglin, County Kerry. It's a place of thatched roofs and stone walls, where the River Laune ends its journey from the MacGillycuddy Reeks and the Lakes of Killarney and spills out into the harbour and the sea.

He is a young man with empty pockets and big hopes.

Born in 1855, in the wake of the Great Famine, the mass-starvation and disease that killed more than one million people in Ireland and caused even more than that to emigrate, Timothy O'Donoghue has been raised around people deeply scarred by what it is to die of hunger. Few counties suffered as badly as Kerry during the famine. In just three years, from 1845 to 1848, almost a fifth of its population either perished, or fled—to America, Canada, Australia.

Many took their chances in the heat and dark and stench of ships where death was so common they were called the coffin ships.

O'Donoghue has a free passage to South Australia. It's a colony of free settlers rather than convicts that is founded on the philosophy of 'civil liberty, social opportunity and equality for all religions'; but it's also the least Irish of the Australian colonies, the most hostile to pauper immigrants, overwhelmingly English in its origins, 'a little dissenting colony, exclusively Protestant evangelical' as its first Catholic priest, William Benson, observed in 1843.

When South Australian authorities engineered an immigration deluge of five thousand single Irish girls in 1848 and 1855, many of them from workhouses crowded with the children of the famine, there was a frenzy of moralising.[1] The first of these girls arrived on a ship called the *Roman Emperor* and when it dropped anchor at Port Adelaide in October 1848 with 238 orphan girls and eight orphan boys on board, the *South Australian Register* lamented the colony was being inundated with Irish orphans, and that further juvenile emigration from the 'ragged schools' would render South Australia 'a receptacle for unfledged thieves, juvenile bastards and incipient prostitutes'.[2] When many more came in 1855, there were chaotic and pitiable scenes as the poor girls arrived in port, clutching at small bundles, their faces filled with despair.

Throughout his life, Timothy O'Donoghue will say he sailed to South Australia on a ship called the *Bencleuch*, although his name does not appear in its passenger lists.

A young man by the name of Timothy Donoghue, a twenty-year-old agricultural labourer from Ireland, is listed as sailing on the *Lady Jocelyn*, which departed from Plymouth twenty days after the *Bencleuch*. The ship's surgeon gave Donoghue a poor report: 'Bad. Gambling contrary to my repeated orders.' But the *Lady Jocelyn*, the fastest and finest clipper in the fleet, a ship so imposing that some of those who saw her remember it as one of the sights of their lives, is never mentioned by Timothy O'Donoghue during his life—nor is it mentioned after it, in his obituary.

If he was on board the *Bencleuch*, he was witness to brave and tragic events. The ship sailed from Plymouth on 8 July 1876, out past the Eddystone Rocks with 443 souls on board—326 adults, 100 children under the age of twelve, and seventeen children under the age of one. It arrived in Port Adelaide on 18 September with 444 on board. Two children, both boys, were born just before arrival. Four children, two boys and two girls, were stillborn during the voyage. One child, a seven-year-old boy by the name of John Kennedy, was lost overboard. The *South Australian Register* reported:

> Lost at Sea—A most melancholy incident occurred on the 19th August, on the voyage of THE BENCLEUCH, which cast quite a gloom over the ship. The vessel was making but little head way, when a child of one of the emigrants, named James Kennedy, was knocked overboard by the flapping of a rope. The alarm was no sooner given than a lifebuoy was thrown over, and one of the passengers named John Testar, in the coolest manner possible, jumped to the rescue, and was overboard in a trice. The ship came to the wind, and a boat was at once lowered, but every exertion proved unavailing, and the brave fellow who so gallantly distinguished himself was the only one rescued. It was a very sad accident, the agonized parents being eye-witnesses of the greater part of the scene which so fatally terminated.

From the deck of the *Bencleuch*, Timothy O'Donoghue looks out on Port Adelaide and a new life, one that he will have to build from nothing. He has just half a sovereign in his pocket and a young wife in Ireland waiting to join him.

Almost eight months earlier, on 26 January, a date that will one day be called Australia Day in his adopted country, he had stood shivering in the Chapel of Killorglin and married Margaret Clifford, who was already pregnant with the first of their thirteen children—a son, Jeremiah Michael, who will be known all his life as Mick.

Illiterate, she signed the wedding certificate with a cross and now awaits word to join her husband.

III

Three years earlier, in July 1873, a party of explorers in central Australia has stumbled upon a sandstone monolith, a rock of immense size and grandeur.

The explorers—five white men, three Afghan camel drivers[3] and an Aboriginal boy named Moses—are led by William Gosse, a man 'of an exceedingly gentle and thoughtful temperament', as his sister Agnes will recall. He is thirty years old and will die young, from a heart attack just eight years later. Gosse has been commissioned by South Australia's surveyor-general, George Goyder, a martinet who suffers from scurvy but is widely regarded as the ablest administrator in the colony, to explore a way from the recently completed Overland Telegraph Line at Alice Springs west across the continent to Perth.

In his diary, Gosse records his astonishment at his first sight of the monolith:

Saturday, July 19—Camp in spinifex sandhills. Barometer, 28.12in, wind, south-east. Continued same course, in direction of hill, over the same wretched country. The hill, as I approached, presented a most peculiar appearance, the upper portion being covered with holes or caves. When I got clear of the sandhills, and was only two miles distant, and the hill, for the first time, coming fairly in view, what was my astonishment to find it was one immense rock rising abruptly from the plain . . .

For millennia, the Pitjantjatjara people have known the monolith as Uluru.

Gosse, with the blithe ethnocentricity of his time, names it Ayers Rock after the South Australian premier, Sir Henry Ayers. The next day, he rides around the foot of the rock, 'in search of a place to ascend'. He finds a large, deep waterhole and names it Maggie's Spring, after Ayers' eldest daughter. Then he climbs it, which the Anangu, for spiritual reasons, do not attempt. Walking and scrambling on bare and blistering feet, he reaches the top, accompanied by one of his Afghan cameleers, Kamran, whose hardened feet do not blister.

To the west, Gosse can see Mount Olga, named the previous year by explorer Ernest Giles after Queen Olga of Württemberg. The Pitjant-jatjara know it as Kata Tjuta. To the north, he glimpses the salt of Lake Amadeus, named by Giles after the Spanish king, at the request of his benefactor Baron Ferdinand von Mueller. To the south-east, he can see mountain ranges. He calls them the Musgrave Ranges, after South Australia's Antiguan-born governor, Anthony Musgrave.

The highest peak in the ranges he calls Mount Woodroffe, Goyder's middle name. The Yankunytjatjara people know it as Ngarutjaranya, the mountain that embodies the great perentie lizard Ngintaka, which helped make the world in the creation time. The Yankunytjatjara call the creation time Wapar and the Pitjantjatjara call it Tjukurpa, which is the basis of all Anangu knowledge. It connects everything in life, including the epic journeys of Ngintaka, of Malu, the red kangaroo, of Tjurki, the nightjar, and of the Napaljarri sisters, who were chased by the Jakamarra man, burning with desire, from Martu country in the west, across the Ngaanyatjarra, Pitjantjatjara and Yankunytjatjara lands, all the way into Warlpiri country, until they turned themselves into fire and ascended to the heavens to become the star cluster known by the Ancient Greeks as the Pleiades.

Three months after William Gosse names the Musgrave Ranges, Ernest Giles explores them, writing in his diary: 'Everything was of the best—timber, water, grass and mountains. In all my wanderings over thousands of miles in Australia I never saw a more delightful and fanciful region than this, and one indeed where a white man might live and be happy.'

Giles believes that the Great Designer of the Universe intends that those who have been placed first among these lovely scenes 'must eventually be swept from the face of the earth by others, more intellectual, more dearly beloved, more gifted than they'.

Two years later, he crosses the desert to Western Australia, bathes in the Indian Ocean, and crosses back again. He is presented with a gold medal. But he is denied an official position because he is 'not always strictly sober', and he dies of pneumonia in obscurity in 1897 in the West Australian goldrush town of Coolgardie, just before the first gramophone was brought to the town's wine and beer saloon.

IV

Timothy O'Donoghue gets work on a railway gang, driving in the spikes on the line from Burra, in the Bald Hills Range, to Hallett in the mid-north of South Australia, and then finds work on a farm. It is a time of prosperity and expansion and rain. Scarcely a day passes when he does not see wagons loaded with families and furniture travelling north. This is despite the warnings of George Goyder, who has drawn a line of demarcation across South Australia, known as Goyder's Line of Rainfall. North of this, he declares, there is insufficient rain for farming.

A year after arriving in South Australia, Timothy O'Donoghue sends for his wife and child.

They sail from Plymouth on a ship called the *Rodney*, on 7 September 1877, travelling steerage with the single women. Margaret signs her name with a cross and gives her occupation as domestic servant. They arrive in Port Adelaide three months later on 7 December. The voyage has gone well. Only three deaths, 'and those were children', as the *South Australian Chronicle* reports.

Early in 1878, Timothy and Margaret O'Donoghue, who is quickly pregnant again, take up three hundred and ninety-six acres (160 hectares) of land in the Hundred of Pinda—tracts of red-brown land and mallee scrub on the edge of the Flinders Ranges that have been opened up for settlement under the inauspicious-sounding Waste Land Amendment Act, which allows all land in South Australia not yet appropriated to become available for selection, including the dismal land beyond Mount Remarkable and Goyder's Line.

Even before Goyder drew his line, South Australia's north had been written about despairingly. In 1803, Robert Brown, a botanist travelling with the explorer Matthew Flinders, had climbed to the top of a rise, looked about and declared it 'a dead, uninteresting flat country'. In 1859, William Jessop, chronicling his travels and adventures, had written that Mount Remarkable marked 'the limits of civilisation':

> South of it is a garden—north of it is a desert. It is the boundary between the farmers and squatters. The country below is fertile; there are hills and valleys, brooks of water, forests, fields, and farms; the finest corn in the London market is grown on these farms; the slightest tillage makes the ground furious, and things grow wild. The land above is sterile; plain after plain, range succeeded by range, small scrub here, a dry creek there, are its features; no art can cultivate it, no ingenuity can coax fertility into it. Naked and bare, dry and stony, a wilderness it has been from the first, a wilderness it will be to the end.

After drought in the 1860s, pioneer pastoralist John Angas had lamented, 'I have visited the deserts of Arabia and Egypt, but never saw anything to compare with the fearful appearance of desolation caused by the recent drought from Mount Remarkable and northwards.'

It took a powerful imagination to see prosperity north of Goyder's Line.

But in the early 1870s, there were abnormally good seasons and the wheat harvests were bountiful. In America a dangerously wrong belief had also begun to spread—that rain would follow the plough and that, with this mastery of nature, clouds would dispense rain and deserts would be converted into gardens and green-growing crops.

Goyder's Line of Rainfall was ridiculed as nonsense and a campaign was waged to remove his 'imaginary line'. Goyder warned in vain against such foolishness, and poor, land-hungry men pushed north into the saltbush plains. Hundreds of them were Irish Catholics. Having arrived in good times, they compared it to the Garden of Eden.

But the good times did not last and most who ventured north of Goyder's Line did not survive the long droughts, and the ironic floods, and the dust storms that filled the sky.

———

Timothy and Margaret O'Donoghue pitch a tent and begin to build their home on their selection at the Hundred of Pinda, on the Willochra Plain, from which the Nukunu and Ngadjuri people have been driven by violence and disease.

A second child, Patrick, is barely walking when he dies in February 1880 in circumstances so sad and horrifying that it is reported in Melbourne, Sydney and Brisbane as well as in Adelaide, where the *South Australian Register* reports:

PROVINCIAL TELEGRAMS
DREADFUL ACCIDENT WITH FIRE.
Wilmington, February 23.
A frightful accident has occurred to the wife of Mr. Donohue, a farmer in the Hundred of Pinda. Mrs. Donohue had lit a fire of bushes, and laying her child, which is about fifteen months old, down, she went outside for a moment. On looking back she saw

the tent, which had a frame of a shed over it, roofed with bushes, all on fire. She rushed in to get the baby, but was so overcome with the smoke and excitement that she could not find it. A man on the place rushed into the flames and got out the child, which was frightfully burned. Mrs. Donohue remembering there was money in the tent, made an effort to get it, but whilst doing so the shed fell upon her. The man rushed into the burning mass to rescue her, and dragged her out from under the ruins, her flesh peeling off in the effort. The child died shortly afterwards. Mrs. Donohue yet lingers, but is in a most critical state.

On the day this story appears, three days after Patrick's death, Margaret O'Donoghue, terribly burned, gives birth to her third child, Timothy.

In April and early May, there are good rains on the Willochra Plain, but the winter months are dry. Heavy rains fall briefly in September, but then it is dry and hot. Red rust infects the wheat, the meagre crops shrivel in their fields and the locusts swarm. By November complete crop failures are reported across the north. It is the beginning of years of drought. Many selections are forfeited, or abandoned.

Newspaper editors, who have been the most ardent of boosters for opening up the land, now castigate the government for ignoring Goyder's Line. The *Port Augusta Dispatch* of 3 February 1882 writes: 'The Government knew that the survey of the "salt-bush" land would inevitably result in the complete ruin of hundreds of families, and yet they consented to work this ruin in order to meet a popular cry.'[4]

The O'Donoghues stay, and their family grows to thirteen children. They see drought and Depression, and women get the right to vote in South Australia.

————

On 1 January 1901, Australia's six separate self-governing colonies unite to form a Commonwealth.

A constitution is agreed to, in which Aboriginal people are mentioned only twice, and then only in terms of exclusion. The federal parliament is given the power to make special laws for the people of any race, 'other than the aboriginal race in any State'; and in reckoning the numbers of the people of the Commonwealth, or of a state or other part of the Commonwealth, 'aboriginal natives shall not be counted'.

No greater symbol of exclusion could have been conceived. Aboriginal people are not to be counted.

In the new parliament, Alfred Deakin, one of the most prominent fathers of Federation, speaks of them as a vanishing race: 'Little more than a hundred years ago Australia was a Dark Continent in every sense of the term. There was not a white man within its borders. In another century the probability is that Australia will be a white continent with not a black or even a dark skin amongst its inhabitants. The aboriginal race has died out in the south and is dying fast in the north and west even where most gently treated. Other races are to be excluded by legislation if they are tinted to any degree.'

Speaking in favour of immigration restriction, Australia's first prime minister, Edmund Barton—'Australia's noblest son', as he will be remembered at the time of his death—says he does not believe 'that the doctrine of the equality of man was really ever intended to include racial equality'.[5]

In 1902, Hugh Mahon—a fighting newspaper editor turned politician, who has previously written of indentured Aborigines being treated like slaves in Western Australia, chained to posts and beaten—writes that the Constitution has left the national parliament powerless to ameliorate the condition of 'the natives'. None of the conventions that fashioned the Constitution 'showed much solicitude for the aborigines', and he can find no satisfactory explanation.

'The Conventions apparently accepted without demur the doctrine of the draughtsman that the control of the aborigines inherently belonged to the State,' he writes:

> It is not clear that the States were unduly desirous of retaining control of the natives. The position is probably due to the reluctance of the Federalists to assume a burden rather than to the determination of the States to preserve a right. A change could not have been resisted on the ground that the State management of the aborigines had been successful or satisfactory. That contention would have conflicted with notorious and well-established facts. That the aboriginal is virtually a slave in one if not in two of the States could have been amply demonstrated and unless it is seriously contended that slavery is the best state for him, or the only state in which he is fit to exist, then the argument for State supremacy must fail . . .
>
> If a nigger be lynched in Georgia or South Carolina we think and talk of it as an American outrage. So when a native is shot or flogged to death in the lonely interior of this continent, the mass of mankind—if the record of the deed ever leaps to light—will debit it to Australia. No geographical lines or constitutional limitations will be taken into account'.[6]

In 1920, Mahon will become the only person to be expelled from the Australian Parliament, for making 'seditious and disloyal utterances' after the death of Irish playwright, poet and hunger striker Terence MacSwiney in London's Brixton Prison.

———

On the Willochra Plain, Timothy O'Donoghue becomes chairman of the local council and the Amyton Agricultural Bureau; the

O'Donoghue boys play football against farm boys from surrounding districts. The *Adelaide Chronicle*, in a column for young people, publishes a poem by Maggie O'Donoghue, who imagines meadows and brooks and shady nooks that are no part of the view from her window.

No place in the world is so dear to me,
And forget it I never will,
As that charming old spot of my early days –
The old farm over the hill.
How often I think of the old wooden bridge
That crosses the swift-rushing brook;
And the golden fields of waving corn,
And my own little shady, loved nook.
Oh, well I recall the dusty mill,
Not far from that dear old farm;
How fast its memory clings to me still,
Like some sweet and beautiful charm.
We played and romped in the meadow,
Tommy and Eddie and I;
We'd startle the birds from the bushes
And watch them soar up to the sky.
We'd drive home the cows from the pasture,
Brindle and Rosy and Lill;
Oh, happy the days that we spent there –
On the old farm over the hill.
I may live in the great grand city,
But my heart with longing will fill
For the scenes and the joys of my childhood,
On the dear farm over the hill.

In 1913, the family suffers another tragedy by fire:

BURNING ACCIDENT.

Hammond, November 25.

A burning accident happened to Miss Johanna O'Donoghue yesterday morning. She was washing and attending to the copper, when her clothes became ignited, and she was badly burnt before the flames could be extinguished. Mrs. O'Donoghue's hands were considerably injured in endeavoring to help her daughter. Miss O'Donoghue had to be removed to the hospital, and is in a critical condition.[7]

She lives for two weeks and dies on 7 December at the age of twenty-nine: 'Hammond, December 8. Johanna O'Donoghue, daughter of Mr. and Mrs. Timothy O'Donoghue, died yesterday from injuries sustained from a burning accident on November 23. From the first little hopes were entertained for her recovery.'

On Thursday 18 December, a public notice in *The Advertiser* states that 'MR. and Mrs. T. O'DONOGHUE and FAMILY wish to THANK their many kind Friends for letters, messages, and telegrams of sympathy received during their recent sad bereavement'.

The following year, Europe plunges into war. Australians die in terrible numbers, at Gallipoli and the Western Front, and the newspapers fill with the names of the dead. In Ireland, the leaders of the Easter Uprising are executed by the British in the stonebreaker's yard at Kilmainham jail and William Butler Yeats writes that a terrible beauty has been born. 'Michael, they've shot them,' the Irish-born Archbishop of Melbourne, Daniel Mannix, says to his caretaker and weeps; in 1916 and 1917 he opposes attempts by Labor Prime Minister Billy Hughes to introduce conscription, an issue that will split the Labor Party and the country.

In 1917, after thirty-nine years, Timothy and Margaret O'Donoghue quit their dry and rocky land and, with their unmarried daughter Margaret, retire to Adelaide.

A farewell social is held in the community hall at the township of Hammond, which will gradually fade away in the years that follow, until it is a ghost town. The guests of honour are presented with reclining Morris chairs, and their daughter is given a gold bangle. The Quorn *Mercury* reports a brief story of their lives and they retire to the Adelaide suburb of Norwood, where Timothy O'Donoghue is listed in the directory as a justice of the peace.

They suffer the death of another child, Daniel, who dies in 1919 at the age of twenty-six of the Spanish flu that sweeps the world after the cataclysm of the war. They bury him at Jamestown: 'Beloved sixth boy . . .' the headstone says.

Timothy O'Donoghue dies, aged seventy-four, on 22 August 1929, on the eve of the Great Depression. The inscription on his grave says that he was born in County Kerry, Ireland, and arrived in Australia in 1876: 'Sacred heart of Jesus, have mercy on his soul'. His obituary states:

Like all early settlers Mr O'Donoghue and his wife endured many hardships, residing in a tent, while their house was being built, and two days before it was finished the tent was burned down and Mr O'Donoghue lost all his cash and belongings. His wife was severely burned while rescuing her second son, a baby, who died a few hours afterwards. They also lost their second daughter through a burning accident in 1913, and death claimed their sixth son in 1919. Like all settlers in the north, Mr O'Donoghue suffered many setbacks through droughts and bad luck, and was more than once on the verge of ruin. But by hard work and the dauntless spirit of his race, he won through . . .

In July 1931, he is followed to the grave by his wife, Margaret, who is seventy-five.

V

August 1915

At Gallipoli on 7 August, at a murderous ridge called the Nek, line after line of the 3rd Light Horse Brigade clamber out of their trenches and run towards a certain death, hoping to reach green and open country, but falling in a hail of bullets 'like corn before a scythe'.[8] The machinegun fire they run towards sounds to journalist Charles Bean like 'one continuous roaring tempest'.

In Central Australia, on 11 August, an Aboriginal man known as 'Jack' is convicted and sentenced to twelve months' jail in Port Augusta for assaulting pastoralist Jeremiah Michael 'Mick' O'Donoghue at his property, Granite Downs, in the far north of South Australia, not far from the border of the Northern Territory. It is a lonely frontier for white men, one of the last places of first contact where Aboriginal people walk out of the desert into a changed reality. It is ruggedly beautiful, vast and silent, hot as a forge in the summer months and bursting with life in the rain.

Passing through these parts in the early 1930s, her typewriter dangling from a camel saddle, the journalist Ernestine Hill will be beguiled by the colours, describing it as a new world waiting to be discovered by an artistic Cortez with a palette in his swag: 'Land of fierce lights and desolate distances, this hard-baked desert glows like a rose, hills change like rainbows the whole day long, evening shadows burn and fade across the bluebush, slate blue and winey-red and the windblown gold of sand.'[9]

Born in County Kerry, Ireland, but with no recollection of it, the eldest son of Tim and Margaret O'Donoghue has been speared while getting rations from a storeroom he has built out of stone, horse-hair and clay. He is thirty-nine years old and has been in Central Australia since July 1912. He has little money but, with the backing of wool brokers Goldsbrough Mort, he has secured the leasehold on more than five hundred square miles (1300 square kilometres) of red earth and spinifex. His property is one hundred and sixty kilo-metres north-west of Oodnadatta, a frontier melting pot of drifters and dreamers on a blistering gibber plain, a railhead town where the steam trains end and the camel trains begin for those pressing further into Central Australia.

When he arrived, there were 187 people at Oodnadatta, not counting the Aboriginal people. There was one hotel—the Transcontinental— where men drank and fought; two bakeries; several butchers; a police station; a post office; a school; a doctor; and two boarding houses. The train would take three days to arrive from Adelaide, a thousand kilo-metres away, and it came once every two weeks. An Australian Inland Mission had been established here by the Presbyterian minister John Flynn—Flynn of the Inland. Chinese grocers made gardens near the waterholes; the bearded and turbaned Afghans, who led camels into the desert, had built a small mosque and established themselves in a huddle of tin shanties known as Ghantown, which smelt of curried goat. They worked in and out of the settlement, enduring winds that blew like a furnace and dust storms so thick they had to carry lanterns. Despite the desert all around, a couch-grass lawn was planted outside the hotel and croquet was played for a while.

Mick O'Donoghue bought his lease from 'William Briscoe the Elder' of William Creek, one of the most remote desert townships in Australia, never larger than a few cottages. He picked through the granite rock to find water and so he called his dry kingdom 'Granite Downs'.

Around 1920, a young rough rider by the name of Jack Fox worked for him and, years later, remembered their conversations:

Mick eventually got a well down. He had to pick through granite rock the last ten feet or so. Granite is very hard. He told me some days he could only get down one or two inches. It was a good well with good water. Then he sunk another well, granite again, and that is why he called the place Granite Downs. Blacks came and sat down at these permanent waters and were very troublesome. You could not go five yards without a firearm of some sort with you. He built himself one room with stone, horsehair and clay mixed together as mortar. An iron roof, no window, just a door to go in and out. This is where he kept his rations, flour tea sugar etc. He slept and eat [sic] under a bough shed. [In 1915], he opened the door to get some flour etc out. He did not know the blacks were hiding at [the] back of [the] room, they stormed the door while he was in there and speared him and would have killed him only for one black who stopped them. Part of the spear was taken out of his head in Calvary Hospital.

It was the beginning of a long and uneasy relationship with Aboriginal people. In November 1915, an Aboriginal man named 'Rufus' was jailed for four months for stealing a sheep at Granite Downs and for a further three months for stealing a goat belonging to Thomas Williams at the neighbouring Lambina station. A man called 'Quartpot' was also jailed for three months for 'unlawful possession of a shirt, the property of Jeremiah Michael O'Donoghue'. In July 1920, four Aboriginal men—'Teddy', 'Peter', 'Johnnie' and 'Jackie'—were jailed for three months for the unlawful possession of a quantity of his flour, sugar and tobacco. In 1929, 'Peter' was charged with killing nine of O'Donoghue's sheep. In 1939, 'Angala' and 'Andy' got fourteen days in the police cells for unlawful possession of a quantity of his meat.

———

In 1920, Mick O'Donoghue is joined by his brother Tom, the twelfth of the thirteen O'Donoghue children, younger by almost twenty years. He arrives just as Central Australia plunges into a long drought of fearful severity. At Granite Downs, Jack Fox and Tom O'Donoghue work together, breaking in horses and looking for land with potential. Fox concludes the land will break him and retreats to Oodnadatta, where he manages the hotel for a while, and then returns home to Cockburn, near Broken Hill. Tom O'Donoghue stays. In July 1923, he is granted a permit to search for water and then a pastoral lease on a block at Agnes Creek, a day's walk from Granite Downs—four hundred and fifty square miles (1166 square kilometres) of unpromising land called De Rose Hill.

The O'Donoghues dream the dreams of poor men and rub up against the fringe of a people who have lived in the desert for tens of thousands of years, but are now considered to be on the verge of extinction. White men trade with Aboriginal men: flour, sugar and tobacco for dingo scalps and the company of women. And sometimes there is abuse and sometimes love. By the end of 1926, Mick O'Donoghue has two sons, Parker and Steve, whose blood is Irish and Pitjantjatjara.

At De Rose Hill, Tom O'Donoghue sleeps under a bough shed with 'a wild bush woman', as a grandson will remember her. White men call her Lily.

In 1924, the first of their children is born, Eileen. Between 1924 and 1935, they will have six children. The fifth, born in 1932, is a girl called Lowitja.

In December 1925, Tom O'Donoghue and James Lennon sit down with a reporter from the *Register* newspaper in Adelaide. Lennon, another Irish Australian, fought in the Boer War and was one of the first pioneers of the 'never never' of South Australia's Far North, arriving with his brothers around 1907 and establishing a station called Indulkana. The article paints a picture of courage and isolation:

> Men who have blazed the trail in the back country are doing great service in helping to develop Australia. Little is heard of the initial hardships which they undergo, and of their courage in battling against great odds in isolated parts where white men and women are few and far between, and where mails and papers are only delivered when a person chances to pass that way—and that is not too often. Away out north-west of Oodnadatta is such a place and those who are battling along there deserve all the help and encouragement that can be given them.

Tom O'Donoghue is described as a 'hardy son of the bush' and a 'brave young pioneer' who, with limited capital, has had to 'make haste slowly', sinking wells in his search for water far from the nearest station. The reporter concludes: 'His pluck and doggedness reveal that he is the right type of man to develop any country.'

There is no mention of the children they are having with Aboriginal women, or of Aboriginal people at all. At Granite Downs and De Rose Hill, the Anangu give the O'Donoghue brothers names that resemble their appearance. Mick, a short man with a bulging stomach, they call nganngi, frog, while Tom is called liri purtju, mangy neck.

VI

In April 1924, Annie Lock, a woman of solitary disposition, steps off the train at Oodnadatta. Lock is a missionary with the Australian Aborigines' Mission, later and better known as the United Aborigines' Mission, a faith-based organisation that relies upon unpaid missionaries, sympathetic donations and God's providence.

Twenty years a missionary, Lock is filled with the zealous conviction that God is guiding her steps. In Oodnadatta, she will evangelise, walking across the stony desert to tell 'the natives' that Jesus will wash their hearts with his blood; she will pray for their dark souls to be enlightened by God's word; and she will gather the 'half-caste' children of white men and black women into a mission home where they can be 'saved' from a heathen culture.

With her, is an Aboriginal girl she calls Rita, who has been given to her by a police officer in the railway town of Marree, 'while she was waiting to go on to Oodnadatta'.

On 9 April, Lock writes to her missionary sisters: 'Dear Fellow-workers, You will see by the above address that I am now in the centre of Australia. It is a very lonely looking place; you can look and walk for miles and see nothing but stones . . .'[10]

In June, she writes again: 'Sad, sad! Sadness is the lot of the aborigine, mostly. Here I have seen a young girl, maybe 15 years old, lying on the ground, just a little fire on each side of her; close to her, on an old garment, a quarter caste infant, hardly covered with a red handkerchief. Miles away is the old white father. Just about a quarter of a mile further on, in from the bush, is a camp of real natives. How lovely the dear little dark babies look!'

In August, Lock is joined by missionary Iris Harris, described in a history of the mission, *Pearls from the Deep*, as a lady of culture and refinement. She arrives with a portable folding organ.

In September, with a welcome rain falling outside her window, Lock writes that more than one hundred natives are in corroboree on the outskirts of the town and have come to get young men to put them through their tribal laws. She sees them dance and is entranced: 'They did this dance just as the sun was about to set, and finished just as it set. You can imagine the beautiful scene—an Australian sunset behind this. How beautiful it looked.' She writes that it is terrible to see white men living with black women and heartbreaking to see the children they produce.

By February 1925, Annie Lock and Iris Harris have five children living with them in an iron shed at the back of a boarding house. They eat their meals at a table made of boxes nailed together and covered with oilcloth. It is the beginning of an institution that will be called the Colebrook Home for Half-Caste Children.

The missionaries regard the children as 'Pearls from the Deep', as the secretary of the United Aborigines' Mission, Violet Turner, will describe them when she writes the mission history in 1936: 'The pearls that adorn a king's diadem once lay in the darkness of the deep, until by sacrifice of personal comfort one went down into the waters and brought them up into the light. Pearls to adorn the diadem of the King of kings are these little dark children of Colebrook Home, brought up from the depths of ignorance, superstition, and vice by missionaries who have followed their Master along the path of self-abnegation.'[11]

In her book, Turner will describe the missionaries as messengers of the Cross, who brought 'the sweet story of Jesus' to a 'despised' race that was 'not used to hearing of anyone loving them'. She writes of Annie Lock: 'The more Miss Lock saw of conditions in these far places, the more convinced was she that God was calling her to establish a Home for the unwanted little half-castes.' She describes a white man in tears at the mission table in Oodnadatta saying, as he hands over his two eldest daughters, 'Sister, they are just everything to me. I don't know how I can part with them, but I know it is the best thing for them.' She claims that a young Aboriginal mother, with a newborn baby, has told the missionaries that she killed her four other light-skinned children after they were born by filling their mouths with sand. Such claims fuelled the missionary fire.

By May 1925, the missionaries are in contact with Mick O'Donoghue. In *Pearls from the Deep*, Violet Turner tells how 'a station owner' overcomes his prejudice against the missionaries and goes to Oodnadatta to ask them to take 'his little half-caste son'. They pray about what to do and, after prayer, 'the conviction grew stronger and stronger that this thing was of the Lord'. They wait three days for the man to be sober enough to drive them back to his property.

During the journey 'into wilder and wilder country', the truck breaks down, they visit stations and native camps 'saddened to see poor, ignorant dark people who knew nothing of the Saviour's love'. They sing hymns in the desert and pray and evangelise, 'their own hearts burdened with the need of this race of despised people'. When they finally arrive at Granite Downs, they can hear the sounds of corroboree in the distance and O'Donoghue takes a revolver to bed with him, 'because the natives had threatened to take his scalp'.

Mick O'Donoghue's eldest son, Parker, born 20 August 1923, is handed over to the missionaries on 3 June 1925. The child is living with the missionaries when he is diagnosed with infantile paralysis at the age of three. O'Donoghue's other son, Steve, born 30 November 1926, is handed over on 4 July 1930, when he is three years old. The mission records note: 'Brothers—both parents living but not living together . . . Father sent both children into the home.' Separated from their parents, and with not much memory of them, they grow up in the home together and call each other Joe.[12]

After a year at Oodnadatta, Lock writes in September 1925:

It is just twelve months since I arrived at Oodnadatta in this dry and desert place. A twelve months I shall never forget, with all its heartbreaks and sorrows. Sin, sin, all around. White men with their black wives just camping under the starry sky with their camp sheet, the only dwelling, sometimes under a dray or old shed. Half-caste children and quarter-caste and some almost white run around their camps. What is Australia coming to? Are there no laws to protect the natives, and can these white men do what they like with the black men and women?[13]

The following month, she leaves Oodnadatta on furlough and does not return. She is replaced on New Year's Day 1926 by Ruby Hyde, thirty-six, a graduate of the Melbourne Bible Institute, who is joined by the English-born Delia Rutter, thirty-eight. Rutter arrived in Australia after World War I intending to stay five years, but 'put aside the natural longings for her own home and stayed in the land of her adoption to minister to its primitive people'. Together, the missionaries assume the role of surrogate parents for fifty Aboriginal children who pass through the Colebrook Home between 1927 and 1952.

In 1928, Annie Lock is in the Northern Territory at the time of Australia's last frontier massacre, at Coniston station in the Northern Territory, where the murder of dingo trapper Fred Brooks results in the massacre of at least thirty-one Warlpiri, Anmatyerr and Kaytetye men, women and children—with oral accounts indicating it was many more than this—by a raiding party led by Mounted Constable George Murray, a veteran of Gallipoli and the Western Front.

Lock gives evidence at the subsequent inquiry. She is not popular. A doctor calls her a misguided crank; his wife thinks that she is mad. The inquiry ultimately exonerates Murray and criticises Lock for inciting racial unrest, describing her as 'a woman missionary living amongst naked blacks thus lowering their respect for the whites'. Asked whether he shot to kill, Murray replies, 'Every time.'

In August 1933, Lock travels more than six hundred miles (1000 kilometres) over rough roads in a horse-drawn buggy to establish a mission at Ooldea, on the eastern edge of the Nullarbor Plain, where the enigmatic Daisy Bates is encamped, convinced that Aboriginal people are a dying race and that her mission is to record as much about them as she is able before they vanish.

Bates does not appreciate Lock's presence and requires Lock to correspond with her by letter, if she must, rather than speaking to her.

Also in Central Australia, from 1926, is a restless, enterprising young man by the name of Reginald Murray Williams. In time, he will rise from bushman to millionaire. His name, R.M. Williams, will become an Australian brand. In Oodnadatta, and in the 'sunset country' to the west, he sees the best and the worst of it: stockmen who can shift dying cattle to water across unmarked land that affords no latitude for failure; men shaped by the natural violence of their surroundings who drink heavily and fight often; Ned Chong, the Chinese baker, who married an Irish–Arrernte woman, Minnie Bell, and plays his music on an old gramophone; and the mounted policeman Bill Virgo. Williams describes Virgo as a man of few words, raw-boned, handy with his fists, whose authority 'could stretch a thousand empty miles' and whose chief occupation, it seems to Williams, is catching drought-starved Aboriginal people accused of spearing cattle, and leading them back across the desert, chained neck to neck. On the fringe of the town, Aboriginal people live in wurlies of cast-off rubbish. They are impoverished and dispirited, their skin covered in yaws.

Williams is eighteen years old and working as a camel driver for Bill Wade, a Cockney sailor from the slums of London turned outback evangelist.

For three years, they traverse the Great Sandy, Gibson and Great Victoria deserts with Wade preaching the word of God to bring the tribes to Jesus. He stands in the red dust and sings 'Rock of Ages' and 'Wide, Wide as the Ocean', his favourite hymn, to leather-hard bushmen and spear-carrying natives he regards as God's lost children.

Wide, wide as the ocean,
High as the heavens above;
Deep, deep as the deepest sea
Is my Saviour's love.

Wade, who has trodden the streets of London and Shanghai, where he 'knew the devious ways of depravity', approaches the Anangu with his arms outstretched. At Moorilyanna, the last outpost of settled country, one hundred and ninety miles (305 kilometres) north-west of Oodnadatta on the edge of 'an uninhabited unknown', he shows them Gospel pictures, and teaches them to sing 'Yes, Jesus Loves Me'. He tells them that Jesus's blood will cleanse them, and, pointing to the sky, that Jesus rose from the dead and went to Heaven.

In Oodnadatta, a shy love blossoms between Bill Wade and the missionary Iris Harris. They marry on Easter Saturday 1928, and go west into the Warburton Ranges 'to itinerate among the Aborigines' and establish a new mission. Harris writes in the *Australian Aborigines' Advocate* that 'God has brought us together to work for Him on virgin soil'.

In old age, Williams will look back on Bill Wade as a saint among sinners, who pleaded with his God in a waterless wilderness and was guileless in his Salvationism: 'At any rate my boss Bill attacked every old bushman he met with tracts and a fierce attempt to save him. Old bushmen don't need saving: they mostly have had their share of hell and the only thing they crave is a loyal mate. But this I still had to learn. My crusading mate had a special relationship with God. They talked together for hours, sometimes into the night.'[14]

At the end of the roads, 'where the last of the "need saving" people lived with one or two gins, stocked up with rum, carried guns and used them on blacks who were tricky', Williams meets Mick and Tom O'Donoghue. Tom he remembers as a well-sinker and hell-raiser; Mick as a man who lived 'on the far edge of civilisation, never quite part of it', beyond salvation, 'a hardened soul, ready to make the payment'. After the Coniston massacre, when the frontier was ablaze with rumours of Aboriginal retribution, he found Mick O'Donoghue armed with a .45 revolver night and day. 'Mick was as crude as they come, a true son of the soil,' Williams later writes. 'He was quite a philosopher in his way, yet unsure of himself, carrying a gun. At that time the tribes had no love for such people as Mick O'Donoghue.'

In old age, Reg Williams will recall, without qualm, that he was involved in gathering up as many as twenty-five half-caste children and taking them by mail coach to the missionaries at Oodnadatta. Recalling one mother who lost her children, he says, 'The mother had nothing to say. She was in a dilemma too, because she probably knew that she couldn't go back to the bush. What would she do? She didn't kick up a shindy.'

Asked whether she understood what was happening to her children, he sighs and says, 'That wouldn't be possible would it. How would it be possible? She couldn't possibly know anything about the way Europeans think. I don't doubt that she was very sorry. I don't doubt that.'[15]

VII

March 1927

Tom O'Donoghue follows his brother's lead and hands his first two children—Eileen, who is three years old, and Geoffrey, who is an infant—to the missionaries at Oodnadatta. Handwritten notes in the mission records say the children have been 'living with parents until their father brought children to mission home at Oodnadatta' and that both of the parents are living, 'but not living together'.

The records contain no mother's name. No mother's consent.

In *Pearls from the Deep*, Violet Turner writes:

There came to Oodnadatta Mission House a sunburnt man from one of the cattle stations. He had something on his mind, for out there in the bush from whence he had come were his two little half-caste children, and his conscience was troubled at the thought of their neglected condition. He could see no present or future help for them. Who wanted them, those atoms of humanity? He could do nothing with them himself, out in the open air as he always was; he had nothing to teach them, no good example to set them, not even a home to share with them.

They ran wild with their native mother, but not with the native tribe, for they were not wanted there. They just belonged to the station, like the sheep and the cattle, and were likely to grow up with as little attention to their morals as those animals received.

The father seldom bothered about them, but when he did give them a thought it was with an uneasy mind, as though he would better their condition if he could. Someone told him that the missionaries in Oodnadatta were taking such little ones as his and were giving them just the kind of home that his wildest dreams had desired for them. He went to see for himself if this incredible thing could be true and found that it was even as he had been told.

In this telling, the man sees that the children at the mission are happy, clean, nicely clothed and well fed, their faces 'radiant'. He asks Ruby Hyde whether she will take his children and the missionary agrees, going out in the mail car to collect them. At his station, a 'lubra' holds a whining infant in her arms, while a little girl of three watches warily from her mother's side. The infant is emaciated: 'The tiny, listless face had the worried look of an old man.

'The lubras had told the little girl that a white woman was coming to take them away, and at the first sight of Miss Hyde she had darted off into the bush like a little frightened animal. Her father brought her back and tried to pacify her with sweets, but she was trembling with fear, and it was some time before she would go near the missionary.'

Matron Hyde speaks to the women about God and leaves with the children.

VIII

By March 1927, there are twelve children in the mission house at Oodnadatta. But the missionaries are agitated. The nearness of the mothers bothers them.

'When there were twelve children in the Home, the Lord led the Mission to take a further step in faith, a step that had an important bearing on the future of this work,' Violet Turner records:

> The Mission desired to give the half-caste children such a training as would help them to merge into the white population. This they were unable to do so long as the Home was in close proximity to an aboriginal camp. Some of the little ones had relatives in the Oodnadatta camp, and it was not possible to segregate them from their own people. The only way to do this was by taking them away where they could no longer see the natives or hear the sounds of corroboree. After much prayer for guidance, it was decided to remove the children to a place further south, where there were no aborigines.[16]

They decide on the town of Quorn, in the Flinders Ranges, more than seven hundred kilometres from the seductive sounds of corroboree. The chief protector of Aborigines, Francis Garnett, provides rail passage and, in April, Ruby Hyde gathers up the children and moves them, telling those who are old enough to ask that they are going on a holiday.

One of the children, Ruth McKenzie, will later recall: 'I remember when I saw the sisters packing everything up. I asked them, I wanted to know what they was packing. They said, "Oh, we go for a holiday." That was a long holiday that. We never went back.'[17]

At Quorn, Ruby Hyde steps out of the train carriage and begins handing babies to the waiting townsfolk, including the Scottish-born mayor, Robert Thompson, the 'grand old man of Quorn', who is staunch in his support of the missionaries.

They walk out into the main street, avoiding the gaze of the silent men standing in the doorways of the hotels—the Transcontinental, which boasts the largest and best ventilated billiard room in the north; the Austral; the Criterion; and the Grand Junction. They walk past the post and telegraph office, the town hall, the courthouse and the Catholic church, and soon they are standing on a bare rocky hill above the town, where a small wooden cottage has been rented for their purpose. Nothing grows on the hill but a peppercorn tree.

They name the cottage the Colebrook Home, in tribute to the president of the Australian Aborigines' Mission, Thomas Edward Colebrook, a Sydney Methodist lay worker, alderman—twice mayor of Annandale and twice Worshipful Master of the protestant Loyal Orange Institution—whose evangelising of Aboriginal people began in 1895 at La Perouse. When he died, in May 1928, the mission newsletter, the *Australian Aborigines' Advocate*, recorded that their president had 'passed peacefully home' to God after a short, sharp attack of heart trouble and thirty hours of intense pain.

Quorn welcomes the missionaries and the children, who are described within the United Aborigines Mission and between the missionaries and the chief protector, as 'inmates'. An auxiliary is formed to address their needs and in December 1927, a concert at the local primary school is given 'to provide Christmas cheer for the inmates of the Colebrook Home'.[18]

In May 1928, the Quorn *Mercury* reports that, after a year in the town, 'the number of God's blessings bestowed are beyond enumeration'. In July, it reports that the house is riddled with white ants, the cow has died, and the children are praying for another. 'The neighbours are kindly sending what milk they can spare to tide over the loss.'[19]

In September, four more children arrive from Oodnadatta, the eldest aged twelve and the youngest a baby of two months. The missionaries report that the baby's mother has died, and the baby, 'according to tribal custom', would have been put to death.

The missionaries are careful to thank the town for God's blessings. Reporting in the Quorn *Mercury* of 21 June 1929, 'The Secretary writes: The usual monthly meeting of the committee was held at Colebrook Home on Wednesday, June 12. Quite a number of members were present. All the inmates are well. The dark children are never forgotten by the townspeople, so many gifts are sent along. During last month one of our businessmen sent along a big load of wood. Needless to say, "How welcome it is!" Love never dies.'

But love is tested. In July 1932, at the height of the Depression, a complaint is made about the children attending the local school alongside white children. A new town clerk, John T. MacDiarmid, expresses his fears that infectious diseases might be communicated to the white children by the half-castes, who he believes have a mental capacity at least three years below that of the white children which causes them to be placed in classes with much younger children, 'and as they arrive at sexual maturity at a very early age, they become a definite menace morally, when associated with the younger white children'. He suggests that 'from a health, and more particularly from a moral, standpoint, something should be done in the way of segregating these half-caste children from the white children'. He thinks they should be returned to the desert.

South Australia's chief protector, Milroy Trail McLean, is ordered to investigate. McLean, the Aborigines Department accountant prior to becoming chief protector in 1928, finds that the complaints are based solely on 'colour prejudice'. He also offers the opinion that 'it is a mistake to think that we can take the children of a stone age people and in one generation expect them to fit into our present-day civilisation which has taken centuries to build up'.[20]

To appease the town, the government promises to halt admissions to the home except in extraordinary circumstances, which the missionaries have no difficulty finding.

A man of nervous disposition, troubled by his responsibilities, McLean remains chief protector until September 1938, when he suffers a breakdown and resigns to become a clerk in the Vermin Branch of the Lands Department. He is replaced as chief protector by Methodist lay preacher William Richard Penhall.

———————

In Central Australia, in the first days of 1931, a prospector, Michael Terry, is returning from his latest expedition, which took him west of Oodnadatta. He cuts a romantic figure: English born, he was a prisoner of the Bolsheviks in Russia before the October Revolution, and, according to one admiring journalist, is 'the answer to a modern maiden's prayer'.

Terry and his party, bushmen whom he trusts with his life, have begun their expedition just before the running of the 1930

Melbourne Cup. At Mount Chandler station, they come across Tom O'Donoghue and Charlie Lester, and ask the question that has been weighing on their minds: 'What won the Melbourne Cup?'

'Phar Lap,' they are told and are not surprised.

In the late afternoon, they reach Granite Downs and Mick O'Donoghue, 'that most cheery of corpulent hosts'. Terry sees immediately that he is a ruined man. His brokers have foreclosed on him and red lines are being run through his name on the pastoral maps.

After twenty years of fighting with a dry land, and at the age of fifty-five, like his father before him, he is at the beginning of the end of his dreams.

Yet he is in surprisingly good spirits. 'We could not help marvelling at the nature of this man whose life work had boiled down to nothing, who was indeed ruined, yet as cheery and lighthearted as though a hundred bullocks of his had just fetched top price in the Adelaide market,' Terry records.

In his own homestead, on his own run amid the piteous remnant of his own stock, he was a banished man, there on sufferance as mere caretaker of the pastures he once possessed, for the enduring drought had so reduced his circumstances that Goldsbrough Mort had foreclosed to cover themselves, quite reasonably for the excessive liabilities of the place. [O']Donoghue was getting, so we heard £2 a week until the firm decided what to do with the run—then he would have to shoulder his swag to seek once more the open road and, if remaining years were not too short, some sort of fortune again.

But did [O']Donoghue care? Not he, he laughed and chortled about the place.[21]

In August 1932, somewhere near De Rose Hill, Lowitja takes her first breath.

Her birth is not registered. Not her name, not the day, not the place.

It is just four years after the Coniston massacre, just seven hundred kilometres away.

Australia is in the grip of the Great Depression. The Sydney Harbour Bridge, an engineering marvel that is the widest and tallest steel arch in the world, has been completed and opens in wild scenes as Francis De Groot, an Irish-born member of the fascist New Guard, slashes the ribbon with his sword, upstaging the pugnacious premier, Jack Lang. Phar Lap has died in America. England's cricketers are planning to bowl short, and at the body, to Don Bradman.

Ion Idriess writes *Flynn of the Inland* about an unlikely hero, a Presbyterian minister who is spreading a 'mantle of safety' over the terrors of inland Australia with a flying doctor service. 'My mythic self', Flynn calls it. Aboriginal people are portrayed as threatening shadows in the landscape: 'Then came a savage sound, sudden and menacing, the song of wild men triumphant at some primitive deed.'[22]

In Australia's far north, along the Daly River, a young anthropologist, Bill Stanner, is coming to terms with what he will call 'a rotted frontier, with the smell of old failure, vice and decadence'. A world in which Aboriginal 'high culture' is disappearing, but customary law is still strong; in which Aboriginal people are treated contemptuously by Europeans and Aboriginal women are exchanged for tobacco, sugar and tea. Over time, he comes to understand Aboriginal culture as few white men have done and writes that the Dreaming, the Aboriginal stories of creation, cannot be fixed in time, but 'was, and is, every-when'.

In September 1934, Lowitja is handed over into the care of the Colebrook missionaries at Quorn, along with her sisters Amy, who is four, and Violet, who is six.

By then, the missionaries have quit their house on the hill, with its white ants and dry well, and moved to a farmhouse two miles (just over three kilometres) out of the town on the Hawker road. It has five large rooms and a wide veranda, and the missionaries add rooms to act as dormitories for boys and girls. But the water in the well is only good for stock. Here, Lowitja and her sisters meet their elder sister, Eileen, who is ten, and brother, Geoffrey, who is eight.

If her mother called her Lowitja, it is not the name the missionaries call her. They call her Lois, a Biblical name, the grandmother of Timothy, a woman of faith.

They give her a birthdate—1 August, the birthday of horses. 'I can only go by what the missionaries have told me,' she will say. 'I guess there would be a degree of accuracy about the month and the year. Close enough.'[23]

At Quorn, Lowitja is less than fifty kilometres from the ruins of her father's childhood home—the dry land north of Goyder's Line where Timothy O'Donoghue settled and raised his family and suffered heartache and loss, and where a road opposite the Catholic church in the almost ghost town of Hammond will be called ODonohue Road in misspelled tribute.

Late in life, Lowitja will see a photograph purporting to show her with her parents: a little girl, seated between a white man and an Aboriginal woman on a camel-drawn buggy at a place called Abminga, two hundred kilometres north of Oodnadatta. Her uncle, Mick O'Donoghue, stands holding the halter.

She has no memory of it, or of any other time spent with her parents.

Book Two

Iti (the baby)

IX

At the Colebrook Home for Half-Caste Children, Violet O'Donoghue runs through the house, bare feet padding on the floorboards, calling out for her little sister.

'Iti,' she calls, using the Pitjantjatjara word for baby.

'Iti . . .'

Lowitja is 'the baby', although by now she is a child, the youngest of the O'Donoghue children at the Colebrook Home. Vi is her protector. Their bond will run deep all their lives. It will be Lowitja's earliest memory, the loving sound of her sister running through the house calling for her, and then, as she gets older, riding on her brother Geoffrey's back with her feet tucked into his pockets, all the two miles to school.

It is a crowded house, full of children taken from their parents and told to forget, watched over by spinster missionaries Ruby Hyde, who is short and stout with hazel eyes that see everything, and Delia Rutter, who is small and thin and gentle. The missionaries are devoted to God and to the children; but at night, when the house is quiet, a child is often crying.

Some of the children will carry that ache all their lives, while others will describe Colebrook as 'a loving sanctuary' and say that they were not stolen from their mothers but saved—from violence, or abuse, or poverty. One of the children, Faith Thomas, will remember constant love and attention. Another, Nancy Barnes, will write of her time at Colebrook: 'We didn't miss out on anything as I recall. Except perhaps our mothers.'

Lowitja does not feel loved. For her, Colebrook is a place of rigid discipline and joyless religious observance, bad food and endless hymn singing and praising of the Lord. It is the ringing of the triangle that hangs near the well, and being punished for 'childish things'. The sting of a strap soaked in water and allowed to dry to make it harder.

Lowitja is fond of Sister Rutter, but regards Matron Hyde as cold and stern, and calls her by the Pitjantjatjara name the children give her—kungka pikati—the angry woman.

Lowitja is often in trouble: 'I remember in my very earliest days standing up for what I believed in. One of the earliest memories I have is of coming between the matron and the strap. I would often stand in the way when the strap was intended for others, with the result being that I, too, got a beating.'[1]

The children are told that Aboriginal culture is 'of the devil'. They are forbidden from asking questions about their past—their parents— and they are forbidden from speaking their native languages. So, out of earshot of the missionaries, they make up their own secret 'Aboriginal' words, and cling to those they remember, including the Pitjantjatjara words tjitji tjuta, many children.

When new children come into the home, they huddle around them and ask the questions that the missionaries will not answer: 'Do you know my mother? Do you know where she is?'

In this way, Lowitja learns that her mother's name is Lily, that she is 'a full-blood Aborigine', and that she is living 'up there . . . in the bush': 'Our hearts ached to know who we were, where did we come from, where were our mothers, and who were our fathers, and why wouldn't they tell us . . . These words were never spoken, so the ache continued.'[2]

Two years after she arrives at the home, an article appears in the Adelaide *Advertiser*, marvelling at the transformation of the Aboriginal children: 'Those who have seen the Colebrook Home children are surprised by their charm, their intelligence and the fact that they are "like ordinary children". It is only the training of a Christian home that has made them so. When they were brought in from the bush they were wild, frightened, dirty and ignorant. Few of them had known anything of civilised life.'

A spokesman for the home tells *The Advertiser*: 'The Home training has two objects—first, to make Christians of these children, and second, to merge them into the white population. As they are half white, it is better to develop in them the instincts of Europeans, and to make useful citizens of them, than to leave them in the camps to become Aborigines.'

The missionaries rely on faith and charity—God's provision. Sometimes the baker bakes too much bread, or burns the crusts, or the greengrocer has left-over cabbages, or someone brings them a load of wood, and then the missionaries ring the triangle that hangs by the well and the children have to run to thank the Lord.

For every act of charity they receive, they sing the hymn 'Praise God from Whom All Blessings Flow':

Praise God, from whom all blessings flow;
Praise Him, all creatures here below;
Praise Him above, ye heav'nly host;
Praise Father, Son, and Holy Ghost! . . .

At mealtimes they line up on the veranda and march into the dining room, singing 'Marching Beneath the Banner'. They sing

'Onward Christian Soldiers' and the Colebrook hymn, in which little girls serve Christ and boys are washed from sin.

All her life, the hymn will come quickly to Lowitja's mind:

Christ paid the debt for all the little children,
Christ paid the debt for us all;
Christ paid the debt for all the little children,
in the Colebrook children's home.
Happy is the girl who is serving Him,
happy is the boy who is washed from sin;
Never to a child will the Lord say no,
So let us all to the Saviour go;
For Christ paid the debt for all the little children,
in the Colebrook children's home.

And to be washed of their sins they sing 'Whiter Than Snow':

Whiter than snow, yes, whiter than snow,
Now wash me, and I shall be whiter than snow.

A Colebrook child writes in a diary:

To-day we have made it a special matter of prayer. Every two hours Sister Hyde would ring a bell and we would leave whatever we were doing and go into our room in little separate groups and have a little quiet time in prayer and reading God's Word. We always pray for all the missionaries, and for our Council in Adelaide, and all the kind people in other towns who help us by sending food and clothing. We do feel that we have a lot to thank God for. He is supplying our daily food every day, and He knows just what we need before we ask Him. It is most lovely to think that God loves black boys and girls as well as white ones. We do praise Him because He first loved us. We will never forget you dear, kind people, who are helping us boys and girls in the Home.[3]

On Sundays they go to church, three times. Sometimes they go in Matron Hyde's car, the one she calls Jonah, and then later in the one she calls The Whale: 'We would all climb in, the big girls first and we little ones over the top, sitting on their knees. There was always such a fuss made by the big girls about their stockings. "Don't crease our clothes," they would warn us. "And don't ladder our stockings".'

Some go to the Salvation Army and some to the Methodists, where they play in the band and sing in the choir. No games are played on the Sabbath; but one of the big girls, Miriam McKenzie, has a love and gift for music and plays a steel guitar.

Colebrook is also climbing trees and playing in the creek and games of Kick the Tin and Knucklebones. Sometimes they find wildflowers as they walk to school along the highway into Quorn, scrambling over the dry rocks of the Stony Creek and the equally stony Pinkerton Creek. Or they jump a fence to chase a kangaroo and forget to go to school altogether.

At the edge of the town, where a park will later be created to commemorate the pioneers, the white children at the Catholic school, alongside the Church of the Immaculate Conception, see them coming down the road, all the Colebrook children, and taunt them with a murderous rhyme: 'Nigger, nigger, pull the trigger.' And the Colebrook children chant back at them, 'Catholic dogs, jump like frogs, in and out of the water.'

In the town, they pass a pretty house. To Lowitja, it looks like something out of a picture book. 'That's the best house in Quorn,' she says, over and over. 'One day, when I'm older, I'm going to buy that house.'

And one day, she does.

At night-time, they pray together: 'Gentle Jesus, meek and mild, look upon a little child.' After which, in Violet Turner's pungent expression, they drift into 'the land of forgetfulness'.

In Turner's expurgated telling of it, in *Pearls from the Deep*, there is no sadness, or longing, only the joy of salvation:

> Nothing pleases the children more than to gather around the little organ and sing hymn after hymn. They know by heart dozens of hymns and choruses, and a number of chapters of Scripture. As they sang our eyes wandered around the group, and we pictured each child as he had been when first he came to the Mission Home. We could see again, in memory, the frightened, wild little faces, the dishevelled hair, the expression of blank ignorance, almost stupidity, that had characterised them then.
>
> Now, what a change had been wrought by the grace of God! Faces eager and full of animation, eyes sparkling with health and happiness, voices raised in songs of praise to Him who had called them out of darkness into His marvellous light—such they were now, and our hearts followed their voices in praise for what He had done.[4]

The children are very young. In November 1941, the secretary of the United Aborigines Mission, Reverend A.B. Erskine, writes to South Australia's chief protector of Aborigines, William Penhall, saying the mission prefers children to be seven years of age or under: 'Over this age it becomes increasingly difficult to control them, as they have learned so much of the bush ways and habits.'

In photographs, Lowitja is a little girl in grey second-hand clothes, wishing she had something bright and frilly to wear.

She tries desperately to be noticed and spends hours brooding over how she has come to be here, without a mother and a father, and why no one comes to get her: 'When I was very tiny, I would ask, "Who am I, who is my mother, who is my father, where do I come from?" '

By the time she is seven or eight, she stops asking: 'I wasn't getting any answers. The other children in the Home became my family.'

X

April 1937

At Parliament House, Canberra, federal and state Aboriginal authorities meet to discuss the destiny of the nation's Aboriginal people. It
is the first attempt at a national policy on 'Aboriginal welfare' and is
attended by representatives of the federal government and all of the
states, except Tasmania, which does not accept it has an Aboriginal
population, and where the skeletal remains of Truganini, the 'last'
Tasmanian Aborigine, stand hideously in the museum on public
display.[5]

All of the chief protectors are seated around the table, men who
wield supreme power over Aboriginal people: Auber Octavius Neville,
from Western Australia; John William Bleakley, from Queensland;
Cecil Evelyn Aufrere Cook, from the Northern Territory.

Tall and thin, with one glass eye and a fastidious self-assurance,
a man of keen intellect with a mastery of the mordant phrase, Cook
arranges marriages between white men and half-caste girls who are
capable of being 'uplifted' in order to 'breed out the colour'. In 1933,
he tells a Sunday newspaper that the 'problem of our half-castes will
be quickly eliminated by the complete disappearance of the black

race, and the swift submergence of their progeny in the white'. The writer Xavier Herbert writes of Cook, 'The man is a monster in his attitude to the unfortunate people he is employed to protect. He not only does not understand them, but detests them. Small wonder they hate or fear him.'[6]

For three fine cool days in the nation's capital, eleven white men deliberate on 'the destiny of the race', during which no Aboriginal voice is heard.

They discuss what to do about 'full-blood' Aboriginal people, who are assumed to be dying out, and 'half-castes' and 'quadroons' and 'octoroons'. They discuss conditions in each state and territory; what it is to be a native; laws making it an offence for a white man to have sexual intercourse with 'a coloured girl'; the problem of 'half-breeds', born from the union of Aboriginal girls and 'a low class of white man'. They talk about maternity allowances that are payable 'only to persons in whom black blood does not predominate'; charcoal opium dross being sold to Aboriginal people by Chinese opium smokers; natives begging along the trans-Australian railway line; the desirability of neck chains to bring Aboriginal prisoners to courts; and whether it is preferable to send a native to jail, or to give him a whipping.

Bleakley, speaking first, calls for a uniform national policy, broad enough to cover different conditions in the various states. He says that Aborigines in 1937 can be classified in four ways: primitive nomads, still free to live their lives on inviolable reservations, but requiring 'benevolent supervision' to protect them; those living precariously on their own lands in food poverty, their hunting grounds usurped and their native culture destroyed; detribalised Aborigines, who live mendicant lives on the outskirts of country towns and mining camps, uncontrolled by native laws or 'the moral code of the superior race'; and the 'crossbreed'.

In Queensland, he says, there is 'definite opposition' to the marriage of half-caste girls to white men and that 'none but the lowest type of white man' would be willing to marry a half-caste girl, who would be likely to gravitate to 'aboriginal associations'.

The issue of half-castes dominates.

To Neville, a man known and feared by Aboriginal people across Western Australia as 'Mister Neville', who has the power to take any Aboriginal child from their mother at any stage of their life, the answer is to remove half-caste children from their families and educate them sufficiently 'to enable them to be assimilated into the white community': 'To achieve this end, however, we must have charge of the children at the age of six years; it is useless to wait until they are twelve or thirteen years of age.'

Cook worries that the growth of a 'coloured' race could result in the kind of racial conflict witnessed in the United States, where two coloured men, suspected of being involved in the murder of a white man, had recently been taken from the police and burned to death: 'There is at present no evidence of any such attitude towards the coloured people in Australia, for in this country the Aboriginal native is regarded with contemptuous tolerance,' he says. 'But when he has been elevated to a position almost equal to that of a white, conflict may be expected unless that stage is reached only after enlightened development.'

Pathologist and naturalist John Burton Cleland, who will be chairman of South Australia's Aborigines Protection Board for more than twenty years, tells the conference that scientists would vigorously oppose any attempt to hasten the detribalisation of full-blooded Aborigines, 'for they are unique and one of the wonders of the world'. But he proposes an investigation 'to ascertain whether the half-caste is able to take his place in the community under present conditions, or whether, on the average, he will always prove to be only a grown-up child who will have to be protected and nursed'. Years later, Cleland's son-in-law, historian Jack La Nauze, will observe that Aboriginal people existed in Australian history only as 'a melancholy anthropological footnote'.[7]

Described by the Minister for the Interior, Thomas Paterson, as 'an epoch-making event', the conference ushers in a new policy era—assimilation—in which half-castes will be absorbed into the Australian community, while the first Australians fade away: 'This Conference believes that the destiny of the natives of aboriginal origin, but not of the full blood, lies in their ultimate absorption by the people of the Commonwealth, and it therefore recommends that all efforts be directed to that end.'

No Aboriginal voice is heard at the conference. But Aboriginal organisations have been forming.

In 1924, the Australian Aborigines Progress Association had been founded in Sydney by Fred Maynard and Tom Lacey, inspired by Jamaican black nationalist Marcus Garvey. It called for the right of Aboriginal people to determine their own lives, the restitution of land, an end to the practice of removing children from their families, and the abolition of the New South Wales Aborigines Protection Board. In the 1930s, activists began emerging from the missions and reserves of New South Wales and Victoria, among them: William Cooper, Bill Ferguson, Margaret Tucker, Doug Nicholls, Jack and Selina Patten, Tom Foster, Pearl Gibbs, Jack Kinchela and Helen Grosvenor.

In August 1937, four months after the gathering of the chief protectors, William Cooper, seventy-six-year-old secretary of the Australian Aborigines League, is interviewed by journalist Clive Turnbull. For the past four years, he has been circulating a petition to the King of England, asking him to 'prevent the extinction of the Aboriginal race', provide better conditions and grant Aboriginal people parliamentary representation. In Western Australia, Neville calls the petition 'a sign of a dawning intelligence'. 'Up until the present time the condition of the aborigines has been deplorable,' Cooper tells Turnbull. 'Their treatment was beyond human reason . . .'[8]

In November, agitators—including Cooper, Ferguson and Nicholls—meet to plan a Day of Mourning, to be held on 26 January

1938, the sesquicentenary of British settlement. A report of the meeting runs on the front page of Melbourne's *Argus* newspaper.

Ferguson, a shearer and organiser with the Australian Workers' Union, the son of a Scottish shearer and an Aboriginal housemaid, has recently helped to establish the Aborigines Progressive Association; he complains bitterly about the treatment of Aboriginal people on settlements in New South Wales. 'It would be better for the authorities to turn a machinegun on us,' he says.

Nicholls, a champion Australian Rules footballer who will one day be governor of South Australia, says that Aboriginal people are not satisfied to be merely kept alive on government rations: 'We do not want chicken food. We are not chickens, we are eagles.'

On a warm summer's morning, 26 January 1938, a 're-enactment' is staged in Sydney, during which the British land and Aboriginal people flee. Sydney's Aboriginal people have refused to take part, so officials have brought Ngiyampaa men from a mission at Menindee, in the far west of New South Wales, to play the part of being conquered. They are told they will be performing a dance. When they discover the truth and also refuse to take part, authorities threaten to cut off their families' rations. They perform, and return home, silent and dispirited.

Huge crowds fill the Sydney streets for a historical parade, after which Aboriginal people, in formal black dress, march silently from the Town Hall to the nearby Australian Hall in Elizabeth Street, to protest one hundred and fifty years of misery and degradation. First to speak is Jack Patten, president of the Aborigines Progressive Association, the son of a blacksmith and police tracker. He has fought professionally in a travelling troupe to make ends meet, under the ring name 'Ironbark', and on Sundays he speaks in Sydney's Domain about the lives of Aboriginal people. He declares:

On this day the white people are rejoicing, but we, as Aborigines, have no reason to rejoice on Australia's 150th birthday.

Our purpose in meeting today is to bring home to the white people of Australia the frightful conditions in which the native Aborigines of this continent live. This land belonged to our forefathers 150 years ago, but today we are pushed further and further into the background. The Aborigines Progressive Association has been formed to put before the white people the fact that Aborigines throughout Australia are literally being starved to death.

We refuse to be pushed into the background. We have decided to make ourselves heard. White men pretend that the Australian Aboriginal is a low type, who cannot be bettered. Our reply to that is, 'Give us the chance!' . . .

At five o'clock in the afternoon, a protest resolution is passed, unanimously: 'We, representing the Aborigines of Australia, assembled in conference at the Australian Hall, Sydney, on the 26th day of January, 1938, this being the 150th Anniversary of the Whiteman's seizure of our country, hereby make protest against the callous treatment of our people by the whitemen during the past 150 years, and we appeal to the Australian nation of today to make new laws for the education and care of Aborigines, we ask for a new policy which will raise our people to full citizen status and equality within the community.'

Five days later, 31 January 1938, an Aboriginal deputation that includes Jack Patten, William Ferguson and Pearl Gibbs, meets with Prime Minister Joe Lyons, his wife Enid, and the Minister for the Interior John 'Black Jack' McEwen. They ask for Commonwealth control of all Aboriginal matters, a Ministry of Aboriginal Affairs, an administration advised by Aboriginal representatives, full citizen status and civil equality with white Australians, including equality in education, labour laws, workers compensation, pensions, land ownership and wages.

Pearl Gibbs, secretary of the Aborigines Progressive Association and one of the architects of the Day of Mourning, tells them, 'I am more proud of my Aboriginal blood than of my white blood' and Enid Lyons never forgets it. When Gibbs dies, in 1983, the Aboriginal author Kevin Gilbert is grief stricken and writes, 'Throughout history, wherever there has been massacre, genocide, deprivation of human right—wherever tyranny ruled—the human spirit objected, often rising to heroic proportion. One such spirit was Pearl Gibbs. Garrulous, cranky, hurt, bitter, defamatorily lashing out in frustration, she held one course: justice, humanity, honour within this country'.[9]

In February 1938, federal Cabinet decides that William Cooper's petition to the King, which has been circulated in Aboriginal communities across the country so people can sign their names or make their mark, should not be forwarded to England. It is marked, 'no action be taken'.

In Germany, in November, Jewish homes, businesses and synagogues are attacked. Kristallnacht, the night of broken glass, ignites the Holocaust.

On 4 February 1939, up to two hundred Yorta Yorta people walk off the Cummeragunja Aboriginal station, on the New South Wales side of the Murray River, and cross into Victoria, saying they have lived for years in a semi-starved condition.[10]

Jack Patten is arrested for 'inciting Aborigines'.

XI

In Central Australia, police inspector Samuel Rabain Parsonage reports that 'immoral intercourse with native women' is common— 'even amongst missionaries':

> In regard to the immoral intercourse with native women, such intercourse is common even amongst missionaries . . . It is an offence against Section 85 (b) of the Police Act for any white person to be found lodging or wandering with aboriginals, but here we have the aboriginals lodging with white men who are the land holders.
>
> The present position in the Musgrave Ranges is that we have missionaries trying to make the tribal native white, a few white men trying to keep him black and a policeman trying to clean up the mess. It seems to me that the only sensible thing to do is to leave the tribal natives alone and perhaps it would have been a wise policy not to lease land in the Musgrave Ranges to settlers unless they were in a position to make a living without trading in dog scalps.[11]

In November 1939, the South Australian government introduces amendments to the Aborigines Act to 'consolidate certain Acts relating to the protection and control of the aboriginal and half-caste inhabitants of South Australia'. Amid lobbying by women's groups, a new section, 34a, is added, making it illegal for white men to consort with Aboriginal women.

Offences against Female Aborigines.

34a. Any male person, other than an aborigine, who, not being lawfully married to the female aborigine (proof whereof shall lie upon the person charged) –

(a) habitually consorts with a female aborigine; or

(b) keeps a female aborigine as his mistress; or

(c) has carnal knowledge of a female aborigine,

shall be guilty of an offence against this Act.

The new law imposes a maximum penalty of £50, or six months imprisonment, and comes into effect in February 1940. The Act is also amended to replace the chief protector with an Aborigines Protection Board, expand the definition of 'Aborigine', and introduce a system of exemptions allowing an Aboriginal person to 'cease to be an Aborigine' for the purposes of the Act if his 'character and standard of intelligence and development' is deemed sufficient. Exemptions may be conditional and revokable, or unconditional and irrevocable.

At Oodnadatta, the O'Donoghue brothers are targeted for prosecution.

They are also on the brink of losing their land.

Mick O'Donoghue's hold on Granite Downs was precarious in 1931, when the prospector Michael Terry saw him in the ruins of his dreams. In 1938, the property passes into the hands of Jim Robb, a lean, straight-backed man. Robb breeds horses for the British army in India: he stands six stallions that have lineage to the great racehorse

Carbine, and he culls heavily for type and temperament, destroying hundreds of horses every year. He also owns the neighbouring Lambina station, on the ephemeral Alberga River. At Lambina, he has built a circular fence around the homestead to protect it from drift sand, but in February 1938 floodwaters wash it all away and Robb takes up Granite Downs.

In November 1938, four Aboriginal men—Yackadi, Aunthar, Conine and Quart Pot—plead guilty in the Circuit Court at Port Augusta to the manslaughter of Tom Maloney, an Aboriginal station hand, at Granite Downs. The court hears that Maloney was suspected of causing the death of Yackadi's elderly mother, Polly, by pointing a bone at her. Quart Pot is sentenced to twelve months' imprisonment and Yackadi, Aunthar and Conine to three months.

In December, a thirteen-year-old boy, Richard Robert Stevens, dies of thirst at Lambina Crossing when his family's truck is stranded in a dry creek.

Robb clashes with Tom O'Donoghue, accusing him of allowing his poor-quality stock, from his barely improved land, to stray onto his breeding property. O'Donoghue responds, disputatiously, warning Robb against a 'policy of obstruction'. In a handwritten letter from De Rose Hill, dated 14 September 1937, O'Donoghue also threatens to 'deal with' any of Robb's Aboriginal workers who might come onto his property 'unaccompanied by a responsible white person': 'Firstly, I am pointing out the vexed question of boundaries,' O'Donoghue writes. 'If you do not know where yours are, it is not within my province to assist you. To make a plain statement plainer, particularly note that I reserve the right to deal with all natives employed by neighbouring runs, or otherwise whilst on my property, unaccompanied by a responsible white person, in strict accordance with the law, as laid down to cover such cases.'

Robb complains to the secretary of the Pastoral Board, K.R. Snell, that he is experiencing 'considerable trouble' with Tom O'Donoghue.

He suggests O'Donoghue's lease be cancelled, and offers to take up the property to keep out 'persons of the O'Donoghue type'.

Robb argues that, although O'Donoghue has held the land for more than five years, he has not complied with the conditions of his lease that require improvements to the value of £10 per square mile. O'Donoghue owns only two cattle, three horses, and no more than two hundred sheep on shares, but gives permission to others to run their poor-quality stock on his land on shares or agistment. This stock, Robb says, is allowed to stray onto his property, where they have the use of his high-class stallions and bulls.[12]

By 1940, stockman Doug Fuller also has his eyes on De Rose Hill.

A man with an acrid turn of phrase, Fuller, in old age, will remember Tom O'Donoghue as 'a good Catholic' who fathered a large family in a desert that would not sustain many children and through a drought so severe that 'lizards were starving to death'.

'When they found out the church would look after the kids, the gins would wait on the side of the road for the mail truck to come along, to hand the kids over to the mail driver,' he says. 'They couldn't feed them, you see.' He remembers 'niggers' and 'gins' who became 'wine dots on fourpenny dark', as alcoholics and cheap wine were called.

In March 1940, Fuller writes from Kulgera station, Finke, to Cecil Goode, an inspector with the Pastoral Board, saying that he has inspected De Rose Hill and found it of no value. He could see no improvements; there was only one well, which contained water that, after floods, was too salty for stock; there were sheep watering on a big swamp, but they were not in good condition after their feed had been destroyed by fires. He says he has offered O'Donoghue £50 for the lease, but O'Donoghue would rather see his lease cancelled than sell.[13]

In April, the Pastoral Board demands evidence that O'Donoghue has made the improvements to his land required by the lease or a notice of intended forfeiture will be issued.

O'Donoghue responds in June, writing to the director of Lands, Adelaide, from De Rose Hill via Oodnadatta:

Dear Sir,

In reply to yours of 23/4/40 I would respectfully point out that no previous communication has reached me. This has been redirected from Tieyon Station.

Owing to depression, scarcity of labor and the effort to breed a flock of a thousand sheep from a small beginning, I have not been able to effect the improvements specified by the terms of the lease, but if allowed to carry on would be able to go ahead from next shearing, in August. Rumours that have been circulated over a considerable period by persons who have alleged that they have heard from the Pastoral Board that my lease was to be cancelled has prevented me from getting the necessary finance to effect improvements.[14]

He attaches a list of improvements, including windlass and buckets, and notes that a well was destroyed twice during floods in 1938 and 1939.

On 9 November 1940, Tom O'Donoghue is arrested and charged by Mounted Constable Grovermann with carnal knowledge of an Aboriginal woman named 'Lilly'.

He is convicted and fined five pounds: 'THOMAS GREGORY O'DONAGHUE (45), summons, breach of the Aboriginals Act (carnal knowledge of LILLY an aboriginal), at De-Rose Hill, via Oodnadatta; fined £5 and costs 10s. (paid) MC Grovermann. PC, Oodnadatta, 9/11/40.'[15]

It breaks him. Tom O'Donoghue walks away and he does not look back.

At Oodnadatta, Mounted Constable Cyril Keith Bradey writes to William Penhall, South Australia's chief protector of Aborigines and secretary of the Aborigines Protection Board, advising him of O'Donoghue's conviction. The two are in regular, friendly correspondence.

Five months earlier, in June, Bradey had reported to Penhall that several natives had been sentenced to fourteen days jail for killing O'Donoghue's sheep, and several other younger men had been sent back to the Musgrave Ranges. But he said he was reluctant to take action:

> Several complaints were made by the complainant, and admittedly a large number of his sheep had been killed, but I was loth [sic] to take action in this case, as it is well known that for several years past, he has been living practically with the Natives and owing to several surprise visits I have paid his camp, in the hope of detecting breaches against the Natives, I understand he ordered them all away, with the result that large numbers of his sheep had been stolen. I have taken the liberty of telling Natives on patrols to keep away from these sort of Stations, and if found there I would deal with them. I trust by doing this it will not be considered I have exceeded my duties.[16]

Penhall is pleased to hear of O'Donoghue's conviction. 'If action is taken, when possible, against all offenders, it might be possible to stamp out the offence,' he writes. But on 4 December, he writes again to Bradey, wondering whether it might not be better if O'Donoghue married Lily, if he has lived with her and treated her well. Penhall is worried that, if she is separated from O'Donoghue, she will not be welcomed back among her own people.[17]

Bradey writes in reply:

> I agree he has ... lived with the one lubra for a long period, and we have no direct evidence of him living with any other

lubras or at least nothing we could prove, but I certainly cannot see where or how he has been good and treated her very well; this statement is not made from hearsay, but from personal knowledge and observations.

Since he has been prosecuted he has just sold his place, and walked off and left the lubra, and I have heard although admittedly could not prove it, that he stated, 'I could not marry any of the black bastards.' This, I feel sure will prove how well he has or would treat her.[18]

Bradey adds that he does not believe that any harm would come to Aboriginal women turned away from white men's camps, since they invariably live with the natives, 'and are only treated differently from the other natives in sexual relations'.

In December 1940, Doug Fuller writes to the Land Board that he has heard a rumour that Wallis Foggarty has 'closed' on Tom O'Donoghue and taken his sheep. He asks for permission to sink a well and run his sheep on De Rose Hill until the block is reallocated. When he asks again in August 1941, he is told to contact Mick O'Donoghue, who is living at De Rose Hill on peppercorn rent, to discuss the agistment, while the board arranges to inspect the property. Tom O'Donoghue is said to be 'down country' somewhere.

In February 1941, Mick O'Donoghue is charged under South Australia's consorting laws. The South Australian *Police Gazette* records:

APPREHENSIONS DURING THE WEEK
JEREMIAH MICHAEL O'DONAGHUE (60), summons, breach of the Aborigines Act (consorting with MUNGI, female aborigine); fined £2 and costs 10s., in default seven days. M.C. Brady [*sic*] and P.C Breuer. P.C., Oodnadatta, 8/2/41[19]

In his brief of evidence, Bradey says he interviewed 'Jermiah Micheal O'Donaghue [*sic*]' and a native lubra named Mungi at 'Marlow Bore [*sic*]'.

In the record of interview, O'Donoghue begins the conversation saying, 'I know who you are, and have a fair idea of your inquiries, but thank Christ you have nothing on me.'

He tells Bradey, 'You can see I'm too old to ride anything, even Gins.'

Mungi tells Bradey that she camped with O'Donoghue, in the 'Big rain time', but that he is now too old and his 'Curloo' is small and dead, so when she goes to his camp it is only to rub his legs, which are 'properly bad', and to wash his clothes and dishes.

Bradey asks her, 'What name blackfellows call you?'

Mungi replies, 'They call me Mick O'Donaghue's [*sic*] lubra.'

When O'Donoghue says she is lying, Mungi replies, 'I telling Policeman straight, you telling dam lies, you fucked me alright at Sailor's Well big rain time.'

O'Donoghue says he expects he will plead guilty to consorting, 'but I have no intention of pleading guilty to fucking her, as I have not done so for many years, and then only the once, anyhow she is the worst ride in the district'.

Bradey says, 'Perhaps you could tell me the best.'

O'Donoghue replies, 'I might be able to, but I won't, I'm not saying any more.'

In 1942 Bradey leaves the police force. Also hoping to buy Tom O'Donoghue's lease, he asks chief protector William Penhall for a reference and offers to assist the Aborigines Protection Board in a voluntary and honorary capacity: 'I feel sure that a little understanding of the natives can do much good, and can honestly say that I have tried to understand and respect their beliefs,' he says.

Many years later, Doug Fuller, in a rough and ready telling, recalls how he came to own the lease on De Rose Hill, including a brief but colourful account of the last he saw of Mick and Tom O'Donoghue: 'See, old Mick, he used to have Granite Downs. He knew he was going broke and he took De Rose Hill up in Tom's name so when he went broke on Granite Downs he could shift over there to De Rose Hill. But when he did, Tom was there, and he told him to shove off. Well, he didn't. Then they start shooting at each other. Bang, bang! Must have been buggers of shots.'

He says Tom O'Donoghue went broke, 'got near the booze' he thinks, and sent his brother a letter saying he wanted to sell for '50 quid', but Mick O'Donoghue had no money, so Fuller bought it, expecting they would be partners. But then Mick O'Donoghue died.

'After I bought it, I went back out there, when Mick died,' Fuller remembers. 'There was fourteen or fifteen hundred sheep there. I bought those, cheap—about 10 bob each they were—and a few camels, few horses. Sheared a bit there, I suppose, I've forgotten [laughs]. But I won that one. [Mick], he was a good honest old fellow. He was supposed to be my partner, but he died. He didn't pay me . . . half of the price, he just died.'[20]

XII

At Quorn, the missionaries have decided to move again. Despite many attempts to sink new wells, the water has proven 'unsuitable and inadequate' and constant drought has dried out the rainwater tanks. Over eight months in 1940, the mission paid for water to be carted to the Colebrook Home.

They apply to the government to lease a large rambling house at Eden Hills, on the outskirts of Adelaide. It is called 'Karinya Hall' and was once an inebriates' retreat and, after that, it was used at various times to house returned soldiers, Chinese immigrants and unemployed women.

Over Christmas 1943, the children go to stay at Eden Hills for the holidays and then, by the following April, the government has agreed to lease Karinya to the missionaries for ten years.

The secretary of the United Aborigines Mission, Reverend Erskine, thanks the people of Quorn for sympathetically supporting their work for seventeen years. The local newspaper remarks that the home has done 'magnificent work for these children, whose lot in life otherwise would have been obscure and meaningless', and the town will miss them.[21]

Lowitja is eleven years old and sorry to leave the town—the home she has known the longest, to which she will return time and again, to live and to be married, and where she will be buried.

At Eden Hills, thirty-five children live in nineteen rooms. Many are now a thousand kilometres from the mothers they are supposed to forget.

Joined by children from southern Aboriginal communities and reserves, they strike a deep vein of racism at Eden Hills and are initially barred from attending the local schools.

While the missionaries argue their case, they are taught at Colebrook by a retired teacher who gives some importance to elocution—the art of speech and eloquence.

Lowitja reads the Bible confidently at church services. 'I knew how to read everything that was put in front of me and mostly it was the Bible,' she will recall, many years later.

———

Tom O'Donoghue goes to live in Adelaide.

He works for R.M. Williams, who is building a business making bridles and saddles and riding boots. He drives a 1938 Pontiac.

On 26 August 1942, at St Francis Xavier Cathedral, Adelaide, Thomas O'Donoghue, forty-seven, born in the Hundred of Pinda, labourer, son of Timothy O'Donoghue, marries Gertrude Susan Constable, forty-three years old, spinster, born in Eurelia, tough, dry land not far from the O'Donoghue family home. O'Donoghue's brother Henry, also a labourer, is Tom's best man, while Anne Bacchus, home duties, is Gertie's witness.

Eurelia was also home for another Irish Catholic family that arrived in South Australia on Christmas Eve 1853 on a ship named *Epaminondas* after the ancient Greek general and statesman. On board was a young Irish couple, Thomas and Ann Cummins; in Australia their name changes to Cummings and their great-grandson becomes Australia's most famous horse racing trainer, Bart Cummings.

Lily goes to live in Oodnadatta, where a small portion of a reserve used by bullockies and travelling stock has been resumed as an Aboriginal reserve, to enable police to 'protect the Natives from the attentions of undesirable white men'.

She takes a daughter with her—Bee Bee, born in 1935, the year after Lowitja and two of her sisters were taken away. Lily lives in Billy-goat Lane with Jimmy Woodforde, an Arrernte man who was head stockman at Granite Downs, and has another family with him.

Many years later, in a hospital in Adelaide, Bee Bee, who was not taken away, will be asked whether her mother was happy that the missionaries took five of her children and raised them.

Through a translator, she will reply in Antikirinya-Yankunytjatjara: 'Wiya.'—No. 'Ngunytjunya pulkara ulangu munutjuni kuraringu.'— My mother cried a lot and was sick in her stomach.

She will say she thinks she was allowed to stay with her mother because of Lily's sadness. And that after the other children were taken away, Tom O'Donoghue also went away. 'Paluru wantingu.'— And he left.[22]

On 6 June 1944, Mick O'Donoghue, born in County Kerry, dies of myocardial failure and atherosclerosis at the Royal Adelaide Hospital. He is sixty-eight and has never married. He is buried with his parents, Timothy and Margaret, in the Catholic cemetery at West Terrace. His share in De Rose Hill is transferred to Doug Fuller. At Granite Downs, where Mick O'Donoghue once picked through granite to find fresh water and listened fearfully to the sounds of Aboriginal ceremony, a ration depot is established 'to enable old and infirm Aborigines who live in those districts to be provided with food, without having to travel outside the boundaries of their tribal territory'.

XIII

Just before Christmas 1945, an Aboriginal woman arrives in the town of Quorn with two young children at her side. She has travelled more than five hundred kilometres through desert country from the remote township of William Creek.

She attracts the attention of police sergeant Bill Kitchin, who ascertains that her name is Lily and that she is making her way to the Port Augusta mission, where she believes she will find her five children. She has no means of subsistence.

If Kitchin, a policeman for thirty-three years, knows, or suspects, that Lily's children are at the Colebrook Home, he does not tell her. The home has been a prominent part of the town for seventeen years, and relocated to Eden Hills, on the outskirts of Adelaide, the previous year.

He provides for Lily and her children for two days while they wait for a train, buys her a ticket to Port Augusta, and sends her on her way.

Then he sits down and writes to the chief protector of Aborigines, William Penhall, advising him of what has transpired and asking to be reimbursed for his costs:

Police Station
Quorn
10/12/45
Sir,
I have the honour to inform you that on the afternoon of the 8th just, a native woman named Lily with her children arrived here from William Creek without any means of subsistence and stated that she was on her way to Pt Augusta mission to see her five children.

No trains were available to send her on until 6.30 on this date and I have had to provide for the family during their stay in Quorn and I would like to be able to render an account for same.

I believe the woman's husband is employed at William Creek Hotel.
Yours obediently
W.H. Kitchin
PS I issued her with a ticket and one half to Pt Augusta.

At the Aborigines Protection Board, the chief protector, a life-long Methodist and occasional lay preacher, who routinely refuses to reunite half-caste children with their Aboriginal parents, acknowledges the correspondence:

Dear Sir,
I have your letter of the 10th inst. reporting the arrival of Lily and two children without means of subsistence, and their subsequent transfer to Port Augusta.

I am grateful for your interest and help in this case, and will be pleased to defray all expenses if you will kindly submit a claim.
Yours faithfully,

WRP
Secretary
Aborigines Protection Board

Lily does not find her children.

She goes back to Oodnadatta, where, four years later, a photograph will be taken of a wurlie of scrap iron on a barren flat: 'Old Lily's camp north of Oodnadatta, c 1949', the caption says. Almost a decade after her death, an anthropologist working at Oodnadatta, Jen Gibson, will record Lily's tribal name as Yunamba—a name that Lowitja never heard.[23]

Penhall will retire in August 1953. Under the headline 'The aborigines say he's human', the Adelaide *Mail* will report that Aboriginal people have been making their way along that city's Kintore Avenue to the offices of the Aborigines Protection Board 'to say goodbye to a man whom they had come to look on as a real friend'.[24] This will not be a view shared by anthropologists Ronald and Catherine Berndt, who dealt with Penhall in the mid-1940s and wrote of him, 'The reputation among Aboriginal people of this official Protector of Aborigines was perhaps the worst among all of those we have known.'[25]

Penhall will retire with a leather-bound Bible, an oak writing desk and a gold watch.

XIV

At Eden Hills, Lowitja finishes 7th Grade, gets her Progress Certificate and goes on to Unley Girls' Technical School, where her name is listed as Lois Daisy O'Donoghue.

It is the only time she hears the name Daisy and she puts it down to a whim of the missionaries.

Her school reports speak of a girl who is neat and quiet, finds the work difficult but does her best. Her best subjects are English, Social Studies and Home Science. She likes cooking and dressmaking; when she goes to a school dance, she changes out of her uniform into a dress that she has made. 'I thought it was pretty nice,' she remembers.

In 1948, her final year of school, she is ranked thirty-second in a class of thirty-two students. Her final report remarks, 'Lois is a neat worker, but rather slow.' Where the signature of a parent is required on the reports, the missionary Ruby Hyde crosses out the word parent and signs for her.

With no memory of her mother, she receives a School Certificate in Mothercraft, from the Mothers and Babies' Health Association.

At Colebrook, older children help to take care of the young ones and, when she is thirteen, Lowitja looks after Doris Kartinyeri, whose mother has died a month after giving birth to her in September 1945 at Raukkan, a Ngarrindjeri community at Point McLeay. Removed from her family by welfare authorities, Kartinyeri is admitted to Cole-brook on 12 January 1946 and is there for fourteen years. They were bad years after 1952, when Matron Hyde and Sister Rutter leave amid a split in the United Aborigines Mission.

Kartinyeri is sexually abused at the home and then again when she goes out to work as a domestic servant. She plunges into mental illness, and spends years in and out of institutions. Late in life, she becomes a writer. Her first book is called *Kick the Tin*, a game of hide and seek they played at Colebrook with a tin can, kicking and running and hiding and trying to get home. 'My whole life has been moulded into a statue without liberty,' Kartinyeri writes.

Each morning at Colebrook, Lowitja takes care of baby Doris. She feeds and washes her before she goes to school, and puts her to bed at night. 'She was my baby,' she will say whenever she speaks of Kartinyeri.

But early in life Lowitja decides she will not have children of her own.

Sometimes the missionaries allow church families to take Cole-brook children into their homes for the school holidays. When they show affection, Lowitja pushes them away: 'They wanted to hug and kiss you and tuck you in bed and kiss you good night and that sort of stuff,' she will recall. 'I just didn't like it at all. Shied away from it and didn't really want any part of that.'[26]

In her teenage years, she becomes a Baptist, although all her life she will struggle with the role the church played in her life. In old age, worn out and depressed, she will scribble on a piece of paper that she was converted and baptised 'to please the missionaries, the white fellas who dominated my life'.

———

It is April 1949. In China, Shanghai is in chaos as Communist units advance. But in Adelaide, *The Mail* finds some space on its front page to report that the celebrated Aboriginal tenor Harold Blair has sung for part-Aboriginal children at Colebrook.

Born at the Cherbourg Aboriginal Reserve, in southern Queensland, Blair has become a national celebrity after being discovered on a popular amateur radio show. He is on the verge of leaving for America, where he will study at the Julliard School, with the backing of 'the Negro baritone' Todd Duncan, the first black person to sing in an opera with an otherwise white cast, and the original Porgy in George Gershwin's Porgy and Bess. Duncan is fighting against segregation in America. *The Mail* reports, 'Mr. Blair speaks delightful English, can read Italian and German, and has studied opera and drama to help him in his singing career.'

Before he leaves Australia, Blair marries a fellow student from Melbourne's Conservatorium of Music, Dorothy Eden, who is white. Both families fear for them. The bride wears a wedding gown of white satin, with orange blossoms on the veil. Aboriginal pastor Doug Nicholls performs the ceremony. Inspired by the American civil rights movement, Blair will use his voice to agitate for Aboriginal rights. 'I inherited what voice I have from my mother and as a child I sang at bush concerts and now I would like to feel that I am acting as an envoy for my people, to prove that we can take our place in the world of culture.'

Colebrook children are sent out to work when they turn sixteen. The girls have been raised and trained to be domestic servants and the boys to be station hands or labourers. With their past erased, and their minds filled with hymns, they are released back into the world.

Lowitja will later recall: 'For all the pain created by the removal policies and the disciplines of Colebrook Home, there is no denying the fact that the Colebrook kids became an extended family. It's all we really knew. So, when the time came for one of the older ones to leave the Home it was very difficult indeed ... As each one left on the train—going north or south—we would all rush for a tea towel or a napkin to wave goodbye. It was stressful for those who were leaving and those who were left behind. We felt it terribly and quite often would not see our brother or sister again until well into adult life.'[27]

Lowitja sees her sisters and her brother leave, each a wrench.

As she approaches her time to leave, she attempts to find her own employment. She asks the older girls who are already working, 'Do you know who wants a girl? Find out who wants a girl.' If she works in the city, she thinks, she might be able to meet the other girls at Adelaide's Beehive Corner, have lunch at Myer's basement, and visit the children at Colebrook, 'because it was the only thing you knew, the only home you knew'.[28]

And perhaps she could even go to the movies, or go out dancing.

She begins to think, 'I can make my own decisions now.'

But the missionaries have other plans for her. The night before her seventeenth birthday, August 1949, Lowitja is told she is going to be a domestic servant for Douglas and Joyce Swincer, who have a sheep farm at Waitpinga, near Victor Harbor, on the Fleurieu Peninsula, eighty kilometres from Adelaide. The Swincers are Baptists. Douglas Swincer is on the board of the United Aborigines Mission; Joyce Swincer is pregnant with her fourth child and Lowitja will help with the children.

The missionaries believe Waitpinga is far enough from the bright lights of the city that it will curb the girl's rebellious streak.

'I was told the night before,' she will recall. 'Pikati, Matron Hyde, came to the dormitory and she said, "You're going to work tomorrow, you're going to Victor Harbor".'

'I thought, Victor Harbor, good place. I'd heard about it. Not that we knew much about what was going on outside, because we were kids living in an institution. The only thing we did outside of it was church on Sunday.'[29]

Lowitja packs her bag and says her goodbyes.

Before she leaves, Matron Hyde tells her that she confidently expects she will soon be pregnant and will amount to nothing.

She walks out the door and down the road.

'Bugger them all,' she thinks to herself. 'I'll show you.'

Book Three

An old suitcase and a wedding picture

XV

October 1949

Lowitja stands at the train station at Victor Harbor, clutching a battered suitcase, steam belching behind her and beyond that the blue waters of Encounter Bay.

It was here on 8 April 1802—at the end of the French Revolutionary Wars and a year before the Napoleonic Wars began—that two explorers, the Englishman Matthew Flinders and the Frenchman Nicolas Baudin, encountered one another in their ships, *Investigator* and *Le Geographe,* while charting the southern coast of a continent known speculatively in Europe for many centuries as Terra Australis Incognita, the Unknown South Land, and during the seventeenth century, after the discoveries of Dutch navigators, as New Holland.

Each man's voyage had been fuelled by a hunger for discovery. Both had been at sea from the age of fifteen, the Englishman's imagination having been stirred after reading Daniel Defoe's *Robinson Crusoe.*

Flinders marked his maps *Terra Australis,* although he was coming to the view that *Australia* was a name more pleasing to the ear. On board the *Investigator,* he had an Aboriginal guide, Bungaree, 'a worthy and brave fellow' and the first person to be recorded in print as an 'Australian'—and a ship's cat called Trim, named after the butler in Laurence Sterne's novel *Tristram Shandy*, faithful and affectionate, jet black but with feet that seemed to Flinders to have been dipped in snow.

Baudin had called the southern coast 'Terre Napoleon'. His expedition, approved by Napoleon Bonaparte in the wake of the French Revolution, had been filled with science and art, but also rancour, illness and death.

On board *Le Geographe*, they exchanged information and maps. Flinders named the meeting place Encounter Bay; Baudin named the coastal region Fleurieu. For millennia, it had been home to the Ramindjeri people, whose legends include the Dreaming story of Kondoli, the whale man, who alone has the means of making fire.

As the Ramindjeri tell the story:

When the whale man danced, sparks flew from his body. Everyone at the dance was in awe of his fire and secretly wanted it for themselves, but Kondoli was a large powerful man and most dancers were afraid of him. Ngarankani, the shark man, Mulori, the stingray man, and Pungari, the seal man, asked Kondoli over to where they were dancing. 'Kondoli, come and dance' they called. While Kondoli's back was turned, Krilbalu, the skylark man, and Ritjuruki, the wagtail man, readied their spears. The spears flew from the hands of Krilbalu and Ritjuruki, and lodged deep in the neck of the whale man. Flames shot out from the spear wound. Kondoli dived into the sea to put out the fire and was instantly transformed into a whale, water now spouting from the hole in his back. Ngarankani, Mulori and Pungari all followed him into the sea, turning into their totems: a shark, a stingray and a seal.[1]

In the wake of Flinders and Baudin, whalers and sealers arrived in Encounter Bay and were soon kidnapping and living with Ramindjeri women.

Diseases spread rapidly: smallpox, influenza, chickenpox, tuberculosis, venereal diseases, measles, whooping cough, typhus, typhoid fever and dysentery. In 1837, a whaler by the name of John Driscoll was murdered by a Ramindjeri man called Reppindjeri, after drunkenly molesting one of his wives. Reppindjeri, who was suffering from syphilis, was chained to the deck of a ship called the *South Australian* while inquiries were made.

———

More than a hundred years later, Lowitja steps from the train and grips her suitcase.

Doug Swincer is waiting for her at the station. He puts her bag into the back of his new sedan, a British-made Standard Vanguard, and they drive ten kilometres out of the town to his three hundred-acre sheep farm at Waitpinga, where Lowitja finds Joyce Swincer close to delivering the fourth of her six children. Coming from the pious and maidenly world of the missionaries, the sight of the heavily pregnant woman alarms her. She is also surprised the following morning when a bell does not ring to wake her from her sleep, as it did at Colebrook.

Before the war, Doug Swincer studied at the Melbourne Bible Institute and hoped to go to Papua New Guinea as a missionary, but war came and, in 1940, his father died, so he stayed to manage the farm while his two brothers enlisted. When he applied for missionary work again, after the war, he was told that he was too old to be considered. He stayed a farmer and committed himself to his local Baptist church. On Sundays, his home is often filled with the devout.

Lowitja goes to work, caring for the children, cooking and cleaning. On washing day, she hangs the washing from a long line, a length of wire strung between trees in the yard. At mealtimes, she eats alone, on the veranda. Under the arrangement with the missionaries, her wage is to be thirty shillings a week. She is to receive ten shillings in her hand, and one pound a week will be placed into a trust account held for her by the United Aborigines Mission.

She is shy and lonely. 'I was very shy. I remember when I did go out of the Home into domestic service, not entering into any conversations at all and . . . only answering yes or no to any questions that were put to me,' she will later recall.[2]

The Swincers treat Lowitja with kindness and their children think of her as part of their family. They call her Lo-Lo. But they do not question her separation from her mother and they do not contemplate reuniting them. Long after Lowitja has left them, they will watch her rise with admiration and surprise.

'They were kind people, but all the time I was there I was very lonely. I missed my brother and sisters and I felt isolated. I did what I thought I should do, but apart from that I wasn't a good servant.'[3]

She wants more. She wants to be 'somebody': 'Like many young Aboriginal girls, I was taught to earn a living as a domestic. This was thought to be an appropriate means of livelihood for Aboriginal women at the time. But, I decided that I wanted to be "somebody". That God had given me intelligence and that I was going to use it.'[4]

At a small Congregational church down the road from the farm at Waitpinga and at Baptist fellowship, she meets sisters Alice and Connie Tuck. Politics and religion are deeply ingrained in the Tuck sisters, who live in houses side by side above the railway line. Their mother, Eliza Playford, is part of an old South Australian political family. Their grandfather, 'Honest Tom' Playford, was twice premier of South Australia, in 1887–1889 and 1890–1892; he was elected to Australia's first Senate in 1901 and was defence minister in the government of Australia's second prime minister, Alfred Deakin. Their cousin, Sir Thomas Playford, is South Australia's premier, and is destined to be Australia's longest-serving premier, kept in power for twenty-six years and 126 days by a malapportioned electoral system, but remembered on his gravestone as 'a good man who did good things'.

Connie plays the church organ. Alice is matron of the South Coast District Hospital. In the 1930s, she nursed at Wilcannia, in the far west of New South Wales, at a time when the Paakantji people were being herded onto a mission near Menindee.

At Colebrook, Lowitja had often wondered about becoming a nurse, just as her sister Amy had wondered about becoming a teacher and will fight her own long battle for acceptance after being told 'we do not have Aboriginal people in teacher training'. Lowitja's potential becomes a topic of conversation between Joyce Swincer, a nurse before she married, and Alice Tuck, who says to Lowitja one day after church, 'You want to be a nurse, I hear.'

'Yes, I do,' Lowitja replies.

'You can start now,' Tuck says, and changes the course of her life.

It is May 1950. In August, when she turns eighteen, Lowitja will be eligible to become a trainee nurse. She obtains references from the Swincers and from the United Aborigines Mission—and will keep them all her life. In a handwritten letter, dated 10 May 1950, Joyce and Doug Swincer write:

To whom it may concern,
Lois O'Donoghue has been working in our country home for the past seven months as a general domestic help. She has proved to be clean, capable and conscientious. Lois is an honest and reliable girl and from what we have seen and heard of her, her character is irreproachable.

Her happy disposition and sensible outlook on life have qualified her to be 'one of the family' in our home and amongst our friends.

Lois leaves us of her own choice and with our accord and good wishes. We have pleasure in recommending her for any position of trust suitable to her attainments.

We are, yours sincerely

On 15 May, the general secretary of the United Aborigines Mission, Leonard James Samuels, a blind preacher with a passion for evangelism, writes:

To whom it may concern.

I wish to state that Miss Lois O'Donoghue is a girl that has been trained in our Colebrook Home since she was a child of about 2 years, and has always shown a keen desire to make progress.

Lois has had training at the Unley Technical School and obtained a good final report from that school.

For some years, she has shown a deep interest in becoming a Nurse, with a wish to become useful among her own people.

We have been very pleased with this girl's spiritual standing, and her bright nature has always made her a friend of all.

I have no hesitation in commending her to you for training as a Nurse & I feel sure she will give good service and prove herself worthy of your trust and help.

Yours faithfully

LJ Samuels, General Secretary

She is accepted, exceeding missionary Ruby Hyde's expectations for her.

Excited, she makes her way to the United Aborigines Mission office in Adelaide to draw on her trust account so she can buy a nurse's uniform. After nine months of work, it should contain almost £40, more than enough for new black shoes and stockings. But, standing at the desk, she is told she can't have it until she is twenty-one, but that Mr Samuels—the blind preacher—will escort her to a store and buy her what she needs.

She is indignant: 'I wasn't about to subject myself to that.'

She turns on her heels and never goes back. She buys what she can afford from the money that has been paid to her, borrows a uniform, and then buys more as she can afford it: 'Every day, I'd be in the laundry washing what I'd had on, so that I'd have something for my next shift. I'd be in the laundry and borrowing clothes, until I was paid enough to eventually have my own uniforms.'

At the South Coast District Hospital, she works hard and is popular with patients.

On days off, she rides a borrowed bicycle along the coast and sometimes climbs a rocky escarpment at Rosetta Head that whalers called 'The Bluff'. The Ramindjeri, long before them, called it Longkuwar, created in a fury by Ngurunderi, who shaped the land with his spears and caused the seas to rise with a voice of thunder.

Matron Tuck takes a shine to her. 'She used to ride a horse and trap around the area and I was quickly regarded by the other nurses as "Matron's pet", because she would lend me the horse and trap whenever I asked for it,' Lowitja will recall.

They had a lot of fun teasing me about that. In fact, I was seen in those days as a bit of a Goody Two-Shoes! The other nurses would go to dances in the Town Hall at Victor—but I would go upstairs and watch. We had been taught at Colebrook that activities such as dancing and drinking were sinful.

After these dances the girls (and the boys they had met up with) would say, 'Make sure there's some soft drink for O'Donoghue'! We'd all go off to have our drinks and talk and laugh. But

I was always the one who went back to the nurses' home before curfew and then I would open the door for the rest of them to sneak in at all hours of the night!

From the beginning, she is driven by the conviction that as an Aboriginal woman 'I needed to be better than the others to be seen as equal'.[5]

In Darwin, February 1951, Fred Nadpur Waters, a Larrakia man, organises a lightning strike over poor wages and food at the Bagot Road Aboriginal compound. He is arrested by order of the Native Affairs director, Francis Moy, and transported to Haasts Bluff, seventeen hundred kilometres away, where Kukatja, Pintupi, Pitjantjatjara, Arrernte and Warlpiri people line up at the storehouse for rations of tea, sugar, tobacco and corned beef, and 'Jesus loves you' inscriptions are handpainted on white wooden crosses in the cemetery. He has been sent away from his family under the absolute powers of the Aboriginals Ordinance for 'creating a nuisance'.

Section 15 (1) of the Aboriginals Ordinance states: 'A Protector may if he thinks fit give authority in writing to any person so desiring for the removal of any aboriginal, or any female half-caste, or any half-caste male child under the age of eighteen years, from one district to another, or from any reserve or aboriginal institution to another reserve or aboriginal institution or to any place beyond the Northern Territory . . .'

Section 16 (1) states: 'The Chief Protector may cause any aboriginal or half-caste to be kept within the boundaries of any reserve or aboriginal institution or to be removed to and kept within the boundaries of any reserve or aboriginal institution, or to be removed from one reserve or aboriginal institution to another reserve or aboriginal institution and to be kept therein.'

In Melbourne, the Australian Council for Civil Liberties publishes a shilling pamphlet, 'Not Slaves, Not Citizens—Condition of the Australian Aborigines in the Northern Territory'. While life under the Aboriginals Ordinance may not constitute slavery, it says, it involves 'far too many of the attributes of slavery for tender consciences to rest content'.[6]

XVI

Lowitja completes her preliminary training as a probationer nurse at Victor Harbor in June 1952. Matron Tuck describes her work as very good and her conduct as excellent.

In order to become a fully qualified nurse, she is required to do two years' training at a major teaching hospital. In South Australia, there is only one—the Royal Adelaide Hospital. An interview is arranged with the matron, Kathleen Scrymgour.

Lowitja takes the train to Adelaide. In the formal style of the day, she wears a hat and gloves.

A small, dark-haired, quick-stepping woman, Scrymgour has been a nurse for more than thirty years, and the hospital matron for six. In 1935, she was the first South Australian nurse to receive a Florence Nightingale scholarship to study with students from twelve other countries at London's Bedford College, Britain's first higher education college for women, founded by the social reformer, anti-slavery activist and philanthropist Elisabeth Jesser Reid. Hardworking, conscientious and studious, Scrymgour was one of the founders of the College of Nursing, Australia, and is intent on raising the standard of education for nurses.

At the hospital, Kathleen Scrymgour rejects Lowitja in the corridor: 'She stood me up in the corridor outside of her office and just told me very bluntly . . . that I should go to Alice Springs and nurse my own people. Alice Springs, of course, being a place that I had never been to, and my "own people" being a people that I didn't know.'

Lowitja is hurt, but she is also angry: 'It was completely unjust. I was deeply resentful and determined I wouldn't accept the decision. I'm not a radical. But I certainly wasn't to be walked over.'[7]

More than forty years later, when she is made an honorary fellow of Australia's Royal College of Nursing, she will say of her rejection: 'It was my take-off point.'

She returns to Victor Harbor, where Matron Tuck takes her back. But she also joins the Aborigines Advancement League, the leading organisation advocating for Aboriginal people, where she finds herself surrounded by women and men who burn with the injustice of racial prejudice—Aboriginal people and supporters from churches and unions.

They campaign against discrimination, and for young people to be given the opportunity to enter professions, such as nursing, and to take up apprenticeships. They raise money for a hostel for Aboriginal people coming to Adelaide, who are refused accommodation because of their poverty and the colour of their skin.

With the support of Matron Tuck, Lowitja meets Premier Tom Playford: 'And so here I was on my days off heading down on the bus from Victor Harbor to Parliament House with appointments to see the Premier, Tom Playford, and any other member of parliament that I could possibly get an appointment with to somehow open the door to my entry to the Royal Adelaide Hospital. I met him a few times. I can't remember him being that sympathetic, but I continued to keep lobbying.'[8]

In a speech to women at Port Augusta in 1985, when she is Australian of the Year, she recalls: 'I lobbied high and low. I fought tooth and nail for that right to be trained and employed as a nurse. Protests and public speeches in the city square, letters and visits to premiers and members of parliament.'[9]

———————

In South Australia, the Aborigines Advancement League is dominated by Charles Duguid, a doctor and leader of the Presbyterian Church, and his wife Phyllis, the daughter of a Methodist clergyman, a teacher, an advocate for Aboriginal rights and women's rights and a Christian socialist. Six foot (183 centimetres) tall with a Scottish brogue, Duguid is the grand old man in the struggle for Aboriginal rights. The Pitjant-jatjara call him tjilpi, old man, and tjamu, grandfather, as a mark of respect. He has been a presence in Lowitja's life since childhood.

Duguid's anger and concern were sparked initially by the Coniston massacre, but then they were fuelled by a missionary he treated for leprosy, contracted from Aboriginal people, who told him it was common for Aboriginal women to be raped by 'white intruders who beat up the husbands if they tried to rescue their wives'.[10] He had also followed, with clenched teeth, the disappearance of Yolŋu leader Dhakiyarr (Tuckiar) Wirrpanda. Tuckiar had been convicted of the murder of a policeman and sentenced to death after a one-day trial; but when he was acquitted on appeal by the High Court and was released, he vanished without trace.

In July 1934, two months before Lowitja was handed to mission-aries, Duguid had gone to the Northern Territory to see conditions for himself. He found the Aboriginal people there degraded and despised, and discrimination 'deeply implanted in every aspect of life'. He was appalled by the spread of venereal disease among Aboriginal women, whose babies were being born with eyes damaged by gonorrhoea.

At Hermannsburg (Ntaria), where the German Lutheran missionaries had made a haven for the Western Arrernte, and learned their language and prayed for God (Altjira) to change their souls, he told Pastor Friedrich Albrecht he felt ashamed. He talked about the need for 'an intelligent Christian mission'. In June 1935, as the newly appointed moderator of the Presbyterian Church in South Australia and president of the Aborigines Protection League, Duguid travelled north, guided by Reg Williams. They drove in a gale of wind in a bad season. Along the way, at Quorn, they visited the Colebrook Home, where Duguid invited Ruby Hyde to bring the children to Adelaide at Christmas time. Before he left, eight-year-old Nancy Brumbie asked him, 'If you are going up to the Musgrave Ranges, can you find my mother? Her name is Munyi.'[11]

In the Musgrave Ranges, Duguid was taken to Ernabella, a pastoral lease with a partly built house that had no floor, ceiling or windows. It was a focal point for 'doggers', who made a living shooting dingoes for their scalps, or trading with the Aboriginal people for them, for a handful of flour. In a rough shelter near the house, he found an Aboriginal woman pika puka, very sick, with one side of her nose and part of her cheek eaten away by yaws. He met the Pitjantjatjara and found them to be a people of 'striking dignity', living naked and contented in the rocky outcrops and escarpments, 'uncontaminated by contact with the white man', although he feared this would not be the case for long. He decided that this was the place for a mission, to act as a buffer between the Aboriginal people and the encroaching white man.

At Oodnadatta, on the outskirts of town, he saw the Aboriginal camp alongside the rubbish dump, from which they collected trash to build the hovels in which they lived. 'Any shelter less worthy of human beings would be hard to imagine,' he wrote.

Returning to Adelaide, he discussed the principles that should underpin a Christian mission with his wife Phyllis. The most basic, they agreed, was 'the conception of freedom'.[12]

At Christmas 1935, the Colebrook children stayed at Duguid's home in Adelaide for five weeks. Newspapers were invited to witness the transformation of the children in the loving care of the missionaries. The Adelaide *News* reported:

Shy but grinning, excitedly awaiting unknown wonders, 28 aboriginal and half-caste children have arrived in Adelaide for their first sight of a big city and their first sight of the sea. This morning, they were just beginning to savour the delights of the five weeks holiday which lies before them. Their ages range from one to 17 years, and the one-year-olds were having as good a time as the 17-year-olds.

Accommodation has been provided for them at Dr. C. Duguid's home in Magill Road and for recreation to-day they were playing cricket or diving around in a big sandpit with tireless energy. Father Adelaide Christmas will visit Dr Duguid's home this afternoon to distribute gifts to the children. They have received gifts from the fund in past years, but personal distribution has not previously been possible.

What lay outside the grounds they did not know this morning. Arriving in Adelaide last night, they have not yet formed any impressions of the city, and the sea is something so far outside their experience that they have simply no ideas about it at all. For the moment they were content, and as happy as children on holiday should be. They chattered like magpies, white teeth gleaming in dusky faces. It would be worth a long journey to see those faces when the children make their first round of the city shops, or are stunned by the immensity of water when they go to the beaches.[13]

The *News* reported that Matron Hyde was happy, too, watching her frolicking young charges. 'They are going to have a wonder-time,' she told the paper. 'They attend the State school, and know something of cities from their books, of course. But this visit will be a revelation for them.'

A group photograph was taken of the children. A small girl, Lowitja, sat cross-legged front and centre, hiding her face from the camera.

While the Colebrook children were in Adelaide, King George V died in England and Duguid, as moderator of the Presbyterian Church, held a memorial service. He arranged for the Colebrook children to attend, and also invited a group of white children who had been brought to the city by a padre from the Australian Inland Mission. The padre told him, 'You've insulted these children—asking them to sit with niggers.'

Duguid had also been told by a prominent member of parliament, 'The nigger has got to go, and the sooner the better.' When he later published his memoirs, he accused the director of the Australian Inland Mission—the heroic John Flynn—of telling him, 'You are only wasting your time among so many damned dirty niggers.' Flynn denied saying it.

———

In Adelaide, Lowitja goes to work as a private nurse, tending the elderly father of a family that is involved with the Aboriginal rights movement through the church. She leaves Victor Harbor with references from Alice Tuck and Dr William Henry Collins, who both speak of her reliability and popularity. Matron Tuck says she is particularly capable with children and babies, has made a good theatre nurse and would do well to continue her training. Dr Collins writes that she promises to become 'a nurse of very high calibre'.

In June 1953, Grace Lester, Muriel Brumbie and Faith Coulthard, all former Colebrook girls, arrive at Duguid's surgery highly agitated. Like Lowitja, they have been denied permission to train at the Royal

Adelaide Hospital. Despite having the necessary prerequisite education, the matron has told them, as she has told Lowitja, 'that it would be much better if they went to Alice Springs and nursed their own people'. Duguid flies into a 'wild rage'.[14]

On a cold, wet night on 31 August 1953, more than a thousand people attend a rally at the Adelaide Town Hall, where Duguid calls for a 'new deal' for Aboriginal people, including full citizenship. Five 'part-Aborigines' also speak about 'Our Place in the Community'. Mona Paul, who is training to be a nurse at Murray Bridge, tells the audience that Aboriginal girls training in the country to become nurses get disheartened when their applications to the Royal Adelaide Hospital are rejected because of their colour.[15]

Lowitja does not speak, but sings in a choir.

The Adelaide *News* reports that a capacity audience 'got a shock it won't forget for a long time'.

It reports that Aboriginal people with less than fifty per cent white blood receive no social security benefits, but pay taxes; that most part-Aboriginal girls applying to be nurses are advised to go to Alice Springs, although they may never have been there; that Aboriginal people and part-Aboriginal people may be debarred from dining and sleeping cars on the Alice Springs train; and that many white people in the Northern Territory still believe an Aboriginal person reaches the limit of intelligence at twelve to fourteen years. 'Each of these facts was given more point because it was told, without much rancour, by a part-aboriginal,' the *News* writes.

One of the speakers, Peter Tilmouth, a School of Mines student, is reported to have shocked the audience out of its complacency by saying, 'I am proud of my blood—both black and white. Through each I have inherited a certain intelligence, and I am going to use it.'

On 17 December 1953, Rev. Clive Hutchinson, minister at the Parkside Baptist Church, writes Lowitja another reference:

To Whom it may concern,

This is to certify that I have known Miss Lois O'Donoghue since she was a child. I have watched her development with interest, and testify to her persistent efforts, sometimes against severe odds.

Lois has had nursing experience, and repeatedly I hear, directly and indirectly, of her capability, interest and devotion to the task.

She is a member of the above Church, and is held in the highest esteem as being of excellent character, and exemplary habits. She has a very pleasing personality.

I feel sure that this young lady believes nursing to be her vocation, and I have every reason to assume she would be successful both in study and practice, as she has become even more conscientious in recent months.

I have absolutely no hesitation in recommending her, and to do so affords me great pleasure.

It is our intention to assist Lois all we can, and should any further commendation be required we would be happy to furnish it.

At the Royal Adelaide Hospital, Matron Kathleen Scrymgour relents. She writes to Lowitja, inviting her to start her training at the hospital.

Lowitja will be the first Aboriginal person to train as a nurse there. She is twenty-two years old. It is almost 1954—the year in which a young Queen Elizabeth visits Australia, and Adelaide is hit by an earthquake.

XVII

Lowitja enters the Royal Adelaide Hospital on 4 January 1954.

She is denied credit for the two years she has spent at the South Coast District Hospital at Victor Harbor. She will have to start again at the beginning, as a probationer nurse.

But it is the beginning of the happiest time of her life: 'I wasn't accepted for a long time, and when I was accepted I made a decision I was going to be the best nurse on the ward and I worked at that and I was really happy to be able to be the best nurse on the ward. And I loved nursing.'

She is acutely aware that she is blazing a trail for other Aboriginal girls: 'I really couldn't afford to fail. But I was adamant, and I made sure from the first day, at the Royal Adelaide Hospital, that I was going to be the best nurse that that hospital had ever had, and I worked hard at it, in more ways than one. I made sure that my shoes were shinier, my uniforms were whiter, and that I was always on time, and I did the best, best possible job.'[16]

'I was thinking, every day for almost ten years, about being a better nurse than the other nurses . . . I couldn't fail, there was no way I could fail. If I did there wouldn't be an opportunity for other Aboriginal women to be accepted . . .'[17]

'All our uniforms were washed at the Royal Adelaide, but they weren't stiff enough for me at the collars and cuffs, so I'd take them to the drycleaners and have them done all over again, or I'd iron them myself. This is where I'd get all these names from—"Goody Two-Shoes". I was going to be the best nurse at the Royal Adelaide— and I think I was, as good as anyone else. I never went out at night with boyfriends and all that sort of stuff.'[18]

Colebrook remains Lowitja's extended family, but shadows are falling. Missionaries Ruby Hyde and Delia Rutter leave and establish a home called Tanderra, providing accommodation for older Aboriginal girls, relying, as always, on God to provide. It becomes a meeting place for former Colebrook girls, including Lowitja, who sometimes takes her nurse's uniforms there to wash and iron: 'They were the only people I knew. I didn't know where else I could go.'

The Colebrook Home the two women leave behind at Eden Hills descends into cruelty and abuse. In 1954, the Board of Health inspects it and finds 'insanitary conditions', which the inspectors attribute to lack of staff and lack of funding. Two years later, after another inspection, they write that the 'appalling conditions' are 'a menace to health, of not only the staff and inmates of the home, but to the residents living in the district'.

A staff member regularly wakes children during the night for Bible readings and prayers. Children who wet the bed are sent to school without breakfast.

———

It is February 1954 and the newly crowned Queen Elizabeth II steps onto Australian soil—the first reigning monarch to visit Australia— and the country goes wild for her. As the royal party sweeps through fifty-seven cities and towns in fifty-eight days, more than three-quarters of Australia's population of nine million turn out to catch a glimpse.

In Adelaide, two hundred thousand people line the festooned streets to see the young Queen, and her husband, the Duke of Edinburgh; more than one hundred thousand school children, who have practised for weeks, form a giant tableau that spells out 'Loyalty'.

At the Royal Adelaide, Lowitja, caught up in the excitement of it all, persuades the nurses to wheel patients who are well enough out onto North Terrace so they can watch the Royal Progress. Matron Scrymgour storms from her office and orders the young nurse to return them to their wards. Lowitja refuses.

It is their final altercation. The following year, Kathleen Scrymgour retires, is appointed an Officer of the Order of the British Empire, and spends the next twenty-two years caring for her invalid sisters.

At Ernabella, Aboriginal singers have sold dingo scalps for petrol to travel fifteen hundred kilometres, most of it on dirt roads on the back of a truck, to sing for the Queen—traditional songs and Christian hymns, in the Pitjantjatjara language. At Whyalla, Aboriginal people perform a 'sacred tribal dance' for her. 'Never before had such a demonstration been given in the presence of women, and the Queen is the only woman to be told the explanation for the corroboree, as it is called,' British Movietone declares.[19]

Aboriginal poverty is shielded from her view. At Woomera a test rocket, 'the last word in modern weapons', is fired for the fascination of the Duke.

In Canberra, the Queen is introduced to Albert Namatjira, who wears a white linen suit. The Aboriginal artist is at the peak of his fame, but it has brought him ambiguous rewards. He pays his taxes, but he cannot own land and he cannot travel without permission.

In 1957, he is exempted from the restrictions imposed on other Aboriginal people. He is entitled to vote, to live where he wishes and to purchase alcohol. But his children are still considered wards of the state. He lives in a fringe camp at Morris Soak on the outskirts of Alice Springs.

The following year, he is charged with supplying alcohol to artist Henoch Raberaba, who is a ward of the state and prohibited from drinking alcohol. Namatjira is sentenced to six months' jail. Following a public outcry, he serves two months of 'open' detention at the Papunya settlement from March to May 1959. But he is despondent and a few months later, on 8 August 1959, he dies of hypertensive heart failure complicated by pneumonia.

An inscription is placed on his headstone, a line of scripture.

'Altjiraka nguangiberantama jinga nama nana jinga namanga'

1 Corinthians 15: 10: By the grace of God I am what I am.

In March 1954, Lowitja is a bridesmaid at the wedding of Colebrook friend Myra Taylor. The reception is held at the Duguid home, where Myra has been a housekeeper and where Namatjira watercolours hang on the walls. Charles Duguid gives the bride away.

Under the headline 'Dusky bride wore white satin—Aboriginal wedding had a film star touch', the event is covered by the *Australian Women's Weekly*: 'An unusual wedding with a film star touch, at which the bride, bridegroom, bridesmaids, and groomsmen were all part-aborigines, attracted hundreds of people to a little Baptist church at Magill, South Australia. Only the best man was a white boy.'

The article records that the bridesmaids, Muriel Brumbie and Lois O'Donoghue, 'wore nylon net and honiton lace frocks with short sleeves. Their head-dresses were tiny petalled "Royal" curvettes with short shoulder-length silver threaded tulle veils. Both girls are nursing, one at Royal Adelaide and the other at a private hospital':

It was a smart occasion that combined fashion and tasteful dressing. The popular exotic-flower earrings looked particularly effective worn by dark, young beauties, and sling-back shoes were the vogue. Watercolours by aboriginal artist Albert Namatjira, who recently met the Queen, decorated the walls of the reception room. They depicted scenes from the great inland from which the tribal side of the newlyweds' ancestry was derived. Namatjira's art has done much to lift the status of his kinsfolk in this country. As I looked around and saw the young marrieds with their adorable little dark babies, saw Myra, now changed into her going-away 'blues' toss her bridal bouquet, I felt that here the gap between white and aboriginal had been bridged, that these people no longer belonged to the past but the present.[20]

———————

In July, an Aboriginal man, Jimmy Gwiethoona, dies in a police cell at Nungarin, Western Australia, with a broken jaw and a brain haemorrhage. A police constable is charged with his murder, but the charges are dropped when the Crown accepts that he 'fell over when resisting arrest'. In the Northern Territory, two pastoralists are fined and imprisoned and a drover is fined after horsewhipping Aboriginal men and women.

In America, August 1955, at a place called Money, Mississippi, a fourteen-year-old black American boy, Emmett Till, after, in some way, offending a white woman in a grocery store, is beaten and shot in the head and his mutilated body is dumped in the Tallahatchie River. His mother insists on an open casket for 'the world to see'. In December, in Montgomery, Alabama, Rosa Parks refuses to give up her seat on a bus to a white man and is arrested under Jim Crow laws that enforce racial segregation in America's southern states.

In December 1956, feminist Jessie Street returns to Australia from London to gather material on the situation of Aboriginal people for the British Anti-Slavery Society. An establishment maverick, dubbed

'Red Jessie' by her detractors, Street is a tireless campaigner for peace and human rights; she had been Australia's only female delegate to the founding of the United Nations at the San Francisco Conference in 1945 and she is a colleague of Pablo Picasso on the World Peace Council Executive.

She tells Faith Bandler, whose father was kidnapped at the age of thirteen from the island of Ambrym, Vanuatu, to work in the Queensland cane fields, that nothing will change for Aboriginal people without a change to the Constitution. With Street's support, Bandler and Pearl Gibbs form a new organisation, the Aboriginal-Australian Fellowship, to bring white and black together to agitate for change.

A large meeting is convened at the Sydney Town Hall on 29 April 1957, calling for a 'new deal for Aborigines'. A petition is launched to change the Constitution by deleting that part of section 51 (xxvi) preventing the federal government from making special laws for Aboriginal people, and deleting section 127, to allow Aboriginal people to be counted in the census. It has been drafted by Jessie Street, along with Christian Jollie Smith, one of the first women to be admitted to practise as a lawyer and a founder of the Communist Party of Australia, and radical historian Brian Fitzpatrick, a founder of the Council for Civil Liberties. Bert Groves, who has become president of the new organisation, warns that Aboriginal people are facing extinction. Harold Blair sings. Writer Mary Gilmore, ninety-one years old, speaks about the richness of Aboriginal culture.

A film is shown. William Grayden's *Their Darkest Hour* shows stick-limbed children suffering from malnutrition in Western Australia's Warburton Ranges. It evokes comparisons with wartime newsreels of Nazi concentration camps and the Communist newspaper the *Tribune* reports, 'There were cries of disgust and horror and people openly wept.'[21]

The following year, in the mid-summer heat of February 1958, Aboriginal activists and their supporters, 'ardent Christians and equally ardent Communists',[22] travel to Adelaide, many of them second class by train, sitting up through the night, to form the first national Aboriginal political organisation. The Federal Council for Aboriginal Advancement (FCAA), which from 1964 will be known as the Federal Council for the Advancement of Aborigines and Torres Strait Islanders (FCAATSI), will lead the national campaign for 'equal citizenship rights', including the amendment to the Australian Constitution to give the federal government power to legislate for Aboriginal people as for other citizens. Bert Groves likens the policy of assimilation to extermination.

Charles Duguid—whom *People* magazine describes as the seventy-four-year-old champion of the 'dark-skinned underdog'—chairs the meeting and is elected president of the new organisation. Stan Davey, the non-Aboriginal secretary of the Victorian Aborigines Advancement League, who has resigned from his Church of Christ ministry to work full-time for what he calls 'the cause', is elected honorary secretary and over the next decade he will travel throughout Australia investigating reports of injustice, often hitchhiking when funds are short.

Other non-Aboriginal observers include Gordon Bryant, founding chairman of the Aborigines Advancement League in Victoria, who in the Whitlam government of 1972 will become the first Minister for Aboriginal Affairs with a full department under him; Mary Montgomerie Bennett, seventy-six-year-old author of *The Australian Aboriginal as a Human Being*, who travelled across the country from Kalgoorlie to be at the Day of Mourning in 1938; and aspiring young politician and intellectual aesthete Don Dunstan, a future premier of South Australia, who is working with young Aboriginal men, including Charles Perkins, to repeal the consorting provisions of the state's Police Offences Act.

Dunstan had visited the Point Pearce Aboriginal reserve on Yorke Peninsula in 1956. He was appalled by the poverty of the people and the protection laws governing them. In the late 1950s, he campaigned against the death penalty being imposed on Max Stuart, an Aboriginal man convicted of the rape and murder of a nine-year-old girl, a milestone also in the career of Rupert Murdoch, whose Adelaide *News* also opposed the death penalty. In government, Dunstan will author Australia's first anti-discrimination laws, introduce Australia's first Aboriginal Lands Trust and begin talks on returning land to the Pitjantjatjara and Yankunytjatjara people.

At the meetings of the federal council, civil rights campaigners, some more radical than others, sing 'We Shall Overcome', a gospel song that began in the music of slavery and became the anthem of the American civil rights movement. They sing:

Black and white together,
Black and white together,
Black and white together someday.
Oh, deep in my heart, I do believe,
We shall overcome someday.

And the Christians and the Communists hold hands and put aside their differences.

In Far North Queensland, January 1960, the Cairns Aborigines and Torres Strait Islanders Advancement League is formed, backed by the Communist-led Waterside Workers Federation and with a majority black executive. Its leaders include Gladys O'Shane, who is active in the union's women's committees and is regarded by the Lutheran missionaries at Hopevale as a 'godless communist', and waterside unionist Joe McGinness, the son of an Irish fettler and a Kungarakan mother, who spent five years of his childhood in the deprivation of Darwin's Kahlin Compound. In the dry seasons, they travel together in an old borrowed car over the unmade roads of the far north, meeting Aboriginal people, listening to their troubles and encouraging them to organise.

In October and November 1960, the black American singer Paul Robeson visits Australia. In the Starlight Room at the Hotel Australia in Sydney, Aboriginal activists show him Grayden's film *Their Darkest Hour*. Robeson's eyes fill with tears and he pulls off his black cap and throws it to the ground in a rage. At a press conference a few days later, he says, 'There's no such thing as a "backward" human being. There is only a society which says they are backward.'

In 1961, at Easter in Brisbane, Joe McGinness becomes the FCAA's first Aboriginal president, succeeding Don Dunstan, the last sympathetic white man to lead a national Aboriginal organisation. The executive remains majority white, but Aboriginal members are increasingly talking about land and culture and integration rather than assimilation. Doug Nicholls speaks of the need to 'abolish apartheid in our own country' before Australia resembles South Africa. He talks about segregation in swimming pools and theatres, and discrimination around voting, marriage, drinking and wages.[23]

Charlie Perkins speaks passionately and begins his rise to prominence. Born in 1936, on a table at the Bungalow, an Aboriginal reserve at the old telegraph station outside Alice Springs, he only ever saw his grandmother once, through a fence. His mother, Hetti, taught him to speak his mind. He grew up not knowing his father. In 1945, an Anglican priest, Percy Smith, took him and other boys to Adelaide, with the permission of their mothers, to further their education. At fifteen, having failed every subject, he was sent out to work as a fitter and turner and lived in a boarding house, 'mainly full of drunks and no-hopers'.

When he went to dances at the Port Adelaide Town Hall and asked girls to dance, they would reply, with everyone watching, 'We don't dance with Aborigines.' He went to England to play soccer, trialled with great teams, worked in the Liverpool shipyards and a Manchester coalmine, returned to Australia and moved to Sydney, where he completed his matriculation and entered university.

By the end of 1961, Perkins is in the newspapers saying that the treatment of Aboriginal people by some state governments is a disgrace to the world. The *Sydney Mirror* calls him 'an angry young man with the best of causes, who has proved himself among white people and who is ready to tell the truth as he sees it'. For a generation, he will be Australia's best-known Aboriginal civil rights activist, and until his death will be Lowitja's friend and sometimes rival.

XVIII

At the Royal Adelaide Hospital, the other nurses regard Lowitja as very serious.

'I felt that, because I was the first Aboriginal nurse there, I always had to do things to show that Aboriginal people are as good as everyone else,' she will recall. 'So I had the shiniest shoes and the whitest uniform! I would never go out. I never went out with a boyfriend, ever, at night, and when the girls went out to park with their boyfriends they'd come and knock on my window after curfew and I'd let them in. But I said, "Just remember, six o'clock start in the morning".'

She works in surgical, medical, thoracic, tuberculosis and ophthalmic wards. She does not enjoy or excel at her exams, but she passes.

As she progresses, she is urged, almost weekly, by the Protector of Aborigines to apply for an exemption from the provisions of the Aborigines Act. Once granted, she would carry a small card, like a passport, with a numbered exemption stating that, in the opinion of the Aborigines Protection Board, she is entitled 'by reason of her character and standard of intelligence and development' to be exempted from the Aborigines Act and 'shall cease to be an aborigine'.

Lowitja, who has not previously been made to feel 'all that accepted in the white man's world', declines the invitation. As she will later recall: 'Well I think it was because all our life, of course, we'd been treated like we were Aborigines and we always knew, of course, that we were . . . different and so we really cherished that. And the other aspect of it, of course, we weren't all that accepted in the white man's world and there was always a difference made. So I think we hung on to what we felt comfortable with.'[24]

'I remember every week the Protector of Aborigines would contact me to become exempt. That meant I would become white—just like that. I said, "No, I am an Aboriginal person and would not have a dog medal of any kind".'[25]

And exemption will offer no protection against racism. More than once, a patient waves her away, saying, 'Don't put your black hands on me!' She bites her tongue: 'I remember racism coming from the patients. Some would say they didn't want a black nurse. When that happened I wouldn't make a fuss, but would tell the ward sister who would just transfer my patient's care to another nurse. I never made anything of it. Anyway, I didn't want a patient that didn't want me. I thought they were missing out on getting the very best nurse on the ward.'[26]

'I had to go through that for a long time. But for the most part I think I had more good experiences than bad experiences.'[27]

Lowitja completes her training on 8 February 1958, four years after entering the Royal Adelaide Hospital, and gets her nurse's certificate on 24 March 1958, signed by Matron Zelma Huppatz, as well as the hospital's chairman of the board and the medical superintendent.

It fills her with pride, perhaps more so than anything else she will later achieve. She is invited to stay at the hospital and is appointed a staff nurse on 7 April 1958.

By August 1959, she is promoted to sister. She is in charge of a large medical ward at the Royal Adelaide Hospital and is regarded by the younger nurses as something of a disciplinarian.

Every now and again, at the edge of the hospital, she catches a glimpse of a man watching her. A white man, with red hair that is turning to grey. She asks the hospital priest, Father Thomas Michael O'Rourke, if he knows who it is.

O'Rourke has come to know the young nursing sister well. Every week, he drives her from the hospital to Christian Endeavour meetings at Unley Park Baptist church. He drops her off and stands at the gate talking to pastor Allan Spurgeon Tinsley, a missionary-minded man with a passion for evangelism, whose middle name is a tribute to the Baptist 'prince of preachers', Charles Spurgeon.

Lowitja regards O'Rourke as 'a good man'. But he knows more than he has told her. 'Look,' he replies, 'I think it's your father.' She stands silently as he tells her that Tom O'Donoghue worships at his church, that he is a devout Catholic, and that they have spoken about her.

The words hang heavily in the air, but nothing comes of them. She makes no move to contact her father and he never speaks to her.

'He never spoke to me. Ever,' she will recall, with a hard finality. 'There was time for us to know one another. But he didn't have the courage.'

Tom O'Donoghue dies in the Adelaide suburb of Payneham on 24 May 1960.

'Requiescat in pace', the death notice says. Rest in peace. He is sixty-five. His occupation is carpenter. He dies of the drinker's disease, cirrhosis of the liver, and aortic incompetence, the duration of each being described as 'years'. There are no children from his marriage. A requiem mass for the repose of his soul is celebrated at Adelaide's grandest Catholic cathedral, St Francis Xavier's.

Between them, Mick and Tom O'Donoghue fathered eight Aboriginal children in Central Australia: Parker and Steve; Eileen, Geoffrey, Violet, Amy, Lois and Bee Bee. But on their death certificates, to the question of issue living or deceased, the answer given is 'None'.

In her last years, Tom O'Donoghue's widow, Gertrude, tells family members, 'They should never have allowed Tom to go up to that station. It wasn't right.'

Many years later, someone sends Lowitja a photograph of her father—a wedding picture, in dress suit and bow tie, on the day he married Gertrude Constable.

Lowitja cuts his wife out of the picture and keeps the photograph of her father.

Book Four

Lily's daughter

XIX

February 1962

Lowitja is seated in a bullock cart, bumping along a rough and rutted road from Bongaigaon to Tukrajhar. It is the end of the cold season in India. She is deep in the forests of Assam, in the foothills of the snow-capped eastern Himalayas, and it is not like anything she has seen before.

There are ancient banyan trees, and cattle meandering on the roads, women and men dressed in handwoven dokhna and gamsha, lugging bundles of firewood and pushing thela handcarts down the road. There are lush green paddy fields and feathery kohua, forests of sal and betel nut, and som trees alive with silkworm; it is all splashed with the colours of wild frangipani and the flame of the forest is in bloom. The houses are made from bamboo and jute, caked with mud, straw and cow manure; in every house there is an open fire and a loom for weaving, and in the gardens she can see yellow-flowered chal kumra and kopou phool foxtail orchids that are a symbol of love and fertility. Somewhere in the forest there are elephants and tigers and leopards.

A few months earlier, at the end of 1961, at Adelaide's Unley Park Baptist church, Lowitja was introduced to Flo Horwood, a missionary with the Australian Baptist Missionary Society. Australian Baptists have been sending missionaries to India since 1882, when two young women missionaries, Ellen Arnold and Marie Gilbert, went to do zenana work among secluded women in the low wetlands of the Furreedpore District of East Bengal.[1] Arnold was invalided home with the symptoms of malaria, but returned in 1885 with four more women. Preaching on their departure, the evangelist Silas Mead was reminded of Jesus feeding the multitude and so they became known as 'The Five Barley Loaves'.[2]

Flo Horwood is home on furlough. Her life has been one of missionary sacrifice. Since 1948, she has worked among the Bodo people at Tukrajhar, a remote village in the north-east province of Assam, not far from the kingdom of Bhutan. Horwood tells Lowitja there is a shortage of trained nurses at the mission and suggests she joins her in India as a relief nurse.

Lowitja is ambivalent about missionaries, but India lights a fire in her imagination. 'I decided almost immediately to go,' she tells the Baptist Society's newsletter, *Vision*. 'If I like it, I may stay for five years.'

At the Royal Adelaide Hospital, Matron Zelma Huppatz writes her a reference, on 6 December 1961, saying that Lowitja has resigned 'to enter the mission fields': 'Miss O'Donoghue has a calm, dignified and professional manner, and her interpersonal relationships are good. I am sorry to lose her services, but she takes with her our good wishes.—R.Z. Huppatz'

A report on Lowitja's suitability is prepared by the Missionary Society's Asia Regional Committee, which reports that she is twenty-nine years old, in very good health, with no long illness or surgery, and is available for as long as required in Assam. Expenses are carefully itemised: travelling expenses of £158 (donated by a member of the Unley Park church), an outfit allowance of £25, two weeks' pre-embarkation allowance of £24 and an allowance of 1300 rupees, or £123, covering an initial five-month period from February to June 1962.

Lowitja's next of kin is marked: 'Loco Parentis—Sister R. M. Hyde, UAM'. With no birth certificate, Lowitja is forced to ask the Colebrook missionaries to write a reference verifying her identity so she can obtain a passport as an Australian citizen and a British subject. It is issued in Adelaide on 9 January 1962, and is valid for five years. She gives her profession as trained nurse, as she will throughout her life, and her place and date of birth as Granite Downs, South Australia, 1 August 1932. She is five foot three inches (160 centimetres) tall with brown eyes, brunette hair, and no visible peculiarities.

Her passport is stamped by the High Commission of India in Canberra on 27 January 1962, and on 8 February she boards the passenger ship *Orion*, bound for Bombay.

Several of the Colebrook girls come to see her off. So too does Graeme Swincer, the eldest of the children she looked after as a domestic servant at Waitpinga; he has stayed in contact with her through the Baptist church at Unley Park. He is struck by how mature and self-assured she seems.

'Goodbye Lois, all the best,' he calls out as the ship draws away.

Lowitja leaves Adelaide with missionary Floss English, who is returning to her mission at Jorhat, in Assam's lush Brahmaputra Valley. In Fremantle they are joined by the Reverend Peter Ewing, his wife, Win, and their children. Ewing has preached at Tukrajhar since 1949.

From on board the ship, on 20 February, she writes to the secretary of the Missionary Society's Asia Regional Committee, Reverend Albert (Alby) Roberts and his wife Rachel:

Dear Mr and Mrs Roberts,
It is very hard to believe that I am really on my way, in fact almost to the end of my journey. I will be very pleased to arrive at last at Tukrajhar. Tomorrow will be the last day on board ship. I have

enjoyed the ship since leaving Fremantle, it has been calm, but the weather very hot and sticky. Floss English has been real good company and we have got on very well together, Floss moved to the cabin opposite me after Fremantle, so it has been much better than it would have been with both of us in the one tiny cabin, we were allowed to do this because there have been so few passengers since Fremantle.

Peter, Winn and family changed their booking to cabin class so I haven't seen them too often, but they have both enjoyed the travel and are both very relaxed and happy to be return-ing. The children have enjoyed swimming most of the time. It has been good to meet and have Fellowship with so many missionaries, the folks in Perth met us and were very kind, we were shown the beauty spots in the afternoon, and then taken to tea, then to the Central Church for evening worship, then out to supper, and finally back to the ship, which sailed at 11pm. Flo Horwood was amongst those to see us off. Peter, Winn and family had a great farewell.

Yesterday we were at Colombo and Floss English, Mrs Eade and Olwyn Gaze from New Zealand and myself took a car and went to Kandy. The countryside is very green and beautiful. The women are very pretty and the clothes very colourful. We all enjoyed shopping at the bazaars, and the fresh tropical fruits were delicious.

How are you both keeping? How is Unley Park, I am missing them all, they have been very good to me. If you are conduct-ing a service there before Mr Tinsley returns will you give the fellowship my greetings. Well, I must hurry on as I have other letters to write before reaching Bombay on Thursday.

Yours in His service, Lois O'Donoghue

She lands in Bombay on 22 February, boards a crowded train and travels two and a half thousand kilometres across India to Bongaigaon, and then finally by jolting cart to Tukrajhar.

––––––

Lowitja will say throughout her life that she went to Assam as a nurse, not as a missionary; but the missionaries claim her as one of their own. In its annual report, the society's Asia Regional Committee notes with satisfaction that to the best of their knowledge Sister Lois O'Donoghue is 'the first Missionary of Australian Aboriginal extraction to go abroad in such a capacity, & she is proving a worthy ambassador for Australia and her own people'; while the Australian Baptist Missionary Society writes in its annual report that Sister O'Donoghue is among those bearing a virile Christian witness at a strategically important mission twelve miles (19 kilometres) from Bhutan, on a road followed by refugees from Tibet after China's invasion.

'It is not without interest that Miss O'Donoghue, whose fares were met by friends in Adelaide, is an aboriginal nurse,' the report adds.

In March 1962, she makes the cover of the society's newsletter *Vision*. She looks into the camera smiling, a poster girl for a virtuous circle—a missionary nurse raised up by missionaries. As with previous reports, the article highlights, in bold type, that 'she is probably the first part aborigine to be appointed from Australia to an overseas Mission'. It also observes that 'Miss O'Donoghue's path to success began as an infant when she was brought into the United Aborigines' Mission Centre at Oodnadatta'. It urges its readers to 'Remember Miss O'Donoghue as she enters this new field of Christian service'.

A shortened version of the article appears in July in the *Australian Evangel*, 'a family missionary magazine' published by the Aborigines Inland Mission of Australia, and then again in August in *Dawn*, a monthly magazine produced 'for the Aboriginal people of NSW' by the Aborigines Welfare Board. The edition features a report on the observance of National Aborigines' Day in Sydney on 13 July, where Sydney Lord Mayor Harry Jensen tells a crowd of three thousand people, 'This demonstration has been organised to stir the conscience of the Australian people. There never was greater justification for conscience stirring.'[3]

Among Aboriginal leaders who speak, Doug Nicholls tells the crowd that Aboriginal people do not want pity or sympathy, but only the hand of friendship.

The Minister for Territories, Paul Hasluck, 'an intellectual politician plagued by a reputation for pomposity', as *The New York Times* will describe him in his obituary, says that of Australia's ten million population, one hundred thousand are of Aboriginal descent. 'About 30,000 have been fully assimilated,' he says. 'Of the other 70,000 some are nomads living in the Northern Territory, Queensland and Western Australia but there are very few in this State where the Government is doing all it can to advance their welfare. Most of these nomads are between the wild state and full acceptance into the community. The policy of assimilation means that these people must get every opportunity to live exactly like every other Australian, to live side by side in the same street and do the same jobs. We are one people in one continent and there are no second-class citizens.'[4]

In India, Lowitja and the Ewings are welcomed to Tukrajhar. The Baptist logbook records, 'Miss O'Donoghue has come for three years, to help in the dispensary.'

Joan Webster is a missionary doctor who will spend ten years at Tukrajhar, until 1968 when the government refuses to renew the permits of the missionaries amid allegations they are inciting the Bodo people to riot over lack of political representation. She sees Lowitja arrive and thinks nothing about her being Aboriginal, one of the first Aboriginal nurses, or the journey of a girl from Central Australia to the foothills of the Himalayas: 'I never thought anything about it. It wasn't whether she was Aboriginal that we cared about, it was whether she was a good nurse—and she was, she was very good.'

For Lowitja, India is long days and long nights. She works at Tukrajhar and at Debitola, close to the Brahmaputra River. Living conditions are rudimentary: kerosene lamps for light, water from the well, a wood stove for cooking. She rides a bicycle along bullock cart tracks from village to village. She grows her hair in a long braid and sometimes wears a sari. She hardly sleeps in her bed, with villagers coming for her late at night, lighting their way through the jungle with jute sticks, and then tying a chicken to her bicycle before she leaves in the morning, in gratitude: 'It was very remote, jungle country and so on and so the people if they wanted a nurse in the village overnight, would come single file through the jungles and get the nurse to come into the village. I can't remember hardly a night that I spent in bed because come sunset there'd be a group of people at the door to escort you back to the village to watch over somebody and you'd walk single file with a jute stick flare in the front and one at the back to ward off any, you know, wild beasts that might be lurking.'

Years later, speaking as the Australian of the Year, she will remember her bicycle:

My memories and images of India are strange. I remember my bicycle. I rode it everywhere, from village to village, carrying it over dhongs and rivers. I must have looked a sight—a young Aboriginal girl riding one-handed, grasping a big, black, British-style umbrella in the other hand.

I remember walking in a procession through the jungle at twilight. A line of people, with jute torches at the front and back of the line. Thoughts of tigers and cobras and the safety of the village that awaited like an oasis in the desert.

But more than all, I remember the people of the village. They lived a simple and ordered lifestyle in harmony with their land. They were warm and friendly. They welcomed me and accepted me.'[5]

Every morning, many people are waiting for treatment. Her patients come from as far away as Bhutan and Tibet, and there are the tall, dark-skinned Santal people, brought to Assam by the British to work in the colonial tea plantations. They remind her of Aboriginal people from northern Australia.

Before the Baptists established a dispensary at Tukrajhar, the nearest hospital was twenty-four kilometres away, within a leper colony. Malaria, dysentery, typhoid fever, cholera, whooping cough, tuberculosis, tapeworms, smallpox and rabies are known to every villager in Assam. And the jungle could be violent, and death could be sudden.

So high is infant mortality that the Bodo have a grim expression for pregnancy—*modom gotoi*, body of death. 'To have a live birth was really wonderful,' Lowitja will recall.[6] In her nine months at Tukrajhar, she delivers a live baby only once, a set of girl twins.

She feels a connection to the Bodo, 'people who were marginalised and having the same experience as I was'.[7] And she sees the lingering impacts of colonialism: 'It gave me a different perspective, that the Australian Aborigines weren't the only people that had been colonised and that they weren't the only people who were dispossessed.'[8] She is made to feel welcome by these people, who form one of the eighteen tribes of Assam.

Years later at Tukrajhar, former politician Khiren Borgoary will sit on the step of a hospital now run by the Bodo people, with a Bodo surgeon, and say, 'I remember her very well. I was only a young boy, in class nine when she came here, but we still remember her and love her. Everyone loved her.' In a long life, Borgoary will be a teacher, a politician and a church minister; he will see the world change: 'When Lois was here, there was forest everywhere and tigers used to come, but now there is no more forest and no more tigers.'

Lowitja has gone to Assam as a nurse, but she is a nurse among Christian missionaries, so prayer is never far away. In an article published by the Missionary Society after her return, she describes their attempts to save a girl who was haemorrhaging. It is September 1962, the end of the monsoon season. The article appears under the headline 'Prayer is Answered':

We were just closing the dispensary at Tukrajhar for the day. Shaulish, our cook, brought his little girl, bleeding from a leech bite. For hours we tried without success to control the haemorrhage and eventually decided to take the patient to the nearest doctor, on the way to Bongaigaon. We started out in the early morning, wondering as usual at this time of the year (September) if we would get through. Well, we got as far as the first bridge before the jeep broke down. After waiting for two hours in the hope that we might be able to continue the journey, we decided to carry the child back to Tukrajhar, as her condition was deteriorating rapidly. Within an hour it was obvious that both parents feared the worst. We determined to commit the matter to God, and in a time of special prayer, the parents re-dedicated their lives to Him, and offered their child back to God, saying 'Thy will be done with this treasure Thou hast given to us'.

Six hours later, Ajen, our Mission driver, arrived to say that the jeep had been repaired, and that we could try again to get through to Bongaigaon. In my opinion, the child was too sick to move! We asked the father for his will in the matter. He said 'No! I've put her in God's Hands. Leave it to Him!'

Within an hour, the bleeding had stopped completely, and it was apparent that the child had taken a turn for the better.'[9]

Lowitja has left Australia expecting to be in India for at least three years. But in September 1962, border conflict between China and India erupts into fighting. The countries are pledged to peaceful coexistence—India has acknowledged Chinese rule in Tibet, and Prime Minister Jawaharlal Nehru promotes the slogan Hindi-Chini bhai-bhai (Indians and Chinese are brothers)—but there has been tension on the Himalayan border since India granted asylum to the Dalai Lama in 1959. In October, the Baptists' logbook at Tukrajhar notes, 'Threat of Chinese invasion'.

In Australia, the Missionary Society tells its followers there are gathering clouds on the northern border of Assam, that Tibet has been mercilessly subjugated under the guise of liberation and that the Chinese armies directed from Peking are pressing across the disputed borderline of northern India. 'What will happen in the next few months may depend in considerable part on how earnestly and effectively we pray,' it advises.

On 20 October, coinciding with the Cuban missile crisis, Chinese troops advance into disputed territory along the crest of the Himalayas, in Ladakh, and across the McMahon Line in the North-East Frontier Agency (NEFA). In an address to the nation on 20 November, his voice choking, Nehru appears to abandon Assam to its fate: 'Huge Chinese armies have been marching in the northern part of NEFA. We have had reverses at Walong, Se La and today Bomdila, a small town in NEFA, has also fallen. We shall not rest till the invader goes out of India or is pushed out. I want to make that clear to all of you, and, especially our countrymen in Assam, to whom our heart goes out at this moment.'

In Assam, there is widespread panic. At Tukrajhar, Lowitja and Joyce McDonald are ordered to evacuate.

They cross the Brahmaputra River and then go by jeep and rail to Calcutta, where, in a city full of people looking for a way out of India, Lowitja feels isolated and abandoned. She books into the Great Eastern

Hotel and contacts her sister Amy, who is training to become the first Aboriginal teacher in South Australia, to wire her some money to fly home. 'Just give me enough money to fly out,' Lowitja tells her.

She leaves Calcutta on 8 December 1962, and flies in to Adelaide, finding a bed at Tanderra, the home established by Colebrook missionaries Ruby Hyde and Delia Rutter. Just as her decision to go to India made news, so does her return:

EVACUEE NURSE RETURNS
A young Adelaide nursing sister is one of the first to return to Australia after having been evacuated from the Indian State of Assam last week.

She is Sister Lois O'Donoghue, a part-aborigine, who was evacuated from an Australian Baptist Overseas Mission in Tukrajhar because of the recent Communist Chinese advance into India.

'Coming home has been like a whirlwind. It seems that one day I was in Assam and the next in Adelaide,' vivacious Miss O'Donoghue, who arrived in Adelaide by air on Sunday, said yesterday . . .

'We didn't leave suddenly. We had time to think about it and left more or less in the ordinary way. We travelled across the Brahmaputra River by ferry and then by jeep and rail to Calcutta, where the missionaries are waiting to be able to return to their work.

'It was not until we reached the railway that we saw military movements and wounded being brought in.'[10]

Soon after returning, Lowitja becomes sick with malaria and is hospitalised for two weeks. But the publicity she has received prompts the Royal Adelaide Hospital to ask her to return there, as soon as she is able, as a night nurse.

She agrees, but India has changed her, and the world of the hospital that she fought so hard to enter seems small to her now: 'Well, very quickly I got some publicity because I was . . . the first evacuee, so the press was very interested in what had happened there, and, of course, the matron of the Royal Adelaide Hospital learnt very quickly that I was back in Australia and phoned me and asked me to come back to the Royal Adelaide Hospital, which, of course, I agreed to do, because I needed a job and I went back, but I didn't stay very long, because everything seemed so small . . . By this time I'd really been involved in something much bigger and I wanted to get involved in community nursing.'[11]

Among the missionaries, there is animated discussion about the circumstances of her evacuation, and whether they can keep her in the missionary fold. On Monday 17 December 1962, missionary Flo Horwood writes to the general secretary of the Australian Baptist Missionary Society, Reverend John (J.D.) Wiggins:

I had quite a yarn with Lois and to me, quite frankly, why she was popped on the plane is still quite a mystery. Lois has enjoyed her job and would like to return . . .

In herself she is cheerful and uncritical and seems to have had a satisfying contribution to make through our work. Since her return, an official conversation made her think she was not perhaps acceptable, which has come as a surprise to her, and has caused her some dismay and doubts. However, I did my best to allay her fears on that account because all correspondence with the field has been to the contrary . . .

We yarned for hours, of all our mutual friends in Tukrajhar. Judging by her knowledge of their movements and character, the lass didn't miss much. Wish she was my working companion at Tukrajhar. I rather hope that some time in the future that will be possible.

Horwood writes that Lowitja plans to accept the job she has been offered at the Royal Adelaide Hospital soon after Christmas 1962, 'as bread and butter is necessary at her Tanderra home', but she has encouraged her to continue missionary work 'as much as I could'. She says she has been unable to discover the answer to questions that have been raised, 'because the lass had no answers or clues to drop'.

In Melbourne, the society's general secretary, Rev. John D. Williams, who has already phoned Lowitja, writes to her on Friday 21 December 1962, suggesting she go to New Guinea:

Dear Miss O'Donoghue,
Since I spoke with you by phone on Friday last I have had a phone conversation with my Sydney colleague, Rev A.G. (Albert) Dube, who informed [me] that good use could be made of a nurse of your qualifications on our New Guinea field. I believe there is an opening for you if you feel that it is the right course for you. I would be glad to have your reaction to this suggestion. Please give the matter prayerful thought. If you were favourably disposed I think we could arrange your passage to New Guinea very soon.

At Tukrajhar, on New Year's Day 1963, Baptist minister Neville Kirkwood writes to Williams in Melbourne. Defensively, Kirkwood describes the panic and confusion that followed China's attack, with half of the wives of the colonial tea planters evacuated by plane to England. He says that he and Peter Ewing had decided not to abandon the mission during the crisis, but claims that Lowitja pleaded to be allowed to go home. Kirkwood also rejects out of hand any suggestion that she was 'unacceptable':

It is a pity Lois denied to ARCS knowledge of the reason for her being sent home. The following are facts which she cannot deny. In tears she begged Joy to go across and ask Pete (Ewing) if she could be sent home, immediately, as she 'couldn't stand it any longer'. Also the day of the ceasefire announcement in the presence of Joy and Win she said, 'I should have gone yesterday'. She felt that the easing of the situation would not give her the excuse to be sent home. It was upon her own pleadings that she was sent home. Rumours that ARCS has passed onto others which have reached us indirectly that she was unacceptable to the staff out here should be squashed immediately. Every member of staff had the highest respect and affection for Lois and were very sorry to see her go.

On 13 January 1963, Joyce McDonald writes to Flo Horwood: 'Whoever put that stupid idea into Lois' head that she wasn't quite acceptable? I don't think the Boros knew any different. They certainly didn't treat her any differently from the rest of us. She was a big help and just ready for the job that she was want to do this year [*sic*]. We were all very sorry that she went home, but felt (and still feel) it was the best under the circs.' McDonald then discusses continuing tensions that are 'like sitting on a smouldering crater. We are not unpacking. We expect a big blow up in the early Spring and no-one should blame Lois for getting out of it while the going was still good.'

XX

Lowitja goes back to the Royal Adelaide Hospital as a night sister, but soon shifts to a repatriation hospital in an old mansion called Birralee, at Belair, not far from the Colebrook Home for Half-Caste Children at Eden Hills. She works there for four years and meets a medical orderly by the name of Gordon Smart.

Born in the fishing port of Robe, early in World War I, Smart is part of a generation shaped by war and hardship. His father, Jim, who trained police horses at Murray Bridge, fought in the Boer War. When he came home, he brought with him a carbine taken from a Boer officer in a daring raid; he had it engraved and gave it to his son. In old age, he would sit in his shed with uniforms and swords hanging from the walls, smoking his pipe and telling stories.

Gordon Smart had fought in World War II with South Australia's 2/10th Battalion, in North Africa and New Guinea, where his weight fell from fifteen stone (95 kilograms) to five (32 kilograms). Wounded twice, at Milne Bay and Buna, the trailhead to the Kokoda Track, he had pulled out his hair from pain. When the war ended and he came home, his mother did not recognise him. He speaks little about what he has seen and done, but says that the New Guinea people the Australians called the Fuzzy Wuzzy Angels saved his life. He no longer goes to church. His children regard him as a distant emotional figure in their lives.

One night at the repatriation hospital, he invites Lowitja to have supper with him.

'I was in the Army with an Aboriginal man,' he tells her.

'Yes . . . well?' says Lowitja.

'A fellow by the name of Tim Hughes.'

'Well, he's my brother-in-law, married to my sister, Eileen.'

Lowitja is thirty years old, raised by missionaries, scarred by abandonment, and on the cusp of a life dedicated to the Aboriginal cause. Smart is forty-seven, white, and married, with five children, four daughters and a son. He also has a child from another relationship his five children know nothing about. He is smitten with the no-nonsense nurse, and tells her so.

She tells him she can have nothing to do with him. She has no intention of ever marrying. He wants to elope.

'It was a real shock,' she will recall. 'He was in love with me. All my upbringing said to me I couldn't possibly have an interest in a married man.'

She goes about her business, nursing and campaigning, but she is attracted to him and he persists; finally she agrees to the possibility of them marrying, later in their lives. 'You discharge your responsibilities to your family and if I'm still about, and you are still interested, we'll talk about it then,' she tells him.

When she leaves the repatriation hospital, they stay in contact, writing letters and seeing one another from time to time. 'But only ever as friends.'

———

After India, Lowitja plunges into Aboriginal politics. Her nights are filled with meetings and campaigns.

In February 1963, the Menzies government announces it will excise land from the Arnhem Land reserve to allow bauxite mining in the vicinity of the Yirrkala Methodist Mission. The Yolŋu will be squeezed into an area measuring one square mile (2.6 square kilometres). The Federal Council for Aboriginal Advancement calls it a breach of faith with Aboriginal people, who are being defrauded of their land.

In July, Labor politicians Gordon Bryant, the council's vice president, and Kim Beazley senior travel to Yirrkala, where Beazley is struck by bark paintings in the church and suggests a bark petition to the parliament.

Typewritten in both Yolŋu Matha and English and mounted on stringybark boards painted with pipeclay, charcoal and ochre, the Yirrkala petition asserts the Yolŋu connection to the land and sacred places 'from time immemorial'.

It begins, Bukudjulni gonga'yurru napurrunha Yirrkalalili—The Humble Petition of the Undersigned Aboriginal people of Yirrkala.

On 15 November 1963, Queensland's Liberal–Country Party government orders the eviction of a Presbyterian mission at Mapoon, on the southern edge of the Wenlock River, eighty kilometres north of the bauxite mining centre and town of Weipa, to accommodate mining expansion. Police haul the people away by truck and barge; they burn their homes and their church to the ground, and shoot their dogs. Most of the people are shifted to Bamaga, on the tip of Cape York, where 'New Mapoon' is created.

In Adelaide, Lowitja becomes involved 'in every Aboriginal movement that there was': 'This was a time, of course, when there wasn't any federal funding for Aboriginal affairs, but we still formed them, these organisations, working . . . on a weekly basis, having meetings and working towards improving the conditions for Aboriginal people in all those areas.'[12]

In August 1964, she is among those who quit South Australia's Aborigines Advancement League, which is overwhelmingly non-Aboriginal in membership, to join an 'all-Aboriginal' breakaway group, the Aborigines' Progress Association. The breakaway is led by a non-Aboriginal member, Laurie Bryan, whose frustration with the Advancement League boils over when he is told by a churchgoing member of the executive that working on a Sunday is a 'violation of the Sabbath'.[13]

At the Advancement League, Charles Duguid protests about test rockets being fired from Woomera over Aboriginal reserves, but he is now regarded as belonging to another time. The new group draws in young Aboriginal men—Malcolm Cooper, Charlie Perkins, Gordon Briscoe and John Moriarty among them—but Aboriginal matriarch Gladys Elphick soon complains that it is dominated by men and that two non-Aboriginal members, Bryan and Eugene Lumbers, are particularly dominant.

Born in 1904, Elphick was raised at the Point Pearce mission on the Yorke Peninsula. Leaving school at the age of twelve, she married a shearer, was widowed with two sons in 1939 and moved to Adelaide. Remarrying, she worked as a domestic and in the railway workshops, making munitions during World War II; she joined the Aborigines Advancement League. Exempted from the Aborigines Act, she is required to apply to the Aborigines Protection Board for permission to visit her relatives.

Elphick's maternal great-grandmother, Kudnarto, a Kaurna-Ngadjuri woman, became the first Aboriginal woman in South Australia to marry a white man, Tom Adams, in 1848. The Protector of Aborigines gave her away. A newspaper reported, 'She is, for one of her race, remarkably good looking, and has a pleasing expression of countenance.'

He was thirty-seven, a shepherd; she was sixteen and, having attended the Native Establishment School, she subsequently taught her illiterate husband to write.

By the beginning of 1965, young Aboriginal women, several of them from Colebrook, including Lowitja, have gathered around Elphick to form the Council of Aboriginal Women of South Australia—the first all-Aboriginal women's committee in Australia—to help their people, often women, in the areas of greatest need. 'We wanted to show people, and show the government, that we could do things for ourselves,' Elphick will recall. 'They couldn't seem to accept us as intelligent adults. Even Dr Duguid, who was such a true friend, saw us as "his children".'[14]

The women's council affiliates with the Federal Council for the Advancement of Aborigines and Torres Strait Islanders (FCAATSI), and Lowitja, as secretary, attends FCAATSI's annual meetings. When more members of the council want to attend than can be afforded, she declares that she will hitchhike from Adelaide to Canberra: 'I was secretary of the Women's Council and I said, "Any money I've got you people can have it, you can get on the train or whatever, but I'm getting on the road". I'd never hitchhiked before and I was terrified, absolutely terrified. But I did it.'

In the summer of 1965, borrowing an idea from the civil rights campaign in the United States, Charlie Perkins leads a group of Sydney University students on a 'freedom ride' into racially segregated towns in New South Wales in a fact-finding protest supported by Wayside Chapel founder Ted Noffs, who says a prayer on the steps before they leave. Perkins aims to expose the level of persecution faced by Aboriginal people and to say to them, 'second class is not good enough'.

At Walgett, on a blistering hot day, the students picket outside the RSL, with signs that say 'Civil Rights for Aborigines' and 'Aborigines Stand Up for Yourselves'. The town erupts 'like an ant heap'. The students are jeered and spat at and told, 'You're stirring up trouble.

The dirty niggers don't deserve any better and they are happy how they are.'[15]

Perkins sees hatred and confusion boiling to the surface, but also displays of courage and principle. With darkness falling, the street is filled with arguing people; when white men yell and swear at the students, Aboriginal women step out of the crowd and yell back that they are 'gin jockeys' who chase after Aboriginal women in the dark. The women call the men out by name, and Perkins thinks that Walgett will never be the same again. They leave the town, followed by a convoy of cars, and a truck runs them off the road.

At Moree, Perkins attempts to buy tickets so a group of Aboriginal children can enter the public swimming pool. He is told, 'Sorry, darkies not allowed in.' The students are pelted with rotten tomatoes, fruit and eggs, stones and bottles. They are kicked and punched and spat on, and angry white men tell reporters following the protest that 'the only good one's a dead one'. But the mayor relents and the children are let into the swimming pool. They all go swimming for a while and then the police ask the protesters to leave the town. Perkins boards the bus 'literally covered in spit'.[16]

The freedom ride attracts national attention and propels Perkins into the national spotlight. 'The problem is out in the open now,' he tells the Federal Council for the Advancement of Aborigines and Torres Strait Islanders conference in Canberra.

———

On 23 August 1966, a softly spoken Gurindji man, Vincent Lingiari, leads two hundred Aboriginal workers—stockmen, house servants and their families—on a walk-off at the Wave Hill cattle station, eight hundred kilometres south of Darwin, where they work for the British pastoral company Vestey. At Wave Hill they are being paid 'maybe six dollars a week, but not every week', and salt beef and bread; but

Lingiari also tells Dexter Daniels, the Aboriginal organiser of the North Australian Workers' Union, they are 'sick and tired of that Vestey mob living in Gurindji country'.[17] Writer Frank Hardy, looking for a story to write, finds one with the Gurindji: 'I had seen white babies starve and not be fed, I had seen white men fall sick and not be treated, I had seen white women sell themselves for a few shillings worth of groceries, I had seen whites debased and robbed of their self-respect. But no white man, even in the depths of the depression, had suffered as much as the black man suffers now in the height of the nation's boom.'[18]

It is not the first walk-off.

In February 1939, the Yorta Yorta people had walked off the Cummeragunja station over mistreatment and abuse and established a strike camp on the river bank at Barmah.

In May 1946, about six hundred Aboriginal stockmen had walked off more than twenty pastoral properties in the Pilbara region of Western Australia over wages and conditions and the laws that governed them. They had been led by Aboriginal lawmen Dooley Bin Bin (Winyirin), who was born in the Great Sandy Desert, and Clancy McKenna, plus a white radical, Don McLeod. The two Aboriginal strike leaders were jailed for inciting 'natives' to strike. But McLeod won an appeal. In Perth, the Committee for the Defence of Native Rights had been formed to support the strikers, but when its secretary, Reverend Peter Hodge, travelled to Port Hedland, he was arrested for visiting 'natives' 'without permission of the Protector'.

However, at Wave Hill, what begins as a wage strike becomes an epic battle of wills between the Gurindji people and the British pastoral company owned by Lord Vestey. And it is about more than just working conditions.

'We want to live on our land, our way,' Lingiari says, and the land rights movement is born.

In Canberra, at the Easter meetings of the Federal Council for the Advancement of Aborigines and Torres Strait Islanders, Lowitja is at the centre of the fight for Aboriginal rights, surrounded by the ageing legends of the cause and an emerging new generation of activists inspired by the civil rights movement.

They are poor and passionate. Lowitja rolls out her swag and sleeps on the floor at a boarding house called Brassey House: 'All of us activists used to stay at the Brassey, sleep on the floor. We had no money.'

She is especially close to Charles 'Chicka' Dixon, who left Wallaga Lake mission on the New South Wales south coast for Sydney in 1945 and was soon 'sneaking off to meetings of the Aboriginal Progressive Association' at the Ironworkers' Hall at a time when the Ironworkers union was controlled by the Communist Party of Australia.[19]

'Oh Chicka, don't go down there, they'll call you "Red",' his mother would say.

'Well, they've been calling me black for years,' he replies.

Dixon is a recovered alcoholic; he campaigns against the Vietnam War and apartheid in South Africa. Over the course of his life, he will be a stevedore, a Tent Embassy protestor and a university lecturer. He will help to establish the Foundation for Aboriginal Affairs in Sydney, which fosters a generation of activists; and Aboriginal legal and medical services in Redfern. He will chair the Aboriginal Arts Board, represent his people around the world, rub shoulders with prison inmates and prime ministers; and address ten thousand Chinese people in the Great Hall of the People. He will die in 2010, struck down by the asbestosis he contracted while working on the Sydney wharves in the 1960s.[20]

There is a spark between the missionary-raised girl from Central Australia and the radical wharfie from Wallaga Lake. Sometimes they walk to meetings hand in hand, and often she sleeps on his floor, but Dixon is married and Lowitja is proper and churchgoing.

'Chicka Dixon was my friend,' she will recall. 'I'd hitchhike to

Canberra, turn up at the Brassey and I'd be sleeping on Chicka's floor. I wasn't the only one though. He was a union man, a strong union man, and it was at that time that he gave up drinking alcohol too. I remember being there, he had a drink and he didn't have another one after that.

'I was a real strong woman on all that stuff, I wasn't sleeping around. I could have been in his bed, but I was on the floor.

'I did see Chicka an awful lot but, because I was a straight-laced woman, I never had sex with men (not that they didn't try). Chicka was a very good friend of mine, right up until his death. I'd sleep on that floor . . . but I never slept with him, ever.'[21]

These are Lowitja's heady days, filled with fire and passion for the cause: 'We seemed to have a lot of solidarity in those days and it was really a very good feeling to work together towards a cause.

'To get to our meetings, we hitchhiked and pooled our money with a tarpaulin or blanket muster. We stayed in caravan parks or, if somebody was fortunate enough to have enough money to pay for a hotel room, we all camped in there together. In Canberra, that was often at Brassey House, now known as the Brassey Hotel, where the staff kindly turned a blind eye to the fact that the numbers in the breakfast room of a morning often far outnumbered the number of guests they had registered! These were interesting and exciting times—hard too—but times of real unity and solidarity amongst our people.'[22]

In later years, when she is a national figure, but still staying at the Brassey Hotel, there will always be flowers waiting for her in her room.

XXI

By the beginning of 1967, Lowitja has decided that she wants to work among Aboriginal people—and she wants to find her mother.

She applies to join the South Australian Department of Aboriginal Affairs:

And so it was then I started to turn my attention to putting my training into some good purpose in working for my people, because I'd always resolved that I would nurse amongst my own people, but earlier I'd not felt ready for it.

I went to the Department of Aboriginal Affairs, which was a department, of course, that had been in touch with me quite regularly since I . . . completed my training. And I'd continuously said no, I wasn't ready for it. So I made the first contact and said that I would like to take a position, but in the remote areas of Australia and, of course, my motive for joining the Department of Aboriginal Affairs was first to find my mother and second, to do a job in a community as close to Pitjantjatjara lands as I could find.[23]

In March, in the offices of the Public Service Commissioner, in Victoria Square, Adelaide, chief recruiting and training officer R.D. Bakewell writes to Miss Lois O'Donoghue at Belair, where she is living close to the Birralee repatriation hospital. She is offered a job as a temporary welfare officer at Koonibba, a former Lutheran mission on the eastern edge of the vast and featureless Nullarbor Plain, crossed in 1841 by the English explorer and colonial administrator Edward John Eyre, and described in 1865 by the novelist Henry Kingsley as a 'hideous anomaly, a blot on the face of Nature, the sort of place one gets into in bad dreams'.[24]

Koonibba had been visited by Charles Duguid in 1956. At that time, he found that a railing separated the playing areas of the white children and Aboriginal children. The Aboriginal homes were dark and overcrowded; many had been condemned, but not replaced. Before he left, an Aboriginal woman begged him to get her baby back, telling him the child had been very ill and taken to hospital, but months had passed and they had heard nothing since. When he returned to Adelaide, Duguid discovered the baby had been 'placed in a good Christian home in Victoria' at the direction of the Aborigines Protection Board, which was regularly exceeding its authority as the legal guardian of every Aboriginal child and removing children from their parents.

Now, in 1967, Bakewell writes to Miss O'Donoghue:

Dear Madam, Further to your application for employment in the Public Service of South Australia, I am pleased to advise that a position of Temporary Welfare Officer is now available at Koonibba in the Department of Aboriginal Affairs. Your commencing salary will be $2308 per annum in the salary range $2308/3040. Please report to the Director, Mr C.J. Millar, 132 Grenfell Street, Adelaide, at 9.00 a.m. ready to commence duty, on Monday, 17th April, 1967.

When reporting for duty, would you please present your Birth Certificate (or extract) for noting in the records and return to you . . . Yours faithfully . . .

Lowitja does not have a birth certificate.

Before she accepts, however, she is offered an alternative. She can go instead to the opal mining town of Coober Pedy, a dry and barren place where desperate men dig for semi-precious stones almost a thousand kilometres north of Adelaide. Suffocatingly hot in the summer, with cold winter nights, many of the miners live underground, in the cool of the sandstone. In 1921, the *Kalgoorlie Miner* reported that the dugout town, with only one galvanised iron structure above ground that served as a lock-up, had been named Coober Pedy after 'Aboriginal lingo', the words kupa and piti, meaning a 'white man in a hole'.

Coober Pedy will take her back to the edge of Pitjantjatjara country. And perhaps her mother.

The thought of Lily has never left her. But the years apart are filled with questions: 'Yes, all the time. I'm not an angry person, but if ever I was angry, I was angry about what had happened, not for my own sake but for my mother's sake, because I'd always thought about what my mother was feeling and whether in fact she cared, and whether in fact, she ever asked the question, where her children might be.'[25]

She accepts this offer and enrols in a course at Adelaide University that teaches the basics of Pitjantjatjara. It gives her a few words of her mother tongue.

———

On 23 February, federal Cabinet decides to hold a referendum in May to increase the size of the House of Representatives—and to give the federal parliament power to make special laws for Aboriginal people and to count them in the census. The Aboriginal question is the secondary issue and is unanimously supported by the parliament. Labor leader Gough Whitlam says a Yes vote on the Aboriginal question would expunge a national disgrace. 'It is essential in the interests of our nation and in the conscience of all of us that this be carried,' he says.

In March, at the tenth annual meeting of the Federal Council for the Advancement of Aborigines and Torres Strait Islanders at the Albert Hall in Canberra, black and white delegates join hands and sing 'We Shall Overcome'.

On 27 May, Faith Bandler, having declared, 'The eyes of the world are on Australia', wakes fearing the worst. But the result is overwhelming, with 90.77 per cent of Australians voting Yes to include Aboriginal people, and only small pockets of opposition. Kim Beazley senior, who four years earlier had stood in a church at Yirrkala imagining a bark petition, calls it 'an explosion of compassion and concern on the part of the Australian people'.[26] Pat O'Shane—who will be the first Aboriginal woman to become a teacher in Queensland, the first to graduate with a law degree, the first woman to head a government department, and the first Aboriginal magistrate—feels a wave of exhilaration, as though all the past might be swept away, and thinks of her mother, Gladys, who plaited her hair on her first day of school, and told her how important it was to get an education, and didn't live to see the referendum.[27]

Lowitja regards the vote as 'powerfully symbolic'.

In September, Prime Minister Harold Holt announces an Office of Aboriginal Affairs will be established. In November he appoints a three-person Council for Aboriginal Affairs, all of them white men: Reserve Bank Governor H.C. 'Nugget' Coombs for his financial expertise; anthropologist Bill Stanner for his Aboriginal expertise; and public servant Barrie Dexter, a diplomat Holt has met in Vientiane,

Laos, who will be head of the Office of Aboriginal Affairs. All three receive assurances from Holt that he is genuine about reform. He tells Dexter the plight of Aboriginal people is 'very distressing'.

On 17 December 1967, Harold Holt disappears while swimming in the sea.

XXII

Lowitja has not long arrived in Coober Pedy when she hears her mother's name. Outside a store, a group of Aboriginal people are sitting looking at her.

'That's Lily's daughter . . .' she hears.

'Lily . . . I could hear Lily over and over,' she will recall.

'You mob know my mother, Lily?' she asks.

'Uwa,' they reply. Yes.

'What your name?' they ask.

She tells them, 'Lois O'Donoghue.'

One of the women shakes her head: 'Your name Lowitja.'

Speaking in broken English, and the few words of Pitjantjatjara she knows, she learns that this woman is her mother's sister. One of the men is her mother's brother.

'They were happy and crying,' Lowitja recalls many years later. 'I think we brought the town to a standstill. We were so excited.'[28]

Then they tell her that her mother is at Oodnadatta: 'You gotta go Oodnadatta now, right now Oodnadatta.'

After more than thirty years of separation, Lowitja is suddenly close, just two hundred kilometres away. Even on a rough dirt road, she can be there tomorrow.

But now she hesitates. She has barely arrived in Coober Pedy and she has work to do, nursing and running a breakfast program for children, bringing them in from the scattered camps to school. And she wants to talk to her eldest sister, Eileen, and the others, to tell them that she has found their mother. To plan, to do it in a proper way, as she has been raised to do things. To ask, 'How do we do this?'

And her mind is flooded with conflicting emotions, questions that have tormented her since childhood: Why were we separated? Why didn't she come for me? What will I find when I get there? After thirty-three years apart, she needs time to think.

'I was nervous. I didn't know how to meet a mother, I never knew a mother, didn't know what it was to be loved, or kissed, or any of that stuff.'[29]

Lowitja tells her new-found relatives that she can't go to Oodnadatta straight away. So instead, in the days and then the weeks that follow, they visit her at the nurses' quarters at the Aboriginal reserve and they tell her about Lily: that after her five children were taken away by the missionaries, she had other children; that her name is now Lily Woodforde; and that she is a drinker.

It is decided that Eileen will join Lowitja for the reunion and that other family members, who live at a small Aboriginal reserve at Indulkana, north-west of Oodnadatta, will introduce Lily to her daughters. At Indulkana, people live on flinty ground in wurlies of scrap iron and tarpaulins and behind a fence separating them from the Granite Downs pastoral station once owned by Mick O'Donoghue.

Knowing that Lily does not have much, Lowitja and Eileen send her clothes. A dress, a scarf, shoes.

In Oodnadatta, Lily hears that her daughter is coming and she waits, at the edge of the town, staring off into the desert, day after day, from early morning until sundown.

'My mother had heard that I was coming and had been waiting along the road every day for weeks, from first light in the morning.'

It is almost dark, twilight, when they arrive. Lowitja's uncles go to find Lily.

Lowitja is thirty-five years old and has not seen her mother for thirty-three of those years.

Interviewed by a sympathetic journalist two years later, she paints a picture of a mother waiting by the road until she sees her daughters coming. 'We ran to meet each other,' she says. 'She recognised us at once and she cried for joy.'[30]

But it is not an easy meeting.

They do not embrace.

'It was very tense. We were looking forward to it, but we were also nervous because we didn't know whether we should embrace her, kiss her, or how to respond to a mother that we had never known.'

Lily does not speak English and they do not speak Yankunytjatjara.

She is wearing the clothes they have sent her.

It seems to Lowitja that Lily is more excited to see Eileen, the eldest of her daughters. After a while, Lily grows restless, anxious to return home, anxious also that her daughters do not see her home. They tell her they will see her in the morning and she walks off into the night.

They stay at Oodnadatta for five days and Lily never lets them see where she lives, and never lets them see her drink. 'We stayed for five days and she picked us up every morning. She came to the hotel every morning and she dropped us back there every night. Taking us proudly around the town, small town. Introducing us to people. She was obviously very proud of us. But she knew she couldn't provide, so that was her way of steering us away from the camp, the fringe camp, for the whole day. We made no attempt to see where she was living on that trip.'[31]

Lowitja's mind is filled with questions and she asks none of them:

By the time I met my mother, of course, it was far too emotional to talk about. We had language barriers to start with and it was too difficult to talk about the relationship, I guess, of my father and my mother, and I didn't really quite know how to broach the subject. But on the other hand, I'd felt that she'd been hurt enough over the years, that really the mysteries of those things was something that I really was going to have to live with.

In a way, I do regret not being fluent enough in the language to ask her the questions I wanted to ask her—to find out about my father and more details of how I was taken and if she was happy about that and if she agreed with it.[32]

After five days, they leave. But Lowitja's work soon brings her back to Oodnadatta, and this time she asks where her mother is and finds her living in a scrap-iron wurlie on a treeless flat.

She sees her brokenness: 'My mother was a broken woman living in appalling conditions and it was obvious the hurt which she suffered by the removal of five of her children.'[33]

Lowitja's other sisters, Amy and Vi, do not visit their mother at Oodnadatta. If their brother Geoffrey visits her, he does not tell them about it.

In the years that follow, Lowitja will bring Lily south to the city to meet them all, and her grandchildren: 'And she enjoyed that, but she didn't want to stay. She was always ready to get on the train and go back. She didn't live with us, but we . . . let's say we knew her.'[34]

Later, when she speaks of the reunion, as she often will, Lowitja will say that it taught her about the limitlessness of hope and the strength of patience: 'I learnt what hope and patience means—how she had never given up hope of seeing her children again. I also learnt what kinship means to Aboriginal people—how in traditional society everyone has a place and a relationship with all other members of the group. From my mother I also realised what it was to be on the receiving end of racist policies and to have basic human rights denied.'[35]

'I guess the thing that upsets me most is what my mother went through, all those years. I feel quite angry at the mission authorities for not at least sending some photographs so that she could know what we looked like.'[36]

Book Five

The wind across the sandhills

XXIII

It is July 1968 and a geologist, Jim Bowler, reaches down into the wind-blown clay of Lake Mungo, south-west New South Wales, and finds fragments of burned bone. 'This is something I'm not going to touch,' he thinks, pegs the location and returns the following year with archaeologists. They unearth the cremated and crushed remains and take them to Canberra, where paleoanthropologist Alan Thorne painstakingly reconstructs the fragments and identifies them as those of 'a young adult woman of gracile build and small stature'—a young woman burned on a funeral pyre on an ancient shoreline. She becomes known as Mungo Lady, or Mungo Woman. At first, the remains are thought to be twenty-five thousand years old, but then more than forty thousand years old, reaching back to the late Pleistocene era, when the dry Willandra Lakes were full of water and teeming with life.

Five years later, in 1974, not far from Mungo Woman, Bowler finds the skeletal remains of a man, ritually buried in a supine position, his hands crossed on his lap, his remains sprinkled with red ochre powder, thought to have been brought from two hundred kilometres away. In the years that follow, many times, in the quiet of the night, Bowler imagines conversations with the ancient man. 'I say to him,

"What is your message?" And I anticipate his message is, "What have you done to my land? What have you done to my people?"[1]

For years, Mungo Lady and Mungo Man are kept by the Australian National University for scientific investigation. After a long campaign by the Paakantji, Mutthi Mutthi and Ngiyampaa peoples, Mungo Lady is repatriated in January 1992 and placed underground in a decorated safe requiring two keys—one held by traditional owners and the other by scientists. Much later, in November 2017, Mungo Man is returned in an Aboriginal hearse, along with the remains of a hundred other Aboriginal people who lived in the Willandra landscape during the last ice age. They are welcomed back with song and dance.

———

At Coober Pedy, in the dusty morning, Lowitja drives around the scattered Aboriginal camps and brings the children into the reserve, where she showers them, feeds them and dresses them for school. At the end of the day, they take off their school clothes, put their camp clothes back on and she takes them home. She sees around her too much alcohol and too little self-respect, and she tells the parents, 'This is your job!'

'You only apa-cacha [half-caste],' she is told.

'Yeah, I'm half you mob and half that other mob,' she replies.

She also goes out on nursing patrols, driving the bush tracks from camp to camp, knowing that a patrol officer will be making a similar journey at about the same time each week. 'We would usually meet in a dry creek bed, where I would run the clinic and he would do the stores,' she recalls. She finds that those who are still living in traditional shelters, wiltjas, are in better health than those who are living in shanties on the town fringes.

All her life, she will remember working in creek beds and listening to the songs of the bush birds.

She sleeps under the stars, in a swag on the back of her ute close to the Anangu camps. She eats from a tuckerbox and shoots kangaroo along the way, so she can arrive with food.

It was my job to take care of Aboriginal people's needs whatever they were. This meant that I did pretty much everything. I delivered babies, helped with money problems, got medicine to people, and fixed up cuts and broken bones. I used to drive a ute into the outback and take supplies to the Aboriginal people who lived there. Sometimes I would shoot a kangaroo on the way, and they would cook it on their campfire.

We had some very happy times sitting under the trees talking and eating together. They said to me, when I first went there, 'You bring us kangaroo and emu.' When I came back with a kangaroo, they said, 'Where emu?'

I said, 'No, I can't shoot emu, you're not going to get an emu from me, wiya (no).'

So they said, 'Two kangaroo then, two kangaroo . . .'[2]

She laughs at the memory of it.

In those days I mostly treated sores. There was no malnutrition; kids were generally healthy. It was a beautiful experience because most people were well. All the confinements went well. It was unusual for things to go wrong, because grandmothers delivered babies. We had contact with the Flying Doctor who would help us with diagnosis and we had a big kit of prescriptions, and made many of the decisions about diagnosis and treatment.

I had a gun with me, and I would shoot a roo, and take it into the camps and sleep under the stars. I remember the station owners on all those properties would have 'high tea'. They

would dress up every night for dinner. I would visit to keep
the medications in their refrigeration and see them all dressed
up. I often thought that they might offer a shower after knowing
I was camping out and doing it rough, but they never did. Nor
did they invite me in for tea. I would always find myself back in
the camp, but I loved it.[3]

———

In Tokyo in February 1968, a young Aboriginal boxer, Lionel Rose,
raised in a small Aboriginal settlement of tumbledown shacks called
Jackson's Track, fights his way to become the Bantamweight Champion
of the World. He returns a national hero, an Aboriginal icon and a
symbol of the emergent Aboriginal citizen freed of protectors and
welfare boards.

In Melbourne Alfred Deakin's grandson, the journalist Rohan
Rivett, who had studied with Manning Clark at Oxford, survived
the Burma Railway and campaigned to save Max Stuart from the
gallows in South Australia, writes, 'The long-neglected Aboriginal
people of Victoria found suddenly that they had produced a national
hero capable of turning the city upside down.'[4] Rose is made an MBE
(Member of the British Empire) and named Australian of the Year,
the first Aboriginal person to receive this award. 'One hundred and
eighty-two years ago one of my mob would have been a dead cert for
this,' he quips.

Australians take him to their hearts, as they will Evonne Goolagong, when she wins Wimbledon in 1971, and Cathy Freeman, when
she runs to glory at the Sydney Olympics a generation later. But in
the 1968 Boyer Lectures, anthropologist Bill Stanner says Aboriginal
people are the subject of a great Australian silence and a cult of forgetfulness: 'It is a structural matter, a view from a window which has
been carefully placed to exclude a whole quadrant of the landscape,'

he says. 'What may well have begun as a simple forgetting of other possible views turned under habit and over time into something like a cult of forgetfulness practised on a national scale. We have been able for so long to disremember the Aborigines that we are now hard put to keep them in mind even when we most want to do so.'[5]

In Darwin in December 1968, the Yirrkala tribes, whose bark petition has been ignored, go to the Northern Territory Supreme Court to put a stop to mining on their land. It is the first 'land rights' claim by Aboriginal people—*Milirrpum v Nabalco Pty Ltd and the Commonwealth of Australia*. Despite his position as chairman of the Council for Aboriginal Affairs, 'Nugget' Coombs condemns the government for its dishonesty and the company for its haste. 'What happened in Sydney Cove in 1788 is being repeated on Gove Peninsula,' he says.[6]

Between 1967 and 1973, Lowitja works with 'tribal, semi-tribal and detribalised Aborigines' for the South Australian Department of Aboriginal Affairs as a welfare officer–nursing sister at Coober Pedy, Oodnadatta, the North-West Aboriginal Reserve (consisting of most of what would become the Anangu Pitjantjatjara Yankunytjatjara Lands) and Point McLeay, birthplace of Ngarrindjeri preacher, inventor and writer David Unaipon, whom she knows as an old man and who will one day be the face on a $50 note.

In 1971, Lowitja returns to Adelaide, where she is given responsibility for Aboriginal welfare needs in country and city areas. A large part of her work involves helping Aboriginal people find employment and housing. She becomes a member of an Aboriginal–Police Liaison Committee and the Aboriginal Legal Rights Movement. She is seconded to the Aborigines Resources Division of the Department for Community Welfare as the Aboriginal liaison officer, advising Aboriginal groups and liaising between state and federal government departments—the first Aboriginal person employed in South Australia in that role. She is the only Aboriginal person in the department.

In March 1969, Charlie Perkins is hired as a research officer in Canberra in the federal Office of Aboriginal Affairs. He finds it shattering, demoralising and degrading. 'People set out deliberately to show me where I belonged (or should belong), and to make me feel completely an inferior person and nonentity in Aboriginal affairs,' he will write in his autobiography, *A Bastard Like Me*.[7] On one occasion, he is told, 'The trouble with you mixed bloods is, you're not much good—you're bastards, the worst of both worlds.'[8] There are just four Aboriginal staff—Perkins and three Aboriginal liaison officers. Just a front, he believes, like a gum tree, picturesque objects for people to gaze upon. Cattle dogs, black messenger boys.[9]

He rises with a match in his hand, provocative, controversial, insisting on being heard.

———

In Easter 1970, the annual meeting of the Federal Council for the Advancement of Aborigines and Torres Strait Islanders (FCAATSI) unravels chaotically. Young activists from Sydney, Melbourne and Brisbane no longer speak of 'black and white together', but black power. They look to the Black Panther Party in the United States, and the Black Consciousness Movement in apartheid South Africa. They soak up the ideas of Stokely Carmichael, Huey Newton, Angela Davis and Steve Biko. The poet Kath Walker, who will later change her name to Oodgeroo Noonuccal, and whose son, Denis Walker, will become founding president of the short-lived Australian Black Panther organisation, argues passionately for Indigenous people to take control of their own affairs.

During a torchlight procession to Parliament House, placards bearing the names of vanished Aboriginal nations are placed against a wall.

Kath Walker recites a poem, a lament:

Here, at the invaders' talk-talk place,
We who are the strangers now,
Come with sorrow in our hearts.
The Bora Ring, the Corroborees,
The sacred ceremonies,
Have all gone. All gone.

The conference is a shambles.[10] Gordon Bryant, the organisation's vice-president, and soon to be the first federal Minister for Aboriginal Affairs with a supporting department, is booed and hissed and derided as a 'great white father'. Barrie Pittock, a non-Indigenous Quaker scientist, proposes amendments to the FCAATSI constitution to create an all-black executive and restrict voting rights to those of Indigenous descent. The motions fail to get the necessary two-third majority, but the organisation splits, with Doug Nicholls and Kath Walker leading a breakaway that becomes the National Tribal Council. It lasts less than three years.

Having harnessed support for the 1967 referendum, the federal council begins its decline. White advocates, including Charles Duguid, now find themselves shunted aside. Duguid blames 'a clamant minority of part-Aborigines': 'In the past, the white newcomers refused to co-operate with the Aborigines; today, a clamant minority of part-Aborigines refuses to co-operate with the white people or with the rest of their own race. There is increasing talk of "Black Power", and propaganda couched in the language used by some Negroes of the United States. Such isolationism will benefit neither the Aborigines as a race nor Australia as a nation,' he writes.[11]

In his memoirs, Duguid will observe: 'In 1930 it was believed that the Aborigines were dying out, and some Australians hoped that they would. To claim at that time that they were people of worth and ability was to be branded a fanatic—as indeed I was.'[12] He writes of great forward steps, but also lingering malevolence and alcoholism.

In Alice Springs in 1934, the drunks he had seen lying in the gutters had been white men; by 1964, they were Aborigines. 'The white man's privilege had become the black man's curse.'[13]

There were also unintended catastrophic consequences from the campaign for equal wages for Aboriginal stockmen. When the Conciliation and Arbitration Commission delivered its historic ruling in 1966, Chief Judge Richard Kirby had believed their decision would be seen as 'the greatest contribution' he and other members of the commission had made to Australian society. 'We do not flinch from the results of this decision which we consider is the only proper one to be made at this point in Australia's history,' the commission ruled. 'There must be one industrial law, similarly applied, to all Australians, Aboriginal or not.'

But when the ruling came into force in 1968, many stockmen and their families were turned off properties—where they had lived and worked, and had strong traditional connections—by owners who refused to pay Aboriginal stockmen the same wages as white men. People drifted into towns and unemployment. Four decades later, Aboriginal lawyer Noel Pearson would say it paved the way for a 'descent into hell', along with social security income and drinking laws.

In April 1971, the Yolŋu people of Yirrkala, having failed to move political hearts with their bark petition, also fail in court when Judge Richard Blackburn rules in the Northern Territory Supreme Court in *Milirrpum v Nabalco Pty Ltd* that the 'doctrine of communal native title does not form, and never has formed, part of the law of any part of Australia'. But Blackburn acknowledges the existence of 'a subtle and elaborate system' of Aboriginal law relating to land.

The Yolŋu's lawyer, Ted Woodward, believes this provides a basis for land rights legislation. But he looks at the composition and disposition of the High Court and does not appeal. His decision is vindicated a few months later when he hears that Chief Justice Garfield Barwick has described the native title claim as 'a lot of nonsense, or words to that effect'.[14]

Judge Blackburn also writes a memorandum seen by both sides of parliament, suggesting a system of land rights might be 'morally right, or socially expedient'.

On 12 July 1971, an Aboriginal flag is flown for the first time, on National Aborigines Day, in Victoria Square, Adelaide. Designed by artist and land rights activist Harold Thomas, a Luritja man born on the banks of the Todd River in Alice Springs, it is tricolour: black for the Aboriginal people, red for the earth, and yellow for the sun. It is flown again on Australia Day 1972 at an Aboriginal tent embassy established outside Parliament House in Canberra by activists Michael Anderson, Billy Craigie, Bert Williams and Tony Coorey.

Prime Minister Billy McMahon is limping impotently to defeat after twenty-three years of conservative government; in his Australia Day address he rejects the idea of Aboriginal land rights in favour of highly conditional special purpose leases. By April, the tent embassy has become a focus for Aboriginal activists from across Australia, including Gary Foley, who says that Aboriginal people are 'aliens in our own land, so like other aliens, we needed an embassy'.

XXIV

Whitlam arrives like a whirlwind.

Impatient and ambitious, for two extraordinary weeks after he is sworn in as Australia's twenty-first prime minister, on 5 December 1972, Whitlam and his deputy, Lance Barnard, govern as a duumvirate, dividing up all the ministerial responsibilities between the two of them, while waiting for final counting to be completed. In the first week, they abolish conscription; they release jailed draft resisters and return the last remaining troops from Vietnam; they remove restrictions on access to the contraceptive pill; they begin talks in Paris to establish diplomatic relations with the People's Republic of China; they reopen the equal pay case to remove discrimination against women, with future High Court judge Mary Gaudron engaged as counsel for the Commonwealth; they abolish the British honours system, including knighthoods in Australia; they ban visits to Australia by racially selected sporting teams, including the Springboks from apartheid South Africa; and they announce $4 million of major grants for the performing arts.

In his policy speech, It's Time, at the Blacktown Civic Centre, Whitlam has promised an unparalleled reform agenda, including a new relationship with Aboriginal people:

We will legislate to give Aborigines land rights—not just because their case is beyond argument, but because all of us as Australians are diminished while the Aborigines are denied their rightful place in this nation . . . All of us as Australians have to insist that we can do so much better as a nation. We ought to be angry, with a deep determined anger, that a country as rich and skilled as ours should be producing so much inequality, so much poverty, so much that is shoddy and sub-standard. We ought to be angry—with an unrelenting anger—that our aborigines have the world's highest infant mortality rate. We ought to be angry at the way our so-called leaders have kept us in the dark—Parliament itself as much as the people—to hide their own incapacity and ignorance.

Whitlam announces, on 14 December, that there will be a royal commission to inquire into appropriate ways to recognise Aboriginal land rights in the Northern Territory. The commissioner will be Ted Woodward, now Justice Woodward, former lawyer for the Yolŋu people of Yirrkala.

On 19 December, a new federal Department of Aboriginal Affairs is established. State governments, with the exception of Queensland, agree to transfer policy planning and administrative functions to the federal government. State public servants become federal public servants without moving their desks and Gordon Bryant becomes the initial Aboriginal Affairs minister: 'He paid his dues and he could sing the blues,' says Charlie Perkins, who regards him as a good man.[15]

In February 1973, Bryant invites eighty Aboriginal people to a conference in Canberra to begin forming a representative body to advise the minister on policy which will ultimately be called the National Aboriginal Consultative Committee (NACC). Addressing them, Whitlam says: 'If there is one ambition my Government places above all others, if there is one achievement for which I hope we shall

be remembered, if there is one cause for which future historians will
salute us, it is this: that the Government I lead removed a stain from
our national honour and brought back justice and equality to the
Aboriginal people.'[16]

———————

Lowitja is living in a cream-brick flat in St Marys, Adelaide, when, in
September 1973, she applies for two roles in the new federal department—senior liaison officer and executive officer. Her referees
include South Australia's director of Aboriginal Affairs, John Millar,
who has allowed the Aboriginal women's council to use his office for
their evening meetings; Matron Irene Kennedy, at the Royal Adelaide
Hospital; and Aboriginal activists Gladys Elphick, MBE, and Natascha
McNamara.

Lowitja transfers from the Aboriginal Resources Division of the
South Australian Department of Community Welfare to the Commonwealth Department of Aboriginal Affairs in Adelaide and is seconded
to Canberra as part of a special working group to coordinate the NACC
elections. Aboriginal staff are engaged across the country to establish an
Aboriginal electoral roll and register voters; they succeed in registering
about forty thousand people. It will be the first time in any election in
Australia that prisoners have been given the vote.

On 23 November 1973, in a broadcast on the eve of these elections,
Whitlam says that nothing like it has been done before. 'Our most
important objective now is to restore to Aboriginals the power to
make their own decisions about their way of life,' he says. 'Already
the Department of Aboriginal Affairs has been transferring responsibility for community affairs from Government superintendents
and managers to Aboriginals themselves.' The guiding principle in
Aboriginal affairs, after the failures and devastations of exclusion,
protection, assimilation and integration, is now self-determination.

The government intends the forty-one-member NACC, the first elected body representing Indigenous Australians, to be 'a forum for the expression of Aboriginal opinion'. It has no statutory authority and is empowered only to offer advice. Once elected, however, 'the black parliament' drafts a constitution, attempts unsuccessfully to rename itself the National Aboriginal Congress, and seeks control of the federal government's $117 million Aboriginal Affairs budget. Their demand is rejected.

The NACC clashes with Jim Cavanagh, who has replaced Gordon Bryant as Aboriginal Affairs minister, and they demand his resignation. Cavanagh blames six dissident 'part-Aborigines'. But he also clashes with Charlie Perkins, who has become Australia's top Aboriginal public servant, following a life-saving kidney transplant.

Drawn back to Canberra in 1973 by the election of the Whitlam government, Perkins has been promoted from a mid-ranking Class 7 position to the level of assistant secretary in the new Aboriginal Affairs department. Opinionated and outspoken, Perkins criticises the department, the government and his ministers and is warned, reprimanded and suspended. In January, he describes the Minister for the Northern Territory, Rex Patterson, as an 'ultra conservative', and a 'hick from the sticks'. He says Cavanagh treats him like a 'black office boy' and is too influenced by a 'white backlash'. In February, he describes the West Australian Liberal and Country parties, which are on the brink of government in that state, as the most racist in the world.

On 28 February 1974, the Queen opens the federal parliament. Perkins, who has been suspended, is among Aboriginal demonstrators outside. 'We are here for the people who are starving and whose kids' bones are turning to chalk,' he says. Police arrive and take him to the Department of Aboriginal Affairs, where three Aboriginal men, Bobby McLeod, Reuben John Smith and Neville Foster, are holding senior staff at gunpoint. McLeod, an activist from Wreck Bay, has told them, 'I'm going to keep you here for four or five days and teach you to starve.' Perkins takes the bullets out of his gun and is hailed a hero, but tensions remain high.

In March 1975, Perkins is ordered to take a year's leave, without pay. He drives to Alice Springs with his three children, does odd jobs, becomes the first chairman of the Central Land Council, and campaigns for land rights. He writes his autobiography, *A Bastard Like Me*, on a Literature Board grant; and goes to the United Nations on what Cavanagh calls an international tour to defame and denigrate Australia.

Lowitja, meanwhile, is rising through the public service with calm and charm rather than volatility, and in June 1974 is promoted to senior liaison officer, Class 8, in the programme consultation section of the federal department. She travels widely, consulting with Aboriginal communities and organisations. But, like Perkins, she finds the department remote from Aboriginal people and reluctant to embrace 'the task of assisting Aboriginal people to manage their own affairs'.

Ultimately she asks to be transferred back to Adelaide. By March 1975 she is regional assistant director there on a salary of $14,653–$15,224 (Class 9). Now in a position of authority that would have shocked Aboriginal protectors, she searches out her file in the sad and dusty records of the department, and is disappointed by its contents: 'About the only thing that was written on it was my name and that I was half-caste,' she later records.[17]

In Adelaide, journalist Stewart Cockburn writes a piece in *The Advertiser* called 'The Saga of Lois O'Donoghue: An Aboriginal leader in a white society':

A little over 40 years ago, Lois O'Donoghue was a bright-eyed, brown-skinned infant, newly-born into a tribe of nomadic Aborigines in the remote North West Reserve of SA. Lois's mother was a full blood of the tribe. Her father was the white manager of a cattle station where the tribe occasionally called for some variation in its staple diet of native animals and plants. Lois's mother still lives with her tribe near Oodnadatta. Her daughter, now a poised, smiling, mature, self-possessed professional woman, has just become Acting Regional Director for SA of the Department of Aboriginal Affairs.

I talked with her for more than an hour yesterday in her comfortable office on the seventh floor of a Grenfell Street insurance building where she administers the work of a dozen or so Aboriginal and white colleagues, including three university graduates. Like the brilliant Margaret Valadian, Australia's first Aboriginal woman university graduate, who was interviewed in an ABC International Women's Year TV programme last weekend, Miss O'Donoghue has helped explode an old, convenient but false white prejudice. She has demonstrated that, given a fair go, tribal Aborigines can not only be fully assimilated or integrated into white society in one generation, but can assume comfortable and undisputed leadership roles in that society.[18]

There is no mention of her mother's grief or alcoholism. Cockburn writes that the missionaries 'persuaded her mother' that it would be best for her daughter to be raised by them and that Lowitja 'drifted into domestic service' after Colebrook, almost carelessly. A 'white colleague' tells Cockburn she has been promoted on the strength of her abilities. 'She can also take a lot of kicks and keep coming with a smile on her face and with a look which tells you she isn't going to be beaten!' he is told.

In the chill winter, in June of its final tumultuous year, the Whitlam government succeeds in passing a Racial Discrimination Act. Three times it was introduced by Attorney-General Lionel Murphy and lapsed. At the fourth attempt, the new attorney-general is Kip Enderby. In his second reading speech introducing the bill, Enderby states the case that 'all human beings are born free and equal in dignity and rights and that any doctrine of superiority based on racial differentiation is scientifically false, morally condemnable, socially unjust and dangerous and without any justification'.

The government also passes the Aboriginal and Torres Strait Islanders (Queensland Discriminatory Laws) Act, releasing Aboriginal people in Queensland from what lawyer and activist Noel Pearson will call—when he delivers Whitlam's eulogy—the vast and cold and capricious powers of the managers and superintendents, 'those discriminations that humiliated and degraded our people'.

In July, Lowitja applies for the position of regional director of the South Australian branch of the Department of Aboriginal Affairs (Class 10), on a salary of $15,800–16,375 and by September she has been provisionally appointed. She is the first Aboriginal person—and the first woman—to head any federal regional office. Department secretary Barrie Dexter believes she brings 'a special quality to the administration of Aboriginal affairs in South Australia'.[19]

In eight years, she has risen from a nurse and welfare officer in the remote opal mining town of Coober Pedy to responsibility for the implementation of Aboriginal policy in South Australia. In twenty-six years, she has risen from the role of domestic servant. She replaces the retiring John Millar, a gentle, quietly spoken man who joined the department 'starry-eyed' in 1954 when—as he tells the Adelaide Advertiser—Aboriginal people were 'regarded as a dying race'.[20]

The newspaper publishes a picture of Lowitja standing beside Millar. He was South Australia's last Protector of Aborigines.

XXV

By August 1975, Gough Whitlam's government is in disarray. But on 16 August he flies to Daguragu, Wattie Creek, to formalise the return of land to the Gurindji people, nine years after they walked off the Vestey-owned Wave Hill cattle station. They had walked to Daguragu, tired of being 'treated like dogs', and there Vincent Lingiari declared, 'We want to live on our land, our way', and told the novelist Frank Hardy, 'This bin Gurindji country long time before them Vestey mob.'

During the flight, 'Nugget' Coombs urges Whitlam to keep his speech short and invest the day with a sense of ceremony; he tells him a story, recounted by anthropologist Bill Stanner, of how Aboriginal elders in 1835 placed a handful of soil into John Batman's hand to formalise the early Australian settler's attempted treaty for the land that became Melbourne. Coombs suggests that the prime minister reverse the gesture when he hands the Gurindji back their land.

On the bank of a small stream, on 6 June 1835, Batman signed a treaty for five hundred thousand acres of land as rich as he had ever seen. He paid the Aboriginal 'chiefs' in goods—twenty pairs of blankets, thirty tomahawks, one hundred knives, fifty pairs of scissors, thirty looking glasses, two hundred handkerchiefs, one hundred pounds of flour and six shirts, and agreed to pay yearly rent or tribute of one hundred pairs of blankets, one hundred knives, one hundred tomahawks, fifty suits of clothing, fifty looking glasses, fifty pairs of scissors and five tons of flour. Colonial authorities declared the treaty void. Batman, who imagined himself the greatest landowner in the world, died four years later, abandoned and wasted by syphilis.

And so Whitlam pours sand into Vincent Lingiari's hand.

'On this great day, I, Prime Minister of Australia, speak to you on behalf of the Australian people,' he declares, 'all those who honour and love this great land we live in. I want to acknowledge that we Australians still have much to do to redress the injustice and oppression that have for so long been the lot of Black Australians. I want to promise you that this act of restitution which we perform today will not stand alone—your fight was not for yourselves alone and we are determined that Aboriginal Australians everywhere will be helped by it.

'Vincent Lingiari, I solemnly hand to you these deeds as proof, in Australian law, that these lands belong to the Gurindji people and I put into your hands part of the earth itself as a sign that this land will be the possession of you and your children forever.'

Lingiari replies, 'Let us live happily together as mates.'

A photograph is taken, and then taken again, and, when the moment has been captured, Lingiari drops the dust behind his back.

The Gurindji call Whitlam judgadi—the big man—while Lingiari's name is written into legend and song.

———

In Adelaide, as she rises through the bureaucracy, Lowitja makes a point of consulting with Aboriginal people, thrashing out with them their areas of greatest need: 'It was the early days of funding of Aboriginal community organisations, and I began early to consult Aboriginal people and the organisations and brought them in annually to talk about the budget that we would put as a state to the federal government and, of course, the budget was always far in excess of what was available to us and so I had to get Aboriginal people to see that our expectations, of course, weren't going to be realised.'[21]

She is also acutely aware of her mother's poverty and it scratches at her conscience: 'My mother was in dire need but so was everyone around her. I wasn't necessarily in the position of being able to make things right for her, and even if I was, I thought about the problems of nepotism. How could I provide for her ahead of others?'[22]

In Canberra, department secretary Barrie Dexter sees her struggling with it. Years later, he will say no one could ever understand the pressures she faced: 'It weighed on her conscience the whole time.'[23]

Just two months after being provisionally appointed as South Australia's regional director of the Aboriginal Affairs department, on 7 November she abruptly resigns. She is frustrated that, after consulting with Aboriginal people about their areas of greatest need, a red line would often be drawn through these plans by bureaucrats in Canberra who 'decided they knew what was better for us'.

Dear Mr Dexter,
I hereby notify you that I am declining my provisional promotion to the position of Director (Class 10) and also wish to tender my resignation from the position of Assistant Director (Class 9), Regional Office, Adelaide, as from the close of business on 31st December, 1975, reasons being those expressed to you in a recent telephone conversation.
Yours sincerely
L. O'Donoghue

She writes in a notebook: 'Resigned out of frustration with the bureaucracy in Canberra.'

Four days later, 11 November, Remembrance Day, and the anniversary of the day they hanged Ned Kelly, Governor-General John Kerr dismisses the Whitlam government, which has been rocked by scandal and chaos. Liberal leader Malcolm Fraser is appointed caretaker prime minister. 'Well may we say God save the Queen,' Whitlam declares on the steps of the parliament, 'because nothing will save the Governor-General.' Applause and cheering. Whitlam urges Australians to maintain their rage and enthusiasm, but Fraser is elected in a landslide.

Lowitja goes back to Quorn, where she lived as a child at the Colebrook Home. She buys a small cottage opposite the hospital, and close to the school.

———

Australia Day, 26 January 1976, Miss Lois O'Donoghue, of Quorn, is made a Member of the Order of Australia (AM) for service to the Aboriginal community—the first Aboriginal woman to be inducted into the new Australian honours system.

In February, she tells the ABC's current affairs program *This Day Tonight* that she resigned from the Aboriginal Affairs department over 'continued frustrations with the bureaucracy in Canberra'.[24] She says she is appalled by the attitudes of 'professional public servants with no knowledge of the needs and aspirations of the Aboriginals'.

In Adelaide, *The Advertiser* editorialises:

The resignation of Miss Lois O'Donoghue as a senior Aboriginal public servant in SA is a sad setback for her people's cause. Since the middle of last year, Miss O'Donoghue had been regional director of the Department of Aboriginal Affairs. The significance of the appointment, made strictly on merit, was its demonstration that, given a fair go, former tribal Aboriginals can not only be fully integrated into white society in one generation, but can assume effective and undisputed leadership roles in that society . . . Miss O'Donoghue was not radical in her attitudes. She was prepared to see both sides of every question, and her personal charm was an immense advantage in administration and negotiation. The fact that she has been driven to the point of resignation by what she has bluntly described as 'continued frustrations with the bureaucracy in Canberra' seems a depressing commentary on white ineptitude . . . It is one thing for a bitter, turbulent Aboriginal leader like Mr Charles Perkins to throw in the towel. It is quite another for a calm and controlled woman like Miss O'Donoghue to feel she must do so.[25]

Lowitja gets a job with the Education department as an Aboriginal liaison officer at Port Augusta, not far from Quorn at the top of the Spencer Gulf, dealing with 'the problems in the town and the problems within the school', revolving around racism.

But it is not long before she returns to Canberra.

Fraser has gone to the election promising 'an urgent inquiry in consultation with the Aboriginal people' into the role of the National Aboriginal Consultative Committee. In March, at a meeting of the NACC, new Aboriginal Affairs minister Ian Viner says he is keenly aware of the organisation's 'unhappy history' and he senses the disillusionment of Aboriginal people.[26]

The inquiry is chaired by anthropologist Les Hiatt. Lowitja is one of three Aboriginal members. Public meetings and hearings are held at forty different locations around Australia from May to July, in cities and towns and remote communities. In August, the review finds the NACC has not been effective in providing advice to the government, in part because of a lack of a clearly defined role, the disinclination of the elected members to accept a merely consultative role, and 'the state of mutual hostility that prevailed between the NACC and the Department of Aboriginal Affairs from the beginning'.

The following year the NACC is replaced by a National Aboriginal Conference (NAC). Where the NACC was comprised of elected representatives from forty-one electorates, representing eight hundred Aboriginal communities, the NAC will have elected state branches and a ten-member national executive whose charter is 'to provide a forum for the expression of Aboriginal views'.

Lowitja, who has grave doubts about popular elections in Aboriginal communities, had suggested a different model, but now decides to run for election herself.

In the winter of 1976, Aboriginal communities from across the Anangu lands—Pitjantjatjara, Yankunytjatjara and Ngaanyatjarra—gather at Amata, established with the name 'Musgrave Park' as a government station in 1961 at the western end of the Musgrave Ranges in South Australia; here they form the Pitjantjatjara Council. They talk about their problems and they talk about land and how to get it back—including Granite Downs, where Mick and Tom O'Donoghue once dreamed the dreams of poor men on land containing ancient songs that they did not understand.

On 1 December 1976, South Australian premier Don Dunstan appoints Doug Nicholls to be the state's governor, the first Aboriginal person to be appointed to a vice-regal role. Dunstan was the last white president of the Federal Council for the Advancement of Aborigines and Torres Strait Islanders, and the architect of South Australia's Aboriginal Lands Trust Act in 1966—Australia's first attempt to legislate for land rights, by ensuring title to reserve land will be held in trust for the benefit of Aboriginal people.

Dunstan believes that Nicholls will be a great figurehead for his state, a role model for Aboriginal people, 'and at the same time an indication to the whole of the community of the value of Aboriginal people to it'.[27] In Cabinet, he has argued forcefully for an Aboriginal governor, and he resists the reservations of the departing governor, scientist Mark Oliphant, who writes to Dunstan, querying Nicholls' capabilities and expressing concern about the pressures which would be put on him from 'tribal associations'. *The Australian* newspaper writes what Dunstan calls 'a vicious piece', which accuses him of trying to 'downgrade the office'. It argues that Nicholls is inexperienced in the areas and skills needed by a governor—law, politics and public life— although his life has in fact been shaped by all of these things.

'The man we chose was Sir Douglas Nicholls—one of the outstanding and most highly regarded members of his race,' Dunstan will write in his memoirs, titled *Felicia*. 'Doug had been a great and successful athlete, a famous Australian Rules footballer, became a Pastor in the Church of Christ and a leading campaigner for his people. I had known him well and admired him for many years, and we had campaigned together often. I knew him to be a man of capability, and with such endearing qualities that South Australians would in a short time take him to their hearts.'[28]

As Dunstan has predicted, Nicholls quickly endears himself to South Australians; but after a few brief months in office he suffers a stroke and never fully recovers from its effects. Lowitja says to Dunstan, whom she knows and loves as a friend, 'You waited too long.'

XXVI

'I am not going to make a lot of promises to you, like white politicians do, but I am going to say that I will work hard for you, to get better conditions for Aboriginal people throughout my electorate . . . On November 12th give your vote to Lois O'Donoghue.'

It is Spring 1977 and Lowitja is an Aboriginal politician on the stump.

In October and November she campaigns across a wide and desolate area of South Australia, covering Ceduna, Streaky Bay, Port Augusta, Quorn, Hawker, Leigh Creek, Marree, Coward Springs, Anna Creek, Oodnadatta and Coober Pedy. She travels by train and wears out the tyres on her car and buys retreads. She campaigns as 'Lois O'Donoghue AM—Your candidate' on a platform of obtaining better housing, employment, health and education.

In her campaign literature, she says she was born at Indulkana, her mother is Lily Woodforde of Oodnadatta, she spent her childhood in the Colebrook Home, has happy memories of her childhood in the area, is a trained nursing sister, has long experience in Aboriginal affairs and was the former regional director of the Department of Aboriginal Affairs in South Australia. She is a home and school liaison officer at Port Augusta, chairman of the Port Augusta Housing Committee, and is involved in a host of other organisations.

On 12 November, thirty-two thousand Aboriginal people around Australia vote to elect thirty-five representatives from three hundred candidates. In her region, Lowitja is elected. When the South Australian branch meets, she is elected chairperson. Then when the national executive meets for the first time in February 1978, she is elected national chairperson. It fills her with pride.

The first meetings of the National Aboriginal Conference (NAC) are volatile, fuelled by events in Queensland where the deeply conservative government of Johannes (Joh) Bjelke-Petersen is attempting to facilitate bauxite mining on the Aurukun Aboriginal reserve. Aurukun people, led by Donald Peikinna, chairman of the Aurukun Council, challenge it in court, but the Queensland government eventually wins on appeal to the Privy Council in London.

Bjelke-Petersen is also attempting to block the sale of the Archer River cattle station to traditional owners led by John Koowarta, because he does not believe Aboriginal people should be able to acquire large areas of land. This matter is also dragged through the courts in a case that tests the validity of the Racial Discrimination Act. Koowarta ultimately wins, but, in a final act of spite, the Queensland government converts his lease into a national park, and he dies a broken man.

NAC members 'new to the game' want to convene at the Aboriginal Tent Embassy outside Parliament House and call for the resignation of Queensland Liberal Party senator Neville Bonner, who is the first Aboriginal man to sit in the national parliament. Lowitja warns them that they are risking their last chance at credibility. In Adelaide, a newspaper profile describes her as 'a new breed of Aboriginal politician'—not screaming with outrage but looking to work within the system, a 'cool-thinking, decisive Aboriginal leader' who wants 'a new deal for Aboriginal politics'.[29]

She comes to know Malcolm Fraser, and to like him. Fraser is despised by Labor voters; 'Kerr's cur', Whitlam had called him. But in December 1976, his government completes the passage of Whitlam's Aboriginal Land Rights (Northern Territory) Act—the first legislation in Australia enabling Aboriginal people to claim land rights and unprecedented for a conservative government with a support base that includes the mining and pastoral industries.

On Sunday 3 December 1978, Lowitja delivers the fourth annual Lalor Address on Community Relations, an event commemorating the Battle of the Eureka Stockade in 1854 and designed to promote the principles of the Racial Discrimination Act. She is introduced by the flamboyant and controversial Commissioner for Community Relations, Al Grassby, who introduces her as a significant nation-builder who occupies 'the position of highest authority in relation to Aboriginal Australia'.

Her address is shaped around the theme 'Australians—We Must Know Who We Are'. 'The fact is that after nearly 200 years Aboriginal Australians and the newcomers have hardly yet come to know each other, to understand each other and, above all, to respect each other,' she says. 'The responsibility for this clearly lies with the conquerors of the continent who took possession of every single hectare and then resettled at will, moved and removed and moved again. The original owners lost the long battle of the frontiers against the invaders. So today we have the victorious and the dispossessed. It is true that significant steps have been taken in recent years to make peace, to rectify some of the worst features of the occupation and expropriation, but despite significant progress and a great deal of goodwill among Australian men and women, it can hardly be said even today that the newcomers since 1788 have come to know us and who we are.'

She speaks of her life:

My own experience has been a mixture of sadness and pleasure. At the age of two years I was removed from my mother during the early 1930s, 'to be given a better chance in life'. The Protector of Aborigines took over guardianship from my mother. I was reared in an institution for half-caste children, administered by the United Aborigines Mission. There I remained until I was 16 years of age.

Never during those years was I told or even allowed to ask questions about my parentage. I was forbidden to speak the language, although during those years we had many opportunities to hear language spoken and to hear the legends as told in secret by the new children coming into the home. But of course, they soon forgot, because they were forced to forget the old ways. Apart from my very basic needs to know and be nurtured by my own mother, to speak my own language and understand my own culture, I was well cared for and received a good education. After all, the only sin my mother committed was that she was a full-blood and she dared to give birth to a half-caste child.

She says her wounds have healed, but the scars remain. And she quotes Kath Walker:

Pour your pitcher of wine into the wide river
And where is your wine? There is only the river . . .

————

One night at her home at Quorn, Gordon Smart, who fell for her when they met at the repatriation hospital at Belair, knocks on her door. She smiles with the memory of it: 'I bought a house at Quorn because I knew Quorn quite well because we grew up there, and he came knocking on the door one night . . . and he never left!'

On 5 January 1979, the two of them stand in a clearing at Pichi Richi Pass, in the hills above Quorn, and marry. Her dress is a shade of coral, with matching chiffon wrap. A white silk horseshoe, wedding bells and a cross hang from her wrist, a pink silk rose forms her corsage. She is forty-six years old, he is sixty, and they have waited sixteen years to be married.

A small organ has been brought from the church on the back of a truck and hymns are sung. Friends joke that the hills that day became 'Lowitja's Cathedral'.

Smart's children do not attend the wedding, or know anything of it. Nor does Lowitja's mother: 'No, she didn't, she didn't . . . she wasn't there for the wedding because it was always difficult to manage the . . . you know, the transport backwards and forwards.'[30]

Thirty-nine years after her white father walked out on his Aboriginal family, she marries a white man, on her terms. She makes sure he understands the importance of her work. He loves the Anangu Pitjantjatjara Yankunytjatjara Lands and is well liked by the people there.

As she will tell the filmmaker Robin Hughes many years later: 'He was a very supportive husband. In fact, I think we had a virtual marriage contract that I would want to continue my involvement in Aboriginal affairs, and he didn't stand in the way of that and he supported me through all that time . . .

'He was very, very well received. He was better received by my people than I was accepted by his family. I wasn't accepted by his family at all. Really the main contact that I had with his family was after his passing, when I notified them, and they came to the funeral.'[31]

At birth, Lowitja had been assigned a promised husband in her mother's Yankunytjatjara culture. When she learned of it, after her reunion with her mother, she felt glad that she was spared a promised marriage. She met the man many years later, after her marriage to Gordon Smart, when she was working for the government, and he was a 'mischievous old man' teaching Aboriginal music at Adelaide University, a senior lawman in the Anangu Pitjantjatjara Yankunytjatjara Lands, a poor man with a wealth of knowledge, greatly respected by his people. When they met, he teased her about his conjugal rights, and she teased him back, saying she was married to a wadjila, a white man, and could not come to his camp. She tells the story laughing.

'I used to see him a fair bit and one day—after quite a long time— he came right up close to me and said, "You my promised one", looking me in the eyes, standing there. "You my promised one."

'I said, "Yes, so what?"

'He said, "I come your camp tonight?"

'I said, "No, I got white one."

'He was a cheeky man. He would always be looking my way when he came to Adelaide.'

———

Lowitja chairs the National Aboriginal Conference for the first year only, February 1978 to March 1979, when she is replaced by the Reverend Cedric Jacobs, a Noongar man who was taken away from his parents when he was a child, grew up at the Mogumber Methodist Mission, married into a missionary family and became an evangelist. He is followed into the chair almost immediately by Lyall Munro, a Kamilaroi man who came out of the discrimination and segregations of Moree.

At the second national meeting of the National Aboriginal Conference, in April 1979, the government's elected Aboriginal advisers request a 'Treaty of Commitment be executed between the Aboriginal nation and the Australian Government', and that the treaty be negotiated by the NAC, as representatives of the Aboriginal people. With the Fraser government open to discussion, but not willing to accept the word treaty, the NAC, with Lowitja playing a leading role, suggests it

be called a makarrata, a Yolŋu word for the restoration of good relations after a conflict.

At the same time, a group of prominent non-Indigenous Australians, led by former Council for Aboriginal Affairs chairman H.C.
'Nugget' Coombs, forms an Aboriginal Treaty Committee, which
includes poet Judith Wright, historian Charles Rowley and anthropologist Bill Stanner among its members. It calls for a treaty 'within
Australia, between Australians'.

In September, Lowitja travels to Canada for the World Council of
Indigenous Peoples' conference. Founded five years earlier, the council
aims to promote unity among a 'fourth world' of indigenous people
who share striking historical and contemporary similarities. At the
conclusion of the first international conference, in October 1975 at
Port Alberni in British Columbia, a Solemn Declaration is adopted:
'We vow to control again our own destiny and recover our complete
humanity and pride in being Indigenous People.'

———

On 17 October 1979, Lowitja's mother, Lily, dies at the Port Augusta
hospital. Lowitja is in northern Australia when she gets the call from
Eileen.

In the twelve years since their reunion, Lowitja and Lily's days
together have been only a handful. She comes home to bury her
mother. They load the casket into the back of a van and drive north
on the Oodnadatta Track, in the late-autumn heat, hoping to give her
a traditional funeral in her home country at Indulkana.

At Oodnadatta, they find the roads blocked by men's business ceremonies. 'You can't get through there,' they are told.

They wait. And then they decide to bury her at Oodnadatta. But
there is no time to dig her a grave in the stony cemetery, so Lowitja
calls the family together and they agree to bury her in the sandhills

outside the town in which she lived in a wurlie of corrugated iron after her children were taken away. This is where she became an alcoholic after the liberalisation of drinking laws, where she waited, where she was reunited with her daughters. And they stand by the grave in the sandhills, the wind blowing, sand pouring back into the hole as fast as they can dig it out, until they are all laughing.

'We laughed all the time, all through the funeral.'

They are burying a woman they barely know, a mother they were encouraged to forget.

'We just got used to the fact we didn't have her. We couldn't say that we really knew her, loved her, and all those other words that people use. No. We were happy to meet her, we were happy to introduce her to all the rest of the family, and that's where it finished.'

No hymns are sung and no prayers are said. There is no ceremony of any kind.

Afterwards Eileen and Gordon drive south to Quorn and Lowitja flies north to Alice Springs, and the wind blows across the sandhills until they can't remember where they buried her.

XXVII

In the remote north-west of Australia, a simmering dispute over oil explodes at a station called Noonkanbah.

Pegged out by the Emanuel family in 1886, by 1920 Noonkanbah station sprawled over one million acres (more than 400,000 hectares) of red earth. The traditional owners, the Yungngora, lived and worked there until August 1971, when they walked off over poor treatment and squalid living conditions, and became fringe-dwellers on the outskirts of Fitzroy Crossing. They stayed there in misery and turmoil for five years and then returned to Noonkanbah when the station was put up for sale and bought by the Aboriginal Land Fund Commission, set up by the Whitlam government to buy back land for Aboriginal people.

But in March 1978, a letter arrives from a multinational mining company, Amax Iron Ore Corporation, informing them of its intention to drill for oil on their land near a sacred site at Umpampurru, or Pea Hill as the Europeans call it. The Yungngora warn that, if the site is disturbed, it will cause sickness and death.

Aboriginal people from more than thirty communities across the Kimberley, and from as far away as Yirrkala, arrive there on the back of utes on 20 May 1978. They dance in celebration of their culture and establish the Kimberley Land Council. The Yungngora go to court, but a magistrate in Broome tells them that the Mining Act must be upheld: 'In coming to Australia, the white man brought this form of law. That law stands and cannot be over-ridden by moral or spiritual arguments.' The Yungngora lock their gates, get court injunctions and build support. In April 1980, West Australian Premier Charles Court, who offers to fence off the most sacred sites, describes their actions as an 'insurrection against legitimate authority'.

At 1 am on 7 August 1980, a convoy of non-union drilling rigs and trucks leaves Perth for Noonkanbah. At a place called Mickeys Pool, the Yungngora and their supporters, including ministers of religion, sit down on the dirt road and, in heartbreaking scenes, the Yungngora sing for their country as police wade in among them and drag them away to jail.

In Geneva, Jim Hagan, a former Queensland stockman who has become chairman of the National Aboriginal Conference, addresses the unwieldily named United Nations Human Rights Commission Sub-Commission on the Prevention of Discrimination and Protection of Minorities. The first elected Indigenous Australian to address a UN committee, Hagan is accompanied by West Australian NAC members Reg Birch and Jimmy Bieundurry. Reg Birch was born at Forrest River, Oombulgurri, where in 1926 Aboriginal people were massacred and their bodies burned, and Jimmy Bieundurry was born near Lake Gregory and was among the last of the Walmajarri to come out of the desert regions into the cattle-station country, where he learned to read, became a lay preacher, and was a founding co-chairman of the Kimberley Land Council.

Hagan's speech, on 3 September 1980, is reported internationally: 'The Noonkanbah community have sought justice, and have been given obstruction. We have sought peace and have been given violence. The Australian Government's acquiescence in this continuing breach of human rights must see it condemned in the eyes of the world.'

Ultimately, no oil is found at Noonkanbah. But out of the dispute, alliances are made that underpin the Aboriginal land rights movement for decades to come.

The Aboriginal Development Commission is established in July 1980 to further the 'economic development of Aboriginals', through loans and grants for housing, businesses and land. Charlie Perkins is the first chairman. Lowitja represents South Australia on a ten-person board.

Lowitja and Perkins are also together on the board of Aboriginal Hostels, a rapidly growing Aboriginal-led government-funded organisation established by the Whitlam government in 1973 to provide low cost, temporary accommodation for Aboriginal people and Torres Strait Islanders in need; these include the homeless and the transient, rehabilitating alcoholics, those in need of medical attention, students, single parents and the elderly poor. Between 1973 and 1986, its annual budget grows from $1.76 million to more than $17 million, with almost four thousand beds in more than one hundred and fifty hostels. A handful of staff becomes more than five hundred, ninety per cent of them Indigenous. It is the nation's largest single employer of Indigenous people. Perkins is the inaugural chairman; Lowitja succeeds him as chairman in November 1981.

A historian, Peter Read, writes a pamphlet about the removal of Aboriginal children from their families in New South Wales between 1883 and 1969. He finishes it in a day, 'fresh from reading the painful archives relating to removed children' and 'full of fury that such things could have happened in our country'. He calls his pamphlet 'The Stolen Generations'.

On 4 November 1981, South Australian Premier David Tonkin presents Anangu Pitjantjatjara Yankunytjatjara leaders with freehold title deeds to 102,650 square kilometres of South Australia—ten per cent of the state—at Itjinpiri, eight kilometres north of Ernabella, where Charles Duguid established a mission in 1937 to act as 'a buffer between the Aborigines and the encroaching white man'. This is the result of protest and long negotiation. There is pride and hope at first, but then, because of sickness and strife in the APY Lands, anniversaries pass without celebration.

In the New Year's Honours announced on 31 December 1982, Lowitja is made a Commander of the Order of the British Empire, for service to the Aboriginal community. She says her dream is to see Aboriginal people controlling their own affairs and undertaking economic enterprises independent of government funding.[32] She is now Lois O'Donoghue, CBE, AM.

She and Gordon sell their house at Quorn and move to Strathalbyn, midway between Adelaide and Victor Harbor, where she once worked as a servant and began her nursing career.

It is 5 March 1983 and Robert James Lee Hawke leads the Labor Party to a landslide election victory and becomes Australia's twenty-third prime minister. He is a man with a deep sense of his own destiny. On the Aboriginal question he is sympathetic; but captive to powerful forces.

He will promise, and renege; but Galarrwuy Yunupingu will remember him fondly.

Labor comes to office promising national land rights. Fraser had introduced land rights laws in the Northern Territory in 1976, with South Australia following with the Pitjantjatjara Land Rights Act in 1981 and the Wran government passing the NSW Land Rights Act in 1983. The New South Wales government described its Act as the 'first step in this State towards redressing the injustice and neglect of real Aboriginal needs since Captain Phillip stepped upon the shores of Port Jackson in 1788'. But in mineral-rich Western Australia there has been great hostility.

Hawke hands Aboriginal Affairs to Clyde Holding, an ally who has followed him to Canberra after fifteen years in the Victorian Parliament, including ten as leader of the Opposition, during which he lost three state elections. Holding says the government will meet the states in 'a spirit of compromise', but outlines five land rights principles: inalienable freehold title for Aboriginal land; full legal protection of sacred sites; Aboriginal control over mining on Aboriginal land; access to mining royalty equivalents; and compensation for lost land.

In July, Holding addresses Aboriginal Hostels' tenth anniversary celebrations. He says the Hawke government, one hundred days old, wants to achieve land rights by consensus, but he warns the government is not prepared to allow Aboriginal rights to be eroded by 'recalcitrant state governments'. He says the government is committed to giving Aboriginal people back 'that which is theirs' with a sense of generosity and compassion, 'and a sense that understands that the occupation of this nation was one of the most brutal and genocidal acts in history'. He says Australia 'can never aspire to greatness until it recognises that simple fact'.[33]

In November, Hawke announces the government has agreed to transfer the title of the Uluru-Kata Tjuta National Park—Ayers Rock and the domes of the Olgas—to the traditional owners, who have agreed to lease it back to the Australian Parks and Wildlife Service for ninety-nine years in joint management. Excluded from the Aboriginal Land Rights (Northern Territory) Act in 1976, as alienated Crown land, Uluru-Kata Tjuta has been the subject of continuing protest, negotiation and stalemate. 'This is an historic decision and is a measure of the willingness of this government, on behalf of the Australian people, to recognise the just and legitimate claims of a people who have been dispossessed of their land but who have never lost their spiritual attachment to that land,' Hawke says.[34]

In the first week of March 1984, on a blistering hot day in Port Augusta—Nukunu country and the starting point of the long

Urumbula songline that weaves through the Flinders Ranges and two thousand kilometres further through deserts and salt lakes to the Gulf of Carpentaria—Governor-General Sir Ninian Stephen opens the Lois O'Donoghue Hostel. Lowitja says that during his vice-regal term, Sir Ninian and Lady Stephen, Val, have made Government House a place where Aboriginal people feel welcome and jokes that their dog, Sadie, seems to recognise her when she visits.[35]

On 29 March 1984, Charlie Perkins is appointed as the first Aboriginal secretary of the Department of Aboriginal Affairs. Holding considers him the only possible choice, although there is some trepidation that he will be a loose cannon. Lowitja, who is part of a portfolio group that meets regularly with Holding to discuss strategies, had been on his short list, along with Pat O'Shane, the first Aboriginal secretary of the NSW Ministry of Aboriginal Affairs, and Perkins' nephew, Neville Perkins, a Labor Party politician in the Northern Territory, a founder of the Central Australian Aboriginal Congress and a public servant.

But Charlie Perkins embodies hope and possibility.

At a press conference, he says, 'It's not usual for a new permanent head to make a statement on his appointment but then it's not usual for Aboriginal people to be appointed to such a position. Some would find it unusual if I did not say something on this very unusual occasion. My appointment . . . marks another significant step in the advancement of Aboriginal people and the relationship between Aboriginal and non-Aboriginal people. Given the opportunity, our people can achieve the highest positions of responsibility and the management of the affairs of this nation. I'm sure that while I'm the first Aboriginal to be appointed to such a position of responsibility and influence I shall not be the last.' He says Australians 'have not yet come to terms with Aboriginal people'.

In May, at a mining conference, Hugh Morgan, executive director of Western Mining Corporation and immediate past president of the Australian Mining Industry Council, describes land rights as 'anti-Christian and a return to paganism'. He argues that the clash of mining companies with environmentalists and supporters of Indigenous land rights is a clash 'between the Christian orthodoxy of those who work, including the miners, who as St. Paul told us, are abiding in the same calling wherein we are called, and must perforce find the best orebodies wherever they may be; and the Manichean-style commitments of those who regard rivers, or trees, or rocks, or Aboriginal sites as belonging to the spiritual world; who regard such sites as incommensurable, and seek to legislate such incommensurability into the statute books.' He argues that Aboriginal people are being given rights—mineral rights—greater than white Australians.

In Western Australia, the state's Chamber of Mines runs a virulent campaign against proposed land rights legislation. A television advertisement shows black hands building a brick wall across a map of Western Australia. 'Keep out—this land is part of Western Australia under Aboriginal land claim,' the advertisement thunders. Fred Chaney—who had been Aboriginal Affairs minister in the Fraser government, had handed out Yes how-to-vote cards at polling booths for the 1967 referendum, and who regarded the breaking of the Aboriginal protest at Noonkanbah as brutal—is appalled. He will later describe it as 'a vicious racist campaign' that was brutally effective.[36] By December, the federal government's commitment to national land rights is in disarray.

Late in 1984, Lowitja is told that Bob Hawke will name her Australian of the Year, 'for her work in bridging the cultural gap between Aborigines and the rest of the community'. She will be the fifth Aboriginal person to receive this award, after boxer Lionel Rose, tennis player Evonne Goolagong, Yolŋu leader Galarrwuy Yunupingu and Senator Neville Bonner.

She hesitates for two weeks, conscious of the inevitable condemnation; then she accepts, saying she is proud to be Aboriginal, a woman and an Australian: 'I took ages and ages to make a decision about whether I would accept that, and I finally did, only on the basis that I thought I could make a difference.'[37]

'To become Australian of the Year is special to me because it recognises the importance of Aborigines and women to our Australian nation,' she says in her acceptance speech, continuing:

But I have not always felt Australian. At times I have felt an outcast in my own land. I was born in the bush in remote South Australia, a member of the Yankunytjatjara tribe. I was a member of the tribe, but I was not officially an Australian. I had no birth certificate. Later, at the age of two, I was taken from my mother by the church for what they called my own moral good.

Since the early 1950s I have worked for my people as a nurse and an administrator. I have worked with many Aboriginal organisations. I have been an adviser to both Commonwealth and State governments. In all those years since being born in the bush, I have never had to question being an Aborigine. But I've had my doubts about being Australian.

She says that, as an Aboriginal woman, she has experienced prejudice—and learned from it: 'Other people's prejudice has given my life a direction.'

In Adelaide, an old adversary, Mary Cooper, of the Kaurna Plains and Narrunga people, calls her a Judas and a traitor for accepting a white man's 'tin medal'.

As Australian of the Year, Lowitja dines at Government House and is in demand as a speaker. She tells the *Australian Women's Weekly* she has never been bitter: 'The truth is that neither the black nor the white communities wanted children of mixed race, like we were. I have only good thoughts about the mission, because without that training I would not be able to help my people as I now can.' She says she is not an activist, but a moderate; she speaks of the need for cooperation not confrontation, and describes herself as the tip of the iceberg among Aboriginal achievers.[38]

In February 1985, the Hawke government abandons key elements of Labor's 'five principles', including veto rights over mining. This abandonment threatens rights already gained in the Northern Territory. It infuriates Aboriginal leaders, who walk out on talks, and it fails to satisfy the miners.

In Western Australia the Burke Labor government fails to gain parliamentary support for land rights legislation drafted by the mining and pastoral industry that would have denied Aboriginal people a right of veto over mining and restricted applications to land with little economic potential. It is re-elected in February 1986 on a promise of no land rights. Premier Brian Burke, Labor's national president, agitates against national land rights and warns Hawke the issue is electoral poison. Caught between miners and Aboriginal people, with his party rancorous and divided, Hawke abandons national land rights.

————

The 'black parliament', the National Aboriginal Conference (NAC), is also rancorous and divided. Labor had come to government in 1983 having pledged to restructure the NAC, but within a year the mood had become antagonistic with the NAC accusing Holding of meddling in its affairs. In April 1984, 'Nugget' Coombs reports to the government that the NAC is ineffective and lacks grassroots support.

Lowitja, the NAC's first chairwoman, is among those calling for change. In a submission to the Coombs inquiry, Aboriginal Hostels, which she heads, says the NAC has been, in essence, 'a European structure, ill-suited to reflect the wide cultural diversity which characterises Aboriginal communities in Australia'. It says it is 'alarmed by frequent reports about factionalism and internecine disputes within the NAC' and 'we know that the view of traditional owners of Aboriginal lands is rarely listened to'. When an audit also finds deficiencies in NAC's financial management, the government axes it, in April 1985, and Lowitja is appointed to consult with Aboriginal organisations and communities on a replacement.

At a women's conference in Adelaide in September 1985, Lowitja speaks about the rapid advances women have made over the past decade, and about racism: 'Sexism is one thing, colour is another,' she says. 'To be a woman, to be an Aboriginal and to want a decent living is a difficult path. I have trod that path. Believe me, it's all been uphill. As John Lennon once sang, woman is the nigger of the world. I am both, I'm proud of it and nobody is going to change that. And I know that every other black woman wants the chance to have control of her own destiny.'[39]

On 26 October 1985, she is at Uluru as an adviser to Holding when Governor-General Ninian Stephen hands the monolith back to its traditional owners, one hundred and twelve years after William Gosse first clambered to the top, with the Afghan Kamran, and gazed out on the plains below.

Stephen calls it a place of wonder and of strange beauty:

Today we stand not merely in the centre of our continent, at its very heart, but beside what has become one of our national symbols, what Aboriginal Australians know as Uluru and what the rest of us think of as Ayers Rock; and in the far distance lies Kata Tjuta, the Olgas. National symbols to all Australians, these great rocks have been places of high significance to Aboriginals for many thousands of years.

The Aboriginal Land Trust will henceforth be the legal owners of this place and Aboriginals will have a real say in the management of this national park through membership of the Uluru-Kata

Tjuta board. Uluru has seen countless generations come and go, and, as a National Park, will long after all of us here today are gone and quite forgotten, remain for future generations of Australians a place of wonder and of strange beauty. I now place in the hands of the Uluru-Kata Tjuta Aboriginal Land Trust the title deeds.

Despite their great poverty, the Aboriginal people are euphoric, singing and dancing into the night. But the Northern Territory government, hostile to the handover, boycotts the ceremony. Chief Minister Ian Tuxworth has travelled the country lobbying against the return, and his government has placed newspaper advertisements declaring, 'The Rock belongs to all Australians (and always has)'. During the ceremony a plane flies over Uluru trailing a banner that reads 'Ayers Rock for all Australians'.

Lowitja's cousin, Yami Lester, blinded by the poisonous cloud that drifted across Aboriginal lands from the atomic tests at Maralinga, becomes the first chairman of the Uluru-Kata Tjuta Aboriginal Land Trust, which, in accordance with the agreed terms, leases the lands back to the Australian National Parks and Wildlife Service for ninety-nine years. He jokes that Uluru, after millions of years, is going to be taken away by the Aboriginal people: 'By tomorrow that Rock will be missing, the Aboriginal people are going to take it away.'

A few days later, Lowitja goes back to Quorn as 'Australia's top citizen' to speak at her old school, in the town she regards as home—the first home she can remember, full of children and prayer and confusion, her memories full of walking to school along the Hawker road, across the Stony Creek and the equally stony Pinkerton Creek. And the Catholic boys at the edge of the town hanging over the fence calling out 'Nigger nigger, pull the trigger' and the Colebrook kids yelling back, 'Catholic dogs, jump like frogs, in and out of the water'.

'I consider Quorn to be home,' she says.

Book Six

'Pagan' woman rises

XXVIII

It is Australia Day, 26 January 1988, the Bicentennial. Tall ships sail into Sydney Harbour in re-enactment of the arrival of the First Fleet of British convict ships, full of fear and wretchedness. At the Opera House, the Prince of Wales says that, as history goes, two hundred years is barely a heartbeat: 'Yet look around you and see what has happened in that time—a whole new free people and a whole new free country, Australia.' The nation celebrates, with fireworks, flag waving and ballyhoo.

Two million people line the shore; but forty thousand, including Aboriginal people from across the country, march in protest. They chant for land rights and Aboriginal leaders speak at Hyde Park. In England, activist Burnum Burnum plants a flag in the white cliffs of Dover and claims England for Aboriginal Australia: 'I, Burnum Burnum, being a nobleman of ancient Australia, do hereby take possession of England on behalf of the Aboriginal people.'

As she assembles her thoughts, Lowitja writes that Australia is at a crossroads:

Behind us lies history and that is what we are supposed to be celebrating. Two hundred years of history. A history written in blood, sacrifice and misunderstanding. And that is what we are supposed to be celebrating. A history which has tested each one of us and found each of us wanting. And that is what we are supposed to be celebrating.

As we stand here today, we should ask ourselves whether this is a righteous cause for celebration. We must question whether it is possible to reconcile the cost of achievement with the cost incurred in terms of the human condition.

I stand here today, in much the same frame of mind as did a young black man in the United States over two decades ago, and I always ask myself, 'What cause is there for celebration?' He too stood at the crossroads of his people's history. He too was concerned as I am today. Like him, I scan the pages of history and find little cause to celebrate, little cause to join the multitudes of citizens who mark this day as one which is the culmination of human achievement, and the realisation of the promise of a fuller, more fruitful, future for my people.

She writes that the lives of older Aboriginal people are manacled to the words blood, separation and sacrifice. She recalls her own story, her battle to be 'somebody' and the price Aboriginal children paid when they were separated from their mothers—'the opportunity to learn the ways of our elders, to become intimately attuned to nature, the joy of speaking our language and the thousands of days, millions of hours and seconds we could have spent with our people'.

'The child walks in the footsteps of strangers and learns a different code of ethics,' she writes. 'The two are disparate. Over the last decade those of us who were lost to our parents through separation are beginning to come together. It is not easy. Sometimes perceptions between us differ. Often we cannot speak to one another because of language difference. Sometimes the depth of what we feel gets lost in translation.'[1]

————

In the lead-up to the Bicentennial year, Bob Hawke, re-elected for a third term on 11 July 1987, holds out the promise of a bold new direction in Aboriginal affairs. At Labor's campaign launch at the Sydney Opera House, he also says it is Labor's achievable goal that, by 1990, 'no Australian child will be living in poverty'.

On 14 July, he summons Charlie Perkins and tells him that Aboriginal Affairs will be abolished and replaced by an Aboriginal and Torres Strait Islander Commission (ATSIC), which will be led by Aboriginal people, but overseen by a government minister. Hawke offers Perkins the chairmanship, with the head of the Aboriginal Development Commission, Shirley McPherson, as his likely deputy. Perkins asks how long he has to consider the offer. Hawke gives him five minutes and Perkins accepts.

A week later, Hawke announces that Gerry Hand will succeed Clyde Holding as Aboriginal Affairs minister. Perkins has been close to Holding but not to Hand, who, as a prickly leader of Labor's Victorian left, has embraced a new generation of Aboriginal leaders, from the north and the west. In the months that follow, Hand is either unavailable to Perkins, or else, in Perkins' account of it, he emerges only briefly from smoke-filled rooms.[2]

Death and poverty cast long shadows. After a race riot in Goondiwindi, on the border of Queensland and New South Wales, Human Rights Commission president Marcus Einfeld goes to the nearby Aboriginal community of Toomelah, where children play in raw sewage that pools between the houses. Einfeld weeps.

On 10 August, Hawke announces a royal commission into Aboriginal Deaths in Custody amid rising anger and concern about the number of Aboriginal people dying in jails, including a sixteen-year-old boy, John Pat, who died at Roebourne, Western Australia, on 28 September 1983 after being knocked unconscious and thrown into the back of a police van 'like a dead kangaroo'. An autopsy revealed he suffered a fractured skull, and haemorrhage, swelling, bruising and tearing of the brain. Fifty-seven witnesses claimed he was savagely bashed by four off-duty police officers and a police aide. Tried for manslaughter, all five were acquitted by an all-white jury.

The poet Jack Davis picks up his pen:

> Write of life
> the pious said
> forget the past
> the past is dead.
> But all I see
> in front of me
> is a concrete floor
> a cell door
> and John Pat[3]

The singer Paul Kelly sings that he has no heart for celebrating Australia's Bicentennial:

> A ship is sailing into harbour
> A party's waiting on the shore
> And they're running up the flag now
> And they want us all to cheer
>
> Charlie's head nearly reaches the ceiling
> But his feet don't touch the floor
> From a prison issue blanket his body's swinging
> He won't dance any more
>
> Take me away from your dance floor
> Leave me out of your parade
> I have not the heart for dancing
> For dancing on his grave

Hunted man out on the Barcoo
Broken man on Moreton Bay
Hunted man across Van Diemen's
Hunted man all swept away

Take me away from your dance floor
Leave me out of your parade
I have not the heart for dancing
For dancing on his grave[4]

In Alice Springs, on 2 September, Hawke unexpectedly announces he wants a treaty, or a compact of understanding, between Aboriginal and non-Aboriginal people. He says the actual word does not matter, but the nation must acknowledge forty thousand years of Aboriginal history and culture and tradition, and the injustices and disadvantages that followed European settlement. Asked his opinion, Perkins says the proposal should go further and include the incorporation of an everlasting treaty into the Constitution.

Liberal leader John Howard says Perkins has far exceeded his role as a public servant and should be sacked or disciplined. Perkins responds that Howard is under the influence of deeply conservative elements within the Liberal Party, including its beer baron president John Elliott.

In December, Gerry Hand sets out the new Aboriginal policy in a policy statement titled *Foundations for the Future*. It includes the establishment of ATSIC, which he calls a proposal of 'great and historic importance for all Australians'.[5]

'It was only 20 years ago that the Australian people voted overwhelmingly in a referendum to give the Commonwealth the power to make laws affecting the lives of the Aboriginal and Islander people,' he says. 'In the light of this history, it is proposed by this Government to acknowledge that the Aboriginal and Torres Strait Islander

peoples were the prior occupiers and original owners of this land.'
It is envisaged that such an acknowledgement would be included in
the preamble to legislation introduced to achieve the aims outlined
in this statement:

> Whilst achievements have been made in recent years, there
> is a need to understand properly and to address seriously the
> vital issue of self-determination for Aboriginal and Islander
> people. In the past there has been a misunderstanding of what
> Aboriginal and Islander people have meant when talking of
> self-determination. What has always existed is a willingness
> and desire by Aboriginal and Islander people to be involved in
> the decision-making process of government. It is the right of
> Aboriginal and Islander people as citizens of this country to be
> involved in this process, as ultimately these decisions will affect
> their daily lives. We must ensure that Aboriginal and Islander
> people are properly involved at all levels of the decision-making
> process in order that the right decisions are taken about their
> lives. Aboriginal people need to decide for themselves what
> should be done—not just take whatever governments think or
> say is best for them.

Hand also stresses, as Hawke has done, the need for Australia to
'come to terms with our history' through some form of 'compact,
agreement, treaty or Makarrata'.

It is the boldest reform in Australia's administration of Aboriginal
affairs, hailed as a world first—handing decision-making power to
Aboriginal people after generations of discrimination, neglect and
failure. But it is a lightning rod for conservative opposition.

Liberal leader John Howard regards it as an act of national lunacy.

———

In January 1988, more than twenty-one thousand copies of the *Foundations for the Future* statement and a thousand copies of a video are distributed to more than a thousand separate Aboriginal and Torres Strait Islander organisations and communities. For six weeks, Hand and Perkins criss-cross the country, travelling over fifty-six thousand kilometres, explaining and cajoling, but drawing no closer to one another. By the time the legislation is introduced, there have been more than five hundred meetings involving fourteen thousand five hundred people—the most extensive consultations ever undertaken on a single piece of legislation in the Australian Parliament's history, Hand boasts.

But among Aboriginal people, there is distrust. On 13 January, the Aboriginal Development Commission (ADC), which has a $140 million budget to provide business and home loans and buy pastoral properties, withdraws from ATSIC discussions and maintains a corrosive opposition.

In February, Shirley McPherson says that ATSIC will be the Department of Aboriginal Affairs by another name; she threatens to take the matter to the United Nations. In March, an ADC media release headlined 'The Bicentennial of Death?' maintains that ATSIC, stitched together by a 'small rump of faceless advisers', is nothing but a Bicentennial gesture designed to keep Aboriginal people quiet. Gerry Hand orders the ADC's commissioners to cooperate; when they refuse and threaten legal action, he sacks them. Shirley McPherson, whose position is appointed by the governor-general, is beyond his power to sack, but their relationship is sour.

In May, Hand appoints a new ADC board and it includes Lowitja. Sacked as a consultant to the ADC, journalist and activist John Newfong comments bitterly, 'Things have not changed since Aboriginal people were put in chains and other blacks were given a saddle or a portion of bully beef to bring them in.'[6]

In June, at the Labor Party conference in Hobart, Hawke seeks and receives the party's blessing to reach 'a proper and lasting reconciliation through a compact or treaty'.[7] After the conference, Hawke, his wife Hazel, and Hand go to a sport and cultural festival at Barunga, a small Aboriginal community eighty kilometres from Katherine in the Northern Territory. Thousands of Aboriginal people are there from across Australia. 'I threw spears with them and saw Pitjantjatjara and Yolŋu people dance together; we were told it was the first time they had done this,' Hawke will recall in his memoirs. 'There was a gift-giving ceremony and then, as we sat on the ground amid the eucalypts, the Aboriginal elders spelled out to us their hopes for the future.'[8]

The chairmen of the Northern Land Council and the Central Land Council, Galarrwuy Yunupingu and Wenten Rubuntja, present Hawke with the Barunga Statement, a painted declaration of rights. It calls on the federal government to pass laws for a nationally elected organisation to oversee Aboriginal and Islander affairs. It also seeks a national system of land rights; a police and justice system that 'frees us from discrimination'; and the negotiation of a treaty 'recognising our prior ownership, continued occupation and sovereignty and affirming our human rights and freedom'.

In response, in what Pat Dodson will call 'a rush of fervour', Hawke declares that 'there shall be a treaty negotiated between the Aboriginal people and the Government on behalf of all the people of Australia'. He hopes the agreement can be concluded by 1990.

The following day, Opposition leader John Howard declares that the idea of a treaty is 'utterly repugnant to the ideal of one Australia' and 'an absurd proposition'. He says it would divide Australia and 'spawn a form of apartheid' and he would rip it up.

———

On 10 June 1988, Lowitja takes her seat at the state funeral of Doug Nicholls, KCVO, OBE, at the Aborigines Advancement League in

Melbourne. They sing the old hymn 'In the Sweet By and By', and he is buried at the Aboriginal cemetery at Cummeragunja.

'As a nation, we stand condemned,' Nicholls once said. 'For years we have been crying out about the depressed situation and the poverty . . . we have built an empire, raised a kingdom, yet we have done nothing. There is so much more to be done. I have bellowed from Parliament House and the ashes of the campfire. I have represented the State six times at football, dined with the Queen, walked with the highest in the land, yet what have we accomplished? What more can be done? What more can I do? Eventide has come. We have finished our course. We have kept faith. Now we press on to the higher calling.'

In August, as the first substantive item of business at the new Parliament House on Capital Hill, Hawke moves a reconciliation motion suggested by the heads of Australian Christian churches. It acknowledges the prior occupation of Australia by Aboriginal and Torres Strait Islander people for thousands of years before British settlement and that they suffered dispossession and dispersal and were denied full citizenship; it affirms the importance of Aboriginal and Torres Strait Islander culture and heritage, and the right to self-management and self-determination subject to the Constitution and the laws of the Commonwealth; and supports 'recognition of their special place in the Commonwealth of Australia'.[9]

Hawke quotes 'Nugget' Coombs: 'It is never divisive to correct injustice.'

In response, opposing the motion, John Howard says the Coalition has 'no desire to deny the facts of Aboriginal history', or the role of symbolism, although of itself it will do nothing to improve Aboriginal health or education standards, but he will not support division in the Australian community and warns against 'the unwisdom of encountering a treaty'.

On Friday 4 November, Perkins is forced to resign as secretary of the Department of Aboriginal Affairs after allegations are raised against him of maladministration, nepotism and cronyism, which ultimately come to nothing. Morose and depressed, protesting he has never stolen a penny in his life, and hurt 'to a depth beyond anyone's imagination', Perkins goes back to his beginnings, Alice Springs, where he only ever saw his grandmother through a wire fence. He submits himself to tribal initiation as a wadi, a man at the beginning of his journey, and becomes chairman of the Arrernte Council.

In December, John Howard launches a manifesto—*Future Directions*—in which he denounces 'professional purveyors of guilt' who have attacked Australia's heritage. In the Senate, the Democrats and the Coalition combine to force a select committee inquiry into the ATSIC proposal. The legislation is withdrawn and then reintroduced with more stringent accountability.

Howard remains unmoved. In April 1989, he tells the parliament:

I take the opportunity of saying again that if the Government wants to divide Australian against Australian, if it wants to create a black nation within the Australian nation, it should go ahead with its Aboriginal and Torres Strait Islander Commission (ATSIC) legislation. In the process it will be doing a monumental disservice to the Australian community. If there is one thing, above everything else, that we in this Parliament should regard as our sacred and absolute duty, it is the preservation of the unity of the Australian people. The ATSIC legislation strikes at the heart of the unity of the Australian people. In the name of righting the wrongs done against Aboriginal people, the legislation adopts the misguided notion of believing that if one creates a parliament within the Australian community for Aboriginal people, one will solve and meet all of those problems.[10]

A month later, in May, Howard is gone as Liberal leader, replaced by his predecessor Andrew Peacock, in a surprise leadership coup.

Asked whether he could become Liberal leader again, Howard says that would be like 'Lazarus with a triple bypass'.

———————

On 21 July 1989, Lowitja delivers the Charles Perkins Testimonial.

At Canberra's Hellenic Club, with Perkins and his wife, Eileen, in the audience, she reminisces about their youth in Adelaide, when he was a boy at the St Francis Boys Home at Semaphore, and she was a girl at the Colebrook Home at Eden Hills. She speaks about their shared struggle for identity, 'which took you into a society which was hostile and not prepared for the likes of you, who challenged a system that denied us the right to equal status and opportunity'.

She tells of how they took separate paths. While she became a nurse, he became a fitter and turner, and played soccer in England, and had a family and went to Sydney University, and struggled to make ends meet but completed his Bachelor of Arts degree. And then there were the stressful years, when his kidneys failed. Then finally his emergence as a dynamic Aboriginal leader, who not only shone a light on discrimination but, in doing so, awoke in Aboriginal people a power of their own. 'He has often been labelled a stirrer,' she says. 'But to Aboriginal people he has always been a national leader and freedom fighter.'

On 2 November 1989, almost two years after the government announced its plans, after more than forty hours of debate in the Senate, and more than ninety amendments, the ATSIC legislation ends its tortuous journey through the parliament. It specifies that ATSIC has been introduced 'in recognition of the past dispossession and dispersal of the Aboriginal and Torres Strait Islander peoples and their present disadvantaged position in Australian society'; but even before it is established, the Coalition is promising to abolish it.

ATSIC will replace the Department of Aboriginal Affairs, the Aboriginal Development Commission and Aboriginal Hostels Limited;

it will commence in March 1990. In the interim, Hand appoints Lowitja the final chairman of the Aboriginal Development Commission (ADC), saying that, as the first chairman of the National Aboriginal Conference, 'the black parliament', and a consultant on its replacement, she has an 'ideal background' to head the ADC during the transition period, while her chairmanship of Aboriginal Hostels shows she has 'the ability to competently and effectively direct a national organisation'.

In Berlin, people stand on the Wall and bring picks and begin to break it up.

On 13 December 1989, Hand announces that Lowitja will be ATSIC's first chairperson, for a two-year term, and that career public servant Bill Gray, who has become secretary of the Department of Aboriginal Affairs after Perkins's banishment, will be the organisation's chief executive officer.

Hand says Lowitja's experience in the administration of Aboriginal affairs over many years, as well as her vast knowledge of Aboriginal and Torres Strait Islander communities across the country, make her well qualified to oversee the major changes that will occur under ATSIC. 'We are about to begin an exciting new era in the administration of Aboriginal Affairs in this country,' he says. 'The changes will not be easy and the Chairperson's position will be an extremely demanding one. Ms O'Donoghue's administrative experience and strength of character will be equal to that demanding task.'[11]

Forty years after she stood at a country railway station clutching a battered bag, waiting to be a servant, Lowitja is now the most powerful black woman in Australia's history.

She is at the mountain top—a place of sadness and storms.

Left: Margaret and Timothy O'Donoghue who left Ireland and raised their family in South Australia's hard, dry country north of Goyder's Line. (Courtesy Michael O'Donoghue) *Right:* On her mother's country, Lowitja holds photographs of her parents, Lily and Tom O'Donoghue. Lily is pictured on the day Lowitja was reunited with her, after more than thirty years apart. Tom is pictured on his wedding day after he had given his children to missionaries and abandoned his family. (Nick Cubbin/Newspix)

A photograph sent to Lowitja purporting to show her with her parents Tom and Lily, in the cart, with Mick O'Donoghue holding the camel halter. Lowitja has no memory of this. (Courtesy Lowitja O'Donoghue)

Women and children receiving rations of food and clothes at Lambina, near Granite Downs, around 1940. (Maise Chettle, courtesy A<u>r</u>a Irititja Archive, AI-0029250)

'Old Lily's camp', north of Oodnadatta, c. 1949.

The Colebrook Children's Home at Quorn, 1927. A cottage riddled with white ants, it sat on a hill where nothing grew but a peppercorn tree. (Lowitja O'Donoghue papers, National Library of Australia).

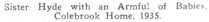

Sister Hyde with an Armful of Babies, Colebrook Home, 1935.

Left: Missionary Ruby Hyde with 'four golden treasures' in her arms, including Lowitja, second from left, 1935. *Right:* At Colebrook, 1936. Lowitja is front left.
(O'Donoghue papers, National Library of Australia)

At Colebrook. Lowitja is front row fourth from right, laughing. Missionary Ruby Hyde is left, and Delia Rutter stands on the right. Lowitja was fond of Sister Rutter, but called Sister Hyde kungka pikati, the angry woman.
(O'Donoghue papers, National Library of Australia)

At Colebrook. Lowitja is in the second row second from the left. (O'Donoghue papers, National Library of Australia)

Gathering wood, Colebrook. (O'Donoghue papers, National Library of Australia)

Lily, with daughters Eva Woodforde (left) and Bee Bee O'Donoghue (right). Just before Christmas 1945, a woman by the name of Lily arrived in the town of Quorn. She had travelled more than five hundred kilometres through desert country. She had two children with her and was searching for her five children who were taken away.

Left: Sisters (left to right) Amy, Lowitja and Vi. (O'Donoghue papers, National Library of Australia) *Right:* On 26 August 1942, when Lowitja was ten, Tom O'Donoghue married Gertrude Constable at St Francis Xavier Cathedral, Adelaide. When he died, his death certificate stated that during his lifetime he had no children.

Lowitja as a domestic servant at Waitpinga, South Australia, 1949, with children Jan and John Swincer. The children called her 'Lo-Lo'. (Courtesy Jan Stevenson)

One day after church, early in 1950, hospital matron Alice Tuck said to Lowitja, 'You want to be a nurse I hear' and changed the course of her life. (O'Donoghue papers, National Library of Australia)

Overcoming low expectations and discrimination, Lowitja trained to become a nurse at Victor Harbor (bottom left, front), became the first Aboriginal nurse at the Royal Adelaide Hospital (top, back row centre), and nursed with missionaries in the foothills of the Himalayas in India, where live births were so rare pregnancy was called *modom gotoi*—body of death. (O'Donoghue papers, National Library of Australia)

Mother and daughters. Reunited after more than thirty years apart, Eileen, Lily and Lowitja, Oodnadatta, December 1967. 'We didn't know whether we should embrace her, kiss her, or how to respond to a mother that we had never known'. (O'Donoghue papers, National Library of Australia)

Working as a nurse and welfare officer for the Department of Aboriginal Affairs, Coober Pedy, 1967. One day outside a store, Lowitja heard a woman say, 'That's Lily's daughter'. (Courtesy Ara Irititja Archive AI-0022866, photographer Betty Culhane)

Marrying Gordon Smart at Pichi Richi Pass, near Quorn, January 1979, after waiting sixteen years. The piano was brought from the church on the back of a truck. Her wedding dress was a shade of coral. Lowitja at the Department of Aboriginal Affairs. Siblings (from left to right) Amy, Violet, Lowitja, Geoffrey, Eileen.
(O'Donoghue papers, National Library of Australia)

With Malcolm Fraser at Parliament House, Canberra, after becoming head of the National Aboriginal Conference, 1978. Fraser would become a lifelong friend. (O'Donoghue papers, National Library of Australia)

Top left: With Bob and Hazel Hawke in Melbourne in February 1985 after becoming the 1984 Australian of the Year. (Mike Arthur/Newspix) *Bottom left:* With poet Oodgeroo Noonuccal. *Right:* First chairwoman of the Aboriginal and Torres Strait Islander Commission (ATSIC), a 'new era' for Aboriginal people, 1990. (O'Donoghue papers, National Library of Australia)

Left: At the podium of the United Nations General Assembly, 10 December 1992, the first Aboriginal person to stand there. *Right*: Last in her class in her final year of school, Lowitja was showered with awards and honorary degrees. (O'Donoghue papers, National Library of Australia)

Deep in conversation with Paul Keating, Brisbane, 18 May 1995. (Patrick Hamilton/ Newspix)

With Noel Pearson at the height of native title negotiations with the Keating government. (Erin Jonasson/ Newspix)

Left: At midnight on 22 December 1993 Native Title passes the Senate, and Lowitja and Noel Pearson embrace. (O'Donoghue papers, National Library of Australia) *Right*: With Paul Keating and members of Aboriginal communities and organisations from Western Australia and Cape York, Parliament House, Canberra, after the native title deal is done, 21 December 1993. (Ray Strange/Newspix)

With Paul Keating and key negotiators and advisers. (O'Donoghue papers, National Library of Australia)

Aboriginal representatives Pat Dodson, Gatjil Djerrkura and Lowitja watch as John Howard addresses the nation on his Wik '10-point plan', 30 November 1997. (David Crosling/Newspix)

Lowitja is distraught after giving evidence to a South Australian government committee about social problems on Anangu Pitjantjatjara Yankunytjatjara Lands, 2 June 2005. (Lindsay Moller/Newspix)

With Faith Bandler, old friend, Aboriginal rights activist and winner of 1997 Human Rights Medal, 9 December 1997. (Chris Pavlich/Newspix)

Pat Dodson (right), Lowitja and Gatjil Djerrkura walking by the gates of Buckingham Palace after meeting with the Queen, 13 October 1999. (Pat Hannagan/Newspix)

Lowitja O'Donoghue, 2006 by Robert Hannaford. He painted her unsmiling, strong but ageing and filled her eyes with loss. (© Robert Hannaford, National Portrait Gallery)

'I like this place,' she said of the remains of her father's camp at Agnes Creek, where she was born. 'I think it would have been a good place to be a child.' (Nick Cubbin/Newspix)

After delivering a national apology to the Stolen Generations in the House of Representatives on 13 February 2008, Prime Minister Kevin Rudd took Lowitja's hands in his and said, 'A long time coming, Lowitja. Sorry us whitefellas are so slow. But we finally got there.' (Gary Ramage/Newspix)

Lowitja, autumn 2018. (Stuart Rintoul)

XXIX

In her new role Lowitja speaks of a 'new era' for Aboriginal people. In the cards and letters she receives after her appointment as head of the Aboriginal and Torres Strait Islander Commission (ATSIC), a constant theme is the confidence that she will be a strong and steady hand in a turbulent time.

When she tells the story of her life, it is without bitterness and strikes a conciliatory tone. 'If I have ever felt angry, I was angry because I was taken away from my mother and my mother never knew from the time we were taken away until the time I made the contact with her, she never had a clue where we were,' she tells the *Age* journalist Mark Metherell.[12]

She remembers the way the Colebrook children would gather around any new child who came into the home—and always ask the same terrible question: 'There were always new children coming in so we would secretly speak the language and secretly ask, "Do you know my mother, where is she?"' ATSIC, Metherell suggests, 'marks the final death knell of assimilation policies pursued by governments and churches for the first half of this century'.

In an article headlined '"Pagan" woman rises from the turbulence', Lowitja tells *The Australian*'s Lenore Taylor she has always tried to be politically bipartisan and hopes she can convince the Coalition to change its mind about ATSIC.[13]

Hawke wins a fourth successive term in March 1990, and Liberal leader Andrew Peacock, twice defeated, is replaced by John Hewson. The government reiterates its support for 'a genuine reconciliation', including a treaty or compact; in May, Hawke writes to Hewson and other political leaders urging a bipartisan approach. He makes it clear the government is not 'wedded' to the word treaty. 'What I believe is important is that there be a process of reconciliation,' he writes. 'In my view the consultation process will be as important as the eventual outcome. But there is little hope of a worthwhile outcome, even to consultations, without the support of the majority of Australians.'

―――――――

Within ATSIC, the mood is hopeful.

New chief executive Bill Gray has had twenty-eight years in the public service, twenty-four of them in Aboriginal affairs. He has deep connections in the Northern Territory. As a young man, in 1962, he hitchhiked from Geelong to Darwin, thinking he might find work on a pastoral station. In Darwin, having only ever met one Aboriginal man—champion boxer, George Bracken—he played for a football team called the Wanderers, which was mostly Aboriginal. He joined the Welfare Branch of the Northern Territory Administration, and became a patrol officer, living and working in Aboriginal communities in north-east Arnhem Land and the Tiwi Islands. An Aboriginal man took him under his wing—Mungurrawuy Yunupingu, cultural leader of the Gumatj people, a signatory to the Yirrkala Bark Petition and father of Galarrwuy Yunupingu.

Gray rose in the Department of Aboriginal Affairs and in 1987 chaired the taskforce planning ATSIC. He watched with growing alarm as Hand and Perkins traversed the nation, drawing lines on maps and creating regions at will, divided by geographical, state or tribal boundaries. When they reached sixty regions, he begged them to stop. In 1989, he was appointed secretary of the Department of Aboriginal Affairs when Perkins was forced to resign.

Gray does not know Lowitja well, but when she is appointed to head the new organisation, he thinks it is a wise choice. In a hostile and volatile political environment, she is matriarchal, respected and disciplined. Gray believes she will give ATSIC its best chance of surviving.

She leads a uniquely challenging organisation. It is democratic, but at its base it is deeply impoverished. It boasts eight hundred regional councillors from cities and remote communities elected to sixty councils in seventeen zones, which each elect one commissioner to a twenty-member national board; but three members, including the chairman, are appointed by the Minister for Aboriginal Affairs. The organisation's chief executive is appointed by the government, but answers to the board.

When ATSIC begins, in March 1990, it has a taxpayer budget of more than $500 million, and this will grow over fifteen years to more than $1 billion; but eighty per cent of the budget is quarantined by the government for expenditure on particular programs, including employment and housing. The poorest people in Australia compete against one another for the remaining pool of funds.

In June, seeking to 'sensitise' white bureaucrats to the idea of Aboriginal control, Lowitja tells the Royal Australian Institute of Public Administration that ATSIC is no ordinary statutory body; it is an attempt to go into uncharted waters and give Aboriginal and Torres Strait Islander people—'who for so long have felt themselves powerless and voiceless in the process of government'—the power to make decisions about government programs that affect them. 'At the heart of these issues are the rights of Australia's Indigenous population and the maintenance of an ancient culture with roots deep in time,' she says.[14]

ATSIC's public servants drink at a bar called the Contented Soul, but they are rarely content. From the beginning, the organisation carries the weight of conservative political hostility, internal tensions and the deep and entrenched poverty of Aboriginal Australia.

———

In July 1990, Lowitja is in Geneva, Switzerland, for the Eighth Session of the United Nations Working Group on Indigenous Populations. She is surrounded by indigenous people from across the globe, and she tells them:

Madam Chair, distinguished members of the Working Group, ladies and gentlemen, my name is Lois O'Donoghue, my language name is Lowitja, I am a member of the Pitjantjatjara language group from the Central Desert area of Australia. I am very pleased, as the Chairperson of the Aboriginal and Torres Strait Islander Commission, to have this opportunity to again address the Working Group. I am proud to indicate to the Working Group that the Indigenous people of Australia are now in an historically unique position and one which bears telling[15]

She says that after twenty years of federal responsibility over Aboriginal affairs, the Australian government has said to Indigenous people 'it is time for you to take over'.

In October, she is standing on red dirt east of Alice Springs, north of the Simpson Desert, for the handback of a cattle station to the Eastern Arrernte people. 'For so long now, you have been fighting to win the right to live on your own land,' she says. 'Land which has always been the land of your people. Today that right is restored to you. I think we can all take heart that such things are happening. For Aboriginal people, there is new hope and new opportunity.'[16]

In the first week of November 1990, thirty-seven thousand people vote in the first ATSIC regional elections, fewer than a third of the hundred and fourteen thousand who are eligible, and similar to the number who voted for its predecessors—the National Aboriginal Consultative Committee and the National Aboriginal Conference. Many Aboriginal people regard ATSIC with suspicion, or indifference, but Lowitja and new Aboriginal Affairs minister Robert Tickner, who has replaced Hand in April, call it 'most encouraging' and 'a promising start'.[17]

In the first weeks of 1991, Lowitja attends regional council meetings across the country, in Broken Hill, Lismore, Brisbane, Perth, Derby, Port Hedland, Darwin, Nhulunbuy, Marla and Alice Springs. 'It was my privilege to see history in the making,' she reports.

When she reports on the achievements of the first year of ATSIC in March 1991, she emphasises the need for accountability. 'Aboriginal and Torres Strait Islander people constitute the most disadvantaged identifiable group in Australia,' she writes. 'To a large extent Aboriginal and Torres Strait Islander people have now been entrusted with the funds and the programs intended to redress these disadvantages. It would be a tragedy if this opportunity were wasted. We must take into account the fact that Aboriginal affairs is an area of government that is subject to intense public scrutiny. There is still a proportion of the Australian population that resents any form of special assistance to us, and that same group has a very low opinion of our managerial ability. In other words, they regard any government funds allocated to Aboriginal affairs as wasted.' She says there are also Aboriginal people who are pessimistic or sceptical. 'The challenge is to prove all of these people wrong.'[18]

She feels 'an overwhelming sense that mainstream Australia is breathing over our shoulder waiting for us to slip up, waiting for us to fulfil certain expectations'.[19]

Also in March, with the three-year Deaths in Custody royal commission set to report, and the government considering how to respond, Lowitja writes to Hawke, asking to address federal Cabinet. He agrees and Lowitja attends with ATSIC commissioners Alf Bamblett and Steve Gordon. It is the first time in the ninety-one-year history of the Australian government that Indigenous people have attended a Cabinet meeting and there is silence as Lowitja tells her life story.

As he sits watching, Aboriginal Affairs minister Robert Tickner thinks her 'magnificent'. 'She was not grandstanding, or dwelling on the past,' he later writes. 'She was simply telling Cabinet about the true history of this country and the terrible toll inflicted on Aboriginal families by those forced separations . . . This was Australian history in the making, Aboriginal people telling the Cabinet what they needed to be reminded of. You could have heard a pin drop. The only other occasion I have seen Cabinet ministers so affected was in the presence of Nelson Mandela.'[20]

The royal commission finds that Aboriginal people do not die at a higher rate than non-Aboriginal people in custody, but the rate at which they are imprisoned is overwhelmingly different, twenty-nine times higher than the non-Aboriginal rate. It finds that of the ninety-nine Aboriginal people who died in custody between January 1980 and May 1989, whose deaths were investigated, eighty-three were unemployed at the date of last detention; only two had completed secondary schooling; forty-three had been charged with an offence at or before the age of fifteen, and seventy-four had been charged with an offence at or before the age of nineteen. Forty-three had experienced childhood separation from their natural families through intervention by state authorities, missions or other institutions; and forty-three had been taken into custody for reasons directly related to alcohol. It found their standard of health varied from poor to very bad; their economic situation was disastrous and they were at the margin of society. Of the twenty-two deaths by hanging in police cells, nineteen had a blood alcohol level of

0.174 per cent or over—mostly much over. Of the other three people, one person's level was not taken and one person was suffering severe withdrawal symptoms.

In his report, Commissioner Elliott Johnston says that, until he examined the files of those who died and listened to Aboriginal people speaking, he had 'no conception of the degree of pin-pricking domination, abuse of personal power, utter paternalism, open contempt and total indifference' that Aboriginal people experienced day to day. The royal commission makes three hundred and thirty-nine recommendations, aimed at redressing not only the circumstances of individual deaths in custody, but underlying social issues of discrimination, disadvantage and neglect.

Lowitja calls the five thousand-page, eleven-volume report 'the most important social document this century', and a challenge to governments at all levels. The government allocates $400 million over five years for reforms of the justice system, for substance abuse programs and for a range of measures to tackle unemployment and economic disadvantage, to be coordinated and monitored by ATSIC.

In the weeks that follow, Lowitja spends long hours at the federal parliament, 'sitting up until the wee hours of the morning', discussing the recommendations with Tickner and others. She likes Tickner; she sees decency in him, where others see weakness. An emotional man by nature, quick to tears, Tickner has a long attachment to the Aboriginal cause. For the five years prior to his entering parliament, he was principal solicitor for the NSW Aboriginal Legal Service. Where others have regarded Aboriginal Affairs as a ministerial graveyard, he has described it as his dream job; he regards it as his responsibility to 'elevate the aspirations of indigenous people to a central place in the national consciousness and debate in the lead-up to the centenary of Australian nationhood in 2001'.[21]

In East Arnhem Land, at a place called Birany Birany, by the Gulf of Carpentaria, Mandawuy Yunupingu and Paul Kelly sit around a campfire and write a scrap of a verse that gradually becomes a song called 'Treaty' to highlight the lack of progress almost three years after Bob Hawke's promise at Barunga. It talks about how Aboriginal people heard the promise on the radio and saw it on the television back in 1988, but that words are easy and cheap and promises can disappear like writing in the sand. The song takes shape and they write the words in English and in Gumatj and it becomes an anthem among Aboriginal people and reminds white Australians that the land was not given up, but was taken, sometimes with violence, and sometimes with barely a glance towards those who had learned its secrets and told its stories for tens of thousands of years:

> Well I heard it on the radio
> And I saw it on the television
> Back in 1988
> All those talking politicians
> Words are easy, words are cheap
> Much cheaper than our priceless land
> But promises can disappear
> Just like writing in the sand
>
> Treaty Yeah Treaty Now
> Treaty Yeah Treaty Now
>
> Nhima djatpangarri nhima walangwalang
> Nhe djatpayatpa nhima gaya' nhe marrtjini yakarray
> Nhe djatpa nhe walang gumurrt jararrk gutjuk

It is 3 June 1991 and Hawke's government is in chaos as Treasurer Paul Keating launches a bid for the prime ministership. He fails, with the one hundred and ten members of the Labor caucus voting for Hawke sixty-six to forty-four. But the die is cast: Keating goes to the backbench and waits to strike again.

On 5 June, as the promise of a treaty turns to a process of reconciliation, the legislation for a Council for Aboriginal Reconciliation is passed unanimously through the federal parliament. In a show of bipartisanship, Robert Tickner and his Liberal counterpart, Michael Wooldridge, shake hands across the parliamentary despatch box.

But even the name of the council is a compromise. Tickner had intended that it would be called the Council for Aboriginal Reconciliation and Justice. Hawke's advisers felt that 'Justice' went too far.

Hawke convinces a reluctant Pat Dodson, drained by his work with the Royal Commission into Aboriginal Deaths in Custody, and whose grandfather has just died, to become the council's inaugural chairman. Over time, Dodson will become known as 'The Father of Reconciliation'.

Lowitja, as head of ATSIC, takes a seat at the table of black and white community leaders. At the first meeting, Dodson invites them to share their stories. Among the Aboriginal members of the council there are common threads, of loss, and of unjust and unfair treatment. At the end of six hours, journalist Ray Martin breaks the emotional silence that has swallowed them up. 'The stories we have heard around this table today are the stories of two worlds, two countries,' he says.

In the Northern Territory, a mining dispute erupts at a place called Coronation Hill, where the mining company BHP wants to mine for gold, palladium and platinum. The Jawoyn people protest that the hill they call Guratba contains the serpent spirit Bula, and if mining is allowed in the 'sickness country', it will 'bring physical disasters which will affect everyone'. Labor powerbroker Graham Richardson, who has switched his support to Keating, calls it 'Bula-shit'.

On 18 June, Cabinet meets to thrash out the issue, over five hours. Keating's leadership ambitions overlay the meeting like a shroud. A majority of Cabinet ministers want the mine to go ahead.

Hawke, 'annoyed beyond measure', accuses them of being innately prejudiced against Aboriginal beliefs. He finds their views abhorrent and discriminatory. He attacks them venomously and spends the last of his authority supporting Aboriginal legend, which he finds no harder to believe than Christian scripture.

'The monumental hypocrisy of this position is mindboggling,' he tells them. 'The same people who denigrate blacks in this way can easily accommodate and embrace the bundle of mysteries which make up their white Christian beliefs—the virgin birth, the holy trinity, God in his question-mark heaven. Where is He? This supercilious, supremacist discrimination is abhorrent to everything I hold most important and to what, in the end, I believe this Party stands for. We can argue about some things, but surely in the end we are at one against discrimination.'

Hawke bans new mining at Coronation Hill and lays the groundwork for its inclusion in the Kakadu National Park.

Angry ministers leave the meeting saying Hawke has lost it.

It wounds him terminally.

XXX

In 1935, a young anthropologist, Ted Strehlow, was camped at Arltunga, east of Alice Springs. He was with Arrernte men, who were entrusting him with their knowledge, filled with foreboding that their way of life was coming to an end. Strehlow had grown up with the Western Arrernte. Born at Hermannsburg mission, Ntaria, where his scholarly father Carl had preached the Lutheran faith but was trusted as an ingkata, a spiritual man, their language had become his, together with English and German, Latin and Greek.

Strehlow had been fourteen when his father died at Horseshoe Bend, stricken with dropsy and pleurisy, and in agony after being carted down the dry bed of the Finke River on a buggy, one hundred and fifty miles (240 kilometres) in an October heatwave. 'God doesn't help!' he said before he died. They buried him in a coffin knocked up out of whisky cases and sang 'Rock of Ages', the hymn that was deemed most likely to be known by the bushmen present.

At university, Strehlow had studied classics and literature and then returned to study the culture of the Arrernte, who shared with him their knowledge and their secret and sacred objects. By 1935, he had already travelled thousands of miles, by train and car and camel back, and collected more than a thousand sacred objects and a thousand song verses. At Arltunga, he writes in his diary:

> It was wonderful to hear chanting again. A group of men, their heads and bodies shaking rhythmically, chanting with the enthusiasm that made them forget age and weakness and become young again in spirit ... the rising and falling of the chant melody, like the breathing that gives us life—what an unforgettable scene! It seems too terrible to think that all that is to pass away in another generation or less unless something is done by the blind stupid white usurpers of the native country of these men. [Kemarre] introduced his half caste wife to me this morning, and proudly showed me his two fat boys ... they were his own sons, he repeated several times, and not the offspring of whites ... His half caste wife looked happier than those unfortunate girls of the bungalow [the 'half caste' institution in Alice Springs] who have grown up without mother love who ... fall an easy prey to syphilitic ruffians as soon as they leave the bungalow. What's the earthly use of education to them without home or affection or kinship while they are yet children! Better let them be happy amongst the blacks, and rear babies whom they can fondle and bring up themselves.

———

At the end of June 1991, Lowitja travels to Alice Springs to open the Strehlow Research Foundation, with its vast collection—created by the anthropologist—of objects and records, film and sound, song verses, myths and ceremonies, all immensely powerful to the Arrernte, and the basis of Strehlow's magnum opus, *Songs of Central Australia*. At the end of his life, Strehlow clashed with a generation he claimed had no knowledge of authentic tribal culture, a world that was finished and would never come back. He said they had no right to atywerrenge, sacred objects, and so, when he died, he left his collection to his widow, Kathleen, who dismissed the claims of 'nouveaux Aborigines'.[22] The collection is returning to Central Australia after years of acrimony and protracted negotiation.

Opening the exhibition, Lowitja says that dispossession had appalling effects, but that language, culture and traditions are being revived with vigour and vitality. She calls the collection 'a comprehensive, precious and surviving record of traditional Aboriginal culture' that has been returned to its home in Central Australia.[23]

The next day, 27 June 1991, Lowitja's husband, Gordon, 'Smarty', dies at the age of seventy-three after suffering a heart attack. She is still in Alice Springs when she is told that he has been admitted to hospital. She charters a plane—but arrives too late.

'I'd hoped to get there. I actually chartered a plane, but I didn't arrive in time and he'd passed away a half an hour before . . . before I got there. But it was something that we'd always prepared ourselves for as well, because we talked about the possibilities that . . . because I was working (in Canberra) and he was home, that there could be a possibility that I wouldn't be there and, once again, you know, we'd sort of prepared the way for any possibility like that.'

They have had twelve years together. Whenever she has been asked about him, she has described him as 'a good bloke' and 'a straight-forward man'.

On 2 July, the funeral service is held in a flower-filled church in the town of Quorn, where they had lived together before and after they married. She takes her seat alongside four of her husband's children. Adults with children of their own, most of them had never met her. But they comfort one another.

And then just as she had done after burying her mother, she flies back to work. In a notebook, she writes, 'Went home to arrange the funeral and to pay my last respects and returned to work, as he would have expected.'

———————

She flies to Darwin, where she speaks at a Harold Thomas exhibition to commemorate the twentieth anniversary of the first raising of the Aboriginal flag he designed. She says it has been a source of unity, strength and pride.

Then she flies to Geneva, to speak at the United Nations Working Group on Indigenous Populations. She speaks about the first year of the operation of the Aboriginal and Torres Strait Islander Commission (ATSIC) and Bob Hawke's controversial decision to ban mining at Coronation Hill because of the spiritual significance of the area to the Jawoyn people. She says it is an illustration of 'how things have changed'.

'The possibility that a development project of this kind and size might be put aside for reasons of indigenous cultural and spiritual significance would have seemed unthinkable in our country not so long ago,' she says. 'I believe it is fair to say that we are making considerable progress in this important area in Australia. There is still much to be done, but things are moving in the right direction.'

Shortly afterwards, she delivers the Sir Robert Garran Oration in Darwin, for the Royal Australian Institute of Public Administration. In a major speech, tying together many of her thoughts, she observes that for the architects of the Australian Constitution, including Garran, 'Aboriginal people were irrelevant':

In 1788, when White Australia was founded, we were a vigorous nation, perhaps one million strong. By 1901, we were a largely dispossessed and demoralised remnant, locked away on reserves or living at the margins of white society, under the control of the government. It was assumed we were a 'dying race', and that whatever problem we posed for the new nation would eventually go away. We haven't gone away ... We are now a political presence in this country; our voices are heard ... We have rolled back 'the great Australian silence' ... the silence that reigned in Sir Robert Garran's time.[24]

She speaks about disadvantage, poverty and despair and quotes David Mowaljarlai, a Ngarinyin man from the Kimberley who has fought a forty-year battle for his people to regain the country from which they were displaced, which he believes has cast them into a kind of spiritual desolation: 'We must give the young ones back their culture, their language and their traditions, otherwise we will be gone,' he has said. 'We have only a little time left before all the old people like me pass away, and when that happens, that's the end of it. The lives of our young people today are like a desert.'[25]

She speaks about 'the thorny path' leading to the establishment of ATSIC, which is a 'tremendous opportunity', empowers Aboriginal people and signals the end of domination of distant administrators. She says that reconciliation will require Aboriginal people 'to stop beating their heads against the now unalterable fact of Australian history'. 'We have, to a large extent, been swept aside by the immensely powerful forces that have occupied our country,' she says. 'Given the history of European domination of the world, it is, in fact, hard to imagine pre-1788 Australia being allowed to remain as it was—though the process of colonisation might have been kinder and more just. We must reconcile ourselves to this fact and to our weakness, our 1.5 per cent, and work towards a realistic accommodation with modern Australia. Some Aboriginal people are fond of pointing to the darker aspects of Australian history, to acts of terrible cruelty against our people. However, it is probable that the most destructive forces have always been invisible—disease, despair, the loss of social structures, of the known universe.'

She talks about the need for Aboriginal people to take responsibility—for alcoholism, child abuse, domestic violence and early death—and notes that, while the Royal Commission into Aboriginal Deaths in Custody investigated twenty deaths in Queensland, in the same period, twenty-three Aboriginal women died as a result of family violence in three Aboriginal communities alone. 'The principle of self-determination must be extended to include self-responsibility,' she says. 'Aboriginal people must take responsibility for their own actions, their own lives, and the lives of their children. We must retrieve the values of our culture and live by them. Role models must emerge like the elders of old. I fear that by constantly invoking the horrors of the past, and by emphasising our present disadvantage, we may undermine our future.'

In December, she speaks at a congress on the impact of alcohol and drugs. 'This issue is a particularly crucial one for my people—almost a life and death one,' she says. 'I am talking not just about the threats to the lives of individuals, which is tragic in itself, but threats to a whole culture, perhaps to a whole people.'[26]

She says that Aboriginal affairs is a policy area that has suffered from 'a confusion of roles and responsibilities', that ATSIC is a radical and necessary change to give Aboriginal and Torres Strait Islander people control over the government decisions that affect their lives, at a time when Aboriginal people live in poor houses, are more likely to be imprisoned, more likely to fail at school, and die twenty years sooner than the average Australian.

Tickner extends Lowitja's two-year appointment, due to end in March, by a further nine months. At a meeting of commissioners and regional council chairpersons, she pronounces ATSIC a success that has 'far exceeded the most optimistic forecasts'.

At ATSIC, a former academic and rising public servant, Peter Shergold, replaces Bill Gray as chief executive. Born in Crawley New Town, England, and with a PhD from the London School of

Economics, Shergold joined the public service in 1987 to establish the Office of Multicultural Affairs. In 1990, he is deputy secretary in the Department of Prime Minister and Cabinet when department secretary Mike Codd asks whether he will go to ATSIC, as deputy chief executive, but with the expectation that he would replace Bill Gray, who goes north. Shergold has no background in Aboriginal Affairs. He gets the sense that because he has worked in Multicultural Affairs, it is assumed he can work in Aboriginal Affairs. He works in an office alongside Lowitja's and forms a high opinion of her political skills, her discipline and her integrity. He thinks he never had a harder job.

More than once he is told that, because of him, 'Aboriginal kids are dying in the desert'.

———

Bob Hawke falls.

With the economy in recession, Paul Keating can no longer be denied. On 19 December, the Labor caucus votes again, and this time Keating narrowly wins, 56 to 51.

On the morning of 20 December 1991, in his last act as prime minister, Hawke unveils the Barunga Statement, which will hang in the halls of the Australian Parliament on permanent display. In a brief ceremony, surrounded by representatives of Northern Territory land councils, he says that he promised at Barunga to hang the statement in Parliament House 'for whoever is Prime Minister of this country, not only to see, but to understand and also to honour'. He urges those who follow him to 'continue efforts to find solutions to the problems, the abundant problems which still face the Aboriginal people of this country'.

One of his greatest regrets, Hawke will say years later, is that he could not do enough for Aboriginal people. 'We did a lot of things, and I was very moved by the tributes I received from representatives of the Aboriginal people when I finished, when we had the Barunga statement in Parliament,' he says. 'But there is still so much to be done and I felt, I wished, I could have done more.'

He says he has no doubt that the antagonism caused by the bitterness of his attack on his colleagues over Coronation Hill, over their 'innate prejudice' and 'cynical dismissal of the beliefs of the Jawoyn people', was an element in his loss of the prime ministership.

After Hawke's death, Galarrwuy Yunupingu describes the former prime minister as 'a friend of the Yolŋu people': 'His efforts to bridge the gap between black and white Australia were always sincere, and continued after the end of his prime ministership. We did not achieve all that was set out in the Barunga statement, but it remains in Parliament, and we continue to pursue its aspirations. We will remember Mr Hawke fondly, a smile on his face.'

In February 1992, Lowitja speaks to federal, state and territory officials about the findings of the Royal Commission into Aboriginal Deaths in Custody: 'They catalogue the terrible history of dispossession and oppression of our people,' she says.

On 20 May, in the lead-up to the twenty-fifth anniversary of the 1967 referendum, she addresses the National Press Club. She speaks about the things that have changed—the redefining of Aboriginal culture, the new art forms, the successful organisations, increasing participation in education, the growing pride in Aboriginal identity. And the things that have not changed, including high unemployment, the 'continued unravelling of the Aboriginal world view', the lack of recognition of the first Australians in the Constitution, and a justice system 'which in some parts of Australia seems unable to treat Aboriginal people as other than a form of human trash to be processed in large numbers'.

She takes this opportunity to reflect on her own life, growing up in a world of protectors and restrictive laws, taken from her mother at the age of two, raised by missionaries who regarded their light-skinned

Aboriginal children as 'pearls from the deep', and then fighting back against discrimination and low expectation and becoming part of a political movement agitating for 'citizen rights'.[27] 'I recall these events because they have undoubtedly shaped my attitudes, which are not ones of protest or of anger—though there is cause for both—but ones of trying not to let them divert me from a sense of purpose in life, not limited nor defined by others,' she says.

In the High Court, a landmark case, a challenge to Australia's understanding of itself, is on the verge of decision. It is known by the name of its principal plaintiff, Eddie Mabo, a gardener who has challenged the injustice and convenient legal fiction—that Australia was unoccupied at the time of European colonisation, that it was terra nullius, nobody's land.

'We are the victims of this doctrine,' Lowitja says. 'The injustice perpetrated by it is now understood.'

She says that reconciliation—and recognition of Aboriginal people—might redefine Australia. 'I think that this is the task of the 1990s,' she says. 'The 1890s, the decade before Federation, was a period of great artistic and political activity, as Australians—white Australians—laid the foundations for a new democracy, a working man's paradise, and created the "legend of the nineties". But Federation barely recognised Australia's indigenous people. In 1901 the prevailing tendency was towards isolation and exclusion: it was a White Australia. It is now within our hands to make the nineties of this century stand out. Australia has an opportunity rarely given twice—to redefine itself as a nation.'

Two weeks later, the High Court rules.

Book Seven

Only she

XXXI

A man of 'flaring imagination, intellect and courage' as Marcia Langton will remember him,[1] Eddie Koiki Mabo was born in June 1936, at Las, on Mer, in the Murray Islands of the Torres Strait, the fourth surviving child of Robert Zesou Sambo and Annie Poipe Mabo. Five days after he was born, his mother died, and he was adopted by his uncle and aunt, Benny and Maiga Mabo, in accordance with island custom. As a boy, he learned the rhythms of the turquoise sea, and that he belonged to the wind. His first language was Meriam Mir, but he also spoke Creole and learned English.

When he was nineteen, he was accused of being drunk with a girl and was exiled from the island for one year. He worked on the sea in luggers, and then as a canecutter and railway fettler in Queensland. He married a gentle and loving woman, Bonita Ernestine Neehow, whose ancestors were blackbirded from Tanna Island, Vanuatu, and they had seven children, and adopted three more, and fought against discrimination. One day, at Townsville's James Cook University, where he worked as a gardener, Eddie sat talking to historians Henry Reynolds and Noel Loos about his land on the island of Mer. They tried to tell him that he did not own it, but that it was Crown land.

'No way. It's not theirs, it's ours,' he said.[2]

In May 1982, Eddie Mabo, Sam Passi, David Passi, Celuia Mapo Salee and James Rice began proceedings in the High Court against the State of Queensland and the Commonwealth of Australia, claiming 'native title' to the Murray Islands.

In 1985, the Queensland government attempted to derail the proceedings by retrospectively extinguishing their rights, backdated to 1879 when the Torres Strait Islands were incorporated into the colony of Queensland. The Queensland Coast Islands Declaratory Act of 1985 declared that 'the islands were vested in the Crown in right of Queensland freed from all other rights, interests and claims of any kind whatsoever and became waste lands of the Crown'. In December 1988, the High Court ruled, by a margin of four to three, that the state Act breached the federal Racial Discrimination Act, and the original case continued.

———————

Wednesday, 3 June 1992, the High Court, Canberra.

After ten years of legal battle, by a margin of six to one, Australia's highest court recognises the existence of a form of 'native title', where the tide of history has not washed it away. The decision overturns two centuries of presumption—the convenient legal fiction that Aboriginal people were too uncivilised, too low in the scale of social organisation, to have rights over land and that Australia at the time of European settlement was terra nullius, no one's land.

In his lead judgment, Justice Gerard Brennan rules that Australian law should not be 'frozen in an era of racial discrimination'. 'The fiction by which the rights and interests of indigenous inhabitants in land were treated as non-existent was justified by a policy which has no place in the contemporary law of this country,' he declares. 'Whatever the justification advanced in earlier days for refusing to

recognise the rights and interests in land of the indigenous inhabitants of settled colonies, an unjust and discriminatory doctrine of that
kind can no longer be accepted.'

In their joint judgment, Justices William Deane and Mary Gaudron
speak of a 'conflagration of oppression and conflict' spreading across
the continent for a hundred years to 'dispossess, degrade and devastate the Aboriginal peoples and leave a national legacy of unutterable
shame'. They declare: 'The acts and events by which that dispposses-
sion in legal theory was carried into practical effect constitute the
darkest aspect of the history of this nation. The nation as a whole must
remain diminished unless and until there is an acknowledgment of,
and retreat from, those past injustices.'

Goliath reels.

In the courtroom, there is silence. And then elation, and sadness
that Eddie Koiki Mabo did not live to hear the judgment. Four and a
half months earlier, the cancer in his spine having spread to his lungs
and throat, he died in Bonita's arms whispering the words 'land claim'.

In the last weeks of his life, he wrote of struggle and hope and love:
'After they had left me the rest of the night was not so bad. I lay in
bed thinking about the future and how I would like it to be even if
I am not there. I thought about the struggles I have been through
over the past years since 1963 to 1992 or to the beginning of 1992,
while the rest of Black Australia awaits with me for the High Court
decision to be brought down at any time . . . I also thought about how
my wife, the most important person in my life, has stuck to me over
many hardships and hurdles in life but somehow we made it, perhaps
better than others. To me my wife has been the most adorable person,
a friend closest in my life, a most wonderful lover, and we loved every
minute of our lives together.'[3]

Lowitja is at an Aboriginal and Torres Strait Islander Commission (ATSIC) board meeting when the court rules. She is jubilant that the untruth of terra nullius has been struck down, but she also knows that most Aboriginal people will have no claim. Native title will exist only where it has not been given away in land grants and where Aboriginal people can prove a continuous unbroken connection. She says that those who have claims should be given the chance to have them recognised, but that there is also a 'strong moral obligation' on governments to provide for the land needs of the dispossessed. She urges all groups to take 'a co-operative and constructive approach to resolving the differing interests in land'. The chairman of the Council for Aboriginal Reconciliation, Pat Dodson, says the decision was received by the council 'in a spirit of joy and celebration'.

Paul Keating welcomes the decision and says Australian law has taken a major step away from injustice by quashing 'the outrageous notion' of terra nullius. 'With this decision one more barrier—historically, perhaps the greatest barrier—has been effectively removed and the foundations of discrimination and prejudice have been kicked away,' he says.[4]

Prior to becoming prime minister, Keating's knowledge of Aboriginal people was slight. He remembered seeing the film *Jedda* at the Hoyts Civic Theatre in Bankstown when he was a boy and being left with a sense that Australia was 'their place'. He also had strong memories of going with his father to the boxing at the Sydney Stadium and Jimmy Sharman's fighting tent at the Royal Easter Show, where Aboriginal fighters fought for a pittance. He remembered that Kim Beazley senior had made a speech about Aboriginal malnutrition so powerful that Billy Wentworth, Australia's first Minister for Aboriginal Affairs, moved that the House adjourn for five minutes to recompose itself. In 1986, Keating urged Bob Hawke to take on national land rights, and knew that the issue couldn't be left in limbo; but he also felt there was a 'phoniness' at the core of statutory land rights, the idea 'of the

Parliament of Australia seeking to give Aboriginal people land that was never ours to give'.

In April, freshly minted as prime minister, Keating had spoken about the need to come to terms with Aboriginal Australia. 'Until we do this—until we start to make some real progress towards closing the gap in both attitudes and living standards—I think there will always be a feeling among us that maybe we don't quite belong, that we're not serious, that we're simply here for the view. Or just here to make forgeries of the Old World.'[5]

Now the High Court's Mabo decision has given his old conviction a new sense of urgency and direction. He views it as 'the crack of light one should crawl through'.

At the start of July, Lowitja speaks at a conference of Liberal Party women about being an Aboriginal woman in Australia, about discrimination, but also about violence against women so common that it is tearing at the fabric of Aboriginal society. 'Our stories haven't been told with bitterness or anger,' she says. 'Rather, we have tried to show how we have come to terms with a society in which, for generations, Aboriginal people in general—and Aboriginal women in particular— have been viewed as second-class citizens.'

At the end of July, she addresses the United Nations Working Group on Indigenous Populations, in Geneva. She says the Mabo decision is one of great significance, and uncertain consequence.

On 1 August, Lowitja turns sixty. That evening she sails on Lake Geneva with friends including Pat Anderson, an Alyawarr woman from the Northern Territory who is an Aboriginal health and social justice advocate. They watch bonfires burning on the shore to mark the Swiss national day and Lowitja jokes that the fires have been lit to celebrate her birthday.

In Australia, among the birthday congratulations she receives is a handwritten note from Charlie Perkins: 'To a friend of mine for over 35 years.' Hazel Hawke writes to Lowitja that she is 'a great credit to

your own Aboriginal people and to all Australia'. Aboriginal activist
Rosalie Kunoth-Monks, who was fourteen years old when filmmakers
Charles and Elsa Chauvel picked her to play the title role in their 1955
film *Jedda*, thanks her for all she has done, 'on behalf of Aboriginal
women and all Aboriginal people'. Former Aboriginal senator Neville
Bonner writes, 'My dear friend, your dedication to the cause is far and
above the call of duty.'[6]

She keeps them all.

On 4 September, Lowitja addresses the Women's Federal Council
of the conservative National Party of Australia, on the subject of the
Survival of the Family: 'Let me say from the outset that there is no
more important issue than this one. The very future of our society
depends on the strength of the family.'

She says that Aboriginal people have had to deal with changes that
they did not want. 'Our recent history has been a terrible and painful
one. It has been a history that has been ignored by history books and
not told until recently. Now, it is not my intention to make you feel
guilty. None of us is responsible for what happened in the past. But
we are responsible, individually and collectively, for what is happening now and if you are to understand how Aboriginal people feel you
need to know that history. It is a history of brutality and bloodshed.
The assault on our people included massacres, disease, dispossession
and dispersal from our lands . . . The most basic of human rights were
denied us.'

She says that Aboriginal people are 'just beginning to pick up the
pieces'.

In October, Keating, Attorney-General Michael Duffy and Aboriginal Affairs Minister Robert Tickner present Cabinet with policy
options, ranging from leaving native title to the courts, to land rights
legislation, or a 'document of reconciliation'. Extinguishing native
title is rejected from the outset, on the basis that 'it would lead to deep
domestic divisions and strong international condemnation'. So too is

amending the Constitution to put it beyond the control of parliament. Cabinet agrees to recognise 'the importance of the threshold across which the High Court has taken the nation and the ultimate need for government decision'.

Keating announces he will legislate a response to the Mabo decision and—for the first time in Australia's history—consult with Aborigines and Torres Strait Islanders, and others.

It is 10 December 1992 and Lowitja walks to the podium of the United Nations' General Assembly in New York for the launch of the International Year of the World's Indigenous People. She is one of a dozen indigenous representatives from across the globe, each of whom speak about colonisation, discrimination and struggle. With her is Torres Strait Islander leader George Mye, lifelong friend of Eddie Mabo, who says a prayer. Mabo—the man and the High Court decision—is in both their thoughts. No Aboriginal person has stood where they are standing.

But it is a sparsely filled assembly. No heads of government attend and, as she arrives at the podium, an Aboriginal activist who is opposed to ATSIC yells out, 'The speaker does not speak for the Indigenous people of Australia, but for the federal government of Australia.' He is escorted out.

She begins with her name: 'Mr President, My name is Lowitja. I am a member of the Yankunytjatjara peoples of northern South Australia. I am an Aboriginal person. I am accompanied on the platform by George Mye, a Torres Strait Islander.'

Of recent events, she says:

It took the Indigenous people of Australia until 1967 to be recognised as Australians under the Australian Constitution. This year we celebrated the twenty-fifth anniversary of that Constitutional recognition. We also were given cause to celebrate this year as a result of a decision by the High Court of Australia in what is now known as the Mabo case. Mabo, a Torres Strait Islander, pursued indigenous rights unrelentingly. As a result, the highest court in the land overturned the doctrine of terra nullius. After 204 years Australian law has finally recognised that indigenous people did own their land at the time of European settlement in 1788. This recognition is greatly welcome. Indeed, it is more than two centuries overdue. But it remains to be seen what its practical effects will be. Our land and our culture are the two things in this world that we cherish above all else. We have been dispossessed and dispersed. Our culture has been threatened as a result of colonisation. Many of our languages have been lost. Our spiritual beliefs have been ridiculed. We have become marginalised in our own country. In this International Year for the World's Indigenous People we proudly celebrate one thing—our survival. But our survival has been against overwhelming odds.

She speaks for ten minutes—about injustice and struggle and hope—and at the end of it she allows herself a small smile, and the years roll back to the little girl who was handed over to missionaries in Central Australia and grew up dressed in second-hand clothes trying to be noticed, and wondered why her mother and father didn't come for her, and the girl who was told to pack her bag because she was leaving the Colebrook Home for Half-Caste Children the next day to be a servant, and the young woman who stood in the corridor of the Royal Adelaide Hospital being told that she could not be a nurse because of the colour of her skin.

Just a small smile for her.

In the hours before she speaks, Paul Keating steps onto a makeshift stage in Sydney's Redfern Park, and delivers a speech of rare quality. A speech of power and poetry. Written by speechwriter and historian Don Watson, who regards Redfern as a sad and angry place, 'not a place to dissemble about Aboriginal Australia', it lays bare the nation's historical truths. They are 'truths that were hitherto unspoken', as the Aboriginal lawyer and activist Mick Dodson will describe it.

As Keating begins, there are catcalls from a restless black audience. Then silence and a murmur of approval and then applause as Keating challenges white Australians to know their history, to know 'what Aboriginal Australians know about Australia':

Ladies and gentlemen
I am very pleased to be here today at the launch of Australia's celebration of the 1993 International Year of the World's Indigenous People. It will be a year of great significance for Australia. It comes at a time when we have committed ourselves to succeeding in the test which so far we have always failed. Because, in truth, we cannot confidently say that we have succeeded as we would like to have succeeded if we have not managed to extend opportunity and care, dignity and hope to the indigenous people of Australia—the Aboriginal and Torres Strait Island people. This is a fundamental test of our social goals and our national will: our ability to say to ourselves and the rest of the world that Australia is a first rate social democracy, that we are what we should be—truly the land of the fair go and the better chance . . .

That is perhaps the point of this Year of the World's Indigenous People: to bring the dispossessed out of the shadows, to recognise that they are part of us, and that we cannot give indigenous Australians up without giving up many of our own most deeply held values, much of our own identity—and our own humanity. Nowhere in the world, I would venture, is the message more stark than it is in Australia . . .

It begins, I think, with that act of recognition. Recognition that it was we who did the dispossessing. We took the traditional lands and smashed the traditional way of life. We brought the diseases. The alcohol. We committed the murders. We took the children from their mothers. We practised discrimination and exclusion. It was our ignorance and our prejudice. And our failure to imagine these things being done to us. With some noble exceptions, we failed to make the most basic human response and enter into their hearts and minds. We failed to ask—how would I feel if this were done to me? As a consequence, we failed to see that what we were doing degraded all of us.

He says the report of the Royal Commission into Aboriginal Deaths in Custody has shown 'with devastating clarity that the past lives on in inequality, racism and injustice', while the Mabo decision has ended 'the bizarre conceit that this continent had no owners prior to the settlement of Europeans', established a fundamental truth, and laid the basis for justice. And he asks for imagination:

'Imagine if ours was the oldest culture in the world and we were told that it was worthless,' he says. 'Imagine if we had resisted this settlement, suffered and died in the defence of our land, and then were told in history books that we had given up without a fight. Imagine if non-Aboriginal Australians had served their country in peace and war and were then ignored in history books. Imagine if our feats on sporting fields had inspired admiration and patriotism and yet did nothing to diminish prejudice. Imagine if our spiritual life was denied and ridiculed. Imagine if we had suffered the injustice and then were blamed for it.

'It seems to me that if we can imagine the injustice we can imagine its opposite. And we can have justice.'

In New York, Lowitja wishes she had been in Redfern Park to see it.

XXXII

It is 13 March 1993. Paul Keating leads Labor to a fifth consecutive term of government. 'This is the sweetest victory of all,' he tells cheering supporters. 'This is a victory for the true believers, the people who in difficult times have kept the faith.' The night before, at the Imperial Peking Restaurant at Sydney's Circular Quay, he has spoken to some of his closest advisers about dreaming big dreams and doing big things, about the country knowing itself better and making peace with Aboriginal people 'to get the place right'.

Barely a month later, Aboriginal footballer Nicky Winmar, after a match in which he has been subjected to prolonged racist abuse by Collingwood fans, lifts his guernsey and stands pointing at his skin. 'I'm black—and I'm proud to be black,' he declares. Press photographer Wayne Ludbey captures the moment, full of strength and grace and pride, heroically defiant.

Keating turns his attention to Mabo.[7] No Australian prime minister previously has ever focused so hard on Aboriginal Australia. Within Cabinet there is great nervousness. As Keating's speechwriter, Don Watson, will observe, 'Designing a legislative response to Mabo was a moral imperative and a political death trap' with 'all the elements of political horror'.[8]

———————

On 27 April, Keating invites twenty-one Aboriginal representatives into the Cabinet room to meet with senior ministers—the eighteen men and three women are drawn from peak Aboriginal organisations, land councils and legal services, some of which have been talking together for months to formulate a response to Mabo.[9] Among them are Galarrwuy Yunupingu, Pat and Mick Dodson, Noel Pearson and Lowitja. Nyikina Mangala leader John Watson, a founder of the Kimberley Land Council, tells Keating, 'Old people are crying, dying . . . We're a sad people trying to preserve our culture.'

This is the first time that Aboriginal people have been brought to the centre of the national executive, and the first time Indigenous languages—Gumatj, Luritja, Alngithi, Nyikina and Meriam Mir—have been spoken at a meeting of Cabinet ministers. Senior people speak of their law, history, culture, language, the brutality of dispossession and their hopes for justice. Noel Pearson, emerging as a precocious intellect and powerful orator, will write that never before had Aboriginal people—'lepers in the Australian democratic process'—been invited in from the woodheap to sit at the main table.[10]

Wenten Rubuntja, an artist who lives in considerable poverty in an Aboriginal community in Alice Springs and a founder of the Central Land Council, presents Keating with a painting and they shake hands. Keating is also presented with a 'peace plan' that has been honed from a Red Centre Statement agreed to by Aboriginal land councils and legal services in Alice Springs the previous week.[11] West Australian Aboriginal leader Rob Riley warns Keating: 'Don't exclude us from the process. Don't attempt to do this without our involvement. Please don't dismiss us. If you do, you can forget about reconciliation.

We will wind people up. We will hit the streets. We will go to international forums.'

In February, Lowitja had written to Keating outlining the view of the Aboriginal and Torres Strait Islander Commission (ATSIC) that the government should not only protect native title rights, but also provide for the majority of Aboriginal people who have been dispossessed by the tide of colonisation and who will have no claim: 'I am extremely conscious of the significance of the issues raised for the nation as a whole, and recognise that governments will need to establish policies which maintain confidence and provide certainty for all holders of interests in land,' she writes. 'It is imperative, however, that as well as doing this, governments recognise and take account of the experience of dispossession suffered by indigenous peoples. The actions of governments to dispossess us have continued up to the present day with obvious consequences. Australia's indigenous peoples will expect no less than that your Government takes up the challenges and opportunities presented by the Mabo decision in a constructive and innovative way.'[12]

At the meeting Keating challenges the Aboriginal representatives to negotiate. 'Have you the sense or the courage to negotiate and accept the burden of that responsibility?' he asks.[13] He knows they are wary. He looks at an unsmiling Mick Dodson and sees a man who has been 'ratted on a hundred times before'. He judges that Central Land Council director David Ross, 'a leader in his own right and a weighty judge of circumstances', is a man he must convince, and that Lowitja is pivotal. As negotiations begin, he appoints her to a nine-member Republic Advisory Committee, to advise on the minimum constitutional changes necessary for Australia to become a republic, chaired by future Liberal prime minister Malcolm Turnbull.

On the other side of the table, Pat Dodson, chairman of the Council for Aboriginal Reconciliation, and before that a director of the Central Land Council and the Kimberley Land Council and a commissioner for the Royal Commission into Aboriginal Deaths in Custody, reaches a similar conclusion. He also regards David Ross as 'the toughest guy in the mix', steady and clear-sighted, with a deep understanding of land and culture. But Lowitja, he says, was a 'benign matriarch', cautious but resolute.

Dodson had been aware of her since the 1960s, when, as a young Catholic seminarian, torn between politics and the priesthood, he attended the annual Easter meetings of the Federal Council for the Advancement of Aborigines and Torres Strait Islanders, and later when they were both members of the Aboriginal Development Commission. What strikes him most about her is her understanding of the workings of power. 'She understood the system far better than any of us—and was keen to understand it,' he says.[14]

The next day, in his H.V. Evatt Memorial lecture, Keating sets out his government's primary goals: to reduce the number of unemployed, 'to remove the stain of dispossession and social injustice which attaches to the relationship between indigenous and non-indigenous Australians', and to create an Australian republic.

'The legacy of injustice towards the indigenous people of Australia shames us in the eyes of the world,' he says. 'Yet feelings of shame and outrage are not necessary to feel that things have to change. Pride should be all it takes.' Mabo, he says, is a unique opportunity. 'Mabo presents us with a more substantial and binding basis for reconciliation—a legal and historical basis which goes well beyond those pious and well-meaning sentiments whose history is just as long as the prejudice and dispossession they seek to correct. We now have a chance to do something real. Because land goes to the core of the dispossession, Mabo may have the potential to work the miracle.'[15]

For Lowitja, 1993 has begun with high hopes and the death of heroes.

In January, at Yirrkala, East Arnhem Land, she spoke at a memorial service for Roy Dadaynga Marika, leader of the Rirratjingu clan. A man with a slight build and a face that seemed to have been chipped from stone, Marika was a father of the Aboriginal land rights movement—a signatory to the Yirrkala Bark Petition, the Magna Carta of the Yolŋu people asserting their rights to the land from time immemorial. 'Mr Marika was one of the outstanding Aboriginal leaders of the 20th century,' she says. 'He played a major role in the struggle for Aboriginal land rights and he worked tirelessly for his people and for the cause of justice. We all owe him an enormous debt . . . His life is an inspiration for all of us. One day his vision of a society where Aboriginal culture is cherished, where people can live in justice and where the rights of all indigenous peoples are respected, will become a reality.'[16]

The following month, she took her seat in St Mary's Cathedral, Sydney, for the Requiem Mass of eye doctor Fred Hollows, who became a friend of the Gurindji people at Wave Hill, appalled by the prevalence of blinding trachoma in their eyes. He treated them and other Aboriginal people, and then poor people in towns and villages far beyond Australia, in Eritrea, Nepal and Vietnam. He is to be buried under coolabah trees.

Meanwhile Mabo has been building slowly into conflict. In the closing days of 1992, Aboriginal activists in Queensland had declared they would claim the Brisbane central business district. Aboriginal Affairs Minister Robert Tickner said they had 'less than a snowflake's chance in hell of ever being taken in any way seriously by the courts'. On 12 January, on Perth radio, National Party leader Tim Fischer had said the Mabo decision could jeopardise mining projects in the Northern Territory and Western Australia. He added, 'I am not going to apologise for the 200 years of white progress in this country. Indeed, I will take on and fight the guilt industry all the way.' Keating accused

Fischer of trying to incite fear and resentment against Aboriginal people.

Within the machinery of government, an interdepartmental committee headed by public service mandarin Sandy Hollway has been given the task of drafting the new native title laws. The committee works from crack of dawn until late at night, sifting the competing claims of interest groups, translating the Mabo principles into law. It meets with state governments, with the powerful mining and pastoral industries, and with Aboriginal representatives, who regard Hollway as the brakeman on their ambitions. One of the toughest negotiators from the states is future Labor prime minister Kevin Rudd, director general of the Queensland Government's Cabinet office.

An Office of Indigenous Affairs has also been established within Prime Minister and Cabinet. As an immediate rival to ATSIC as a source of government advice, Lowitja calls it the Office of Insidious Affairs. To senior public servant Mike Dillon, who transfers from ATSIC to head the office, it all feels like the engine room of a ship: 'Keating is up there on the bridge seeing the lie of the battle, and we're down there, shovelling coal into the engine.'[17]

At the end of May, at Keating's request, the Northern Territory government introduces legislation to protect the development of one of the world's largest zinc, lead and silver mines at McArthur River against land claims. It blindsides Aboriginal leaders. A spokesman for the Northern Land Council, Wes Miller, calls it 'a bombshell'. West Australian Aboriginal leader Rob Riley, who had warned Keating at the 27 April meeting 'don't exclude us from the process', says it is a kick 'in the guts'. Lowitja, furious, says that reconciliation 'may not have much of a future'. But Keating replies that, if the $250 million project had failed, 'you'd have the worst elements of conservative interests in this country up there blackguarding the Mabo decision and all it stands for'.

On 3 June, on the first anniversary of the Mabo decision, the federal government releases a one-hundred-and-six-page discussion paper with thirty-three guiding principles. It satisfies no one. Aboriginal leaders are outraged that it appears to be ambiguous about the integrity of the Racial Discrimination Act. Noel Pearson calls it a 'slimy useless document' that ignores the cultural and spiritual issues underlying Mabo. Mick Dodson suggests that the guns and strychnine used against Aboriginal people in the past have been replaced by the word processors of bureaucrats. But miners and farmers also reject key elements, including the idea that native title might be revived after the expiry of another form of lease, and West Australian Premier Richard Court suggests Mabo is paving the way to a form of apartheid.

In New South Wales, the Wiradjuri people lodge an inflammatory claim for a third of the state and billions of dollars in compensation for trespass. It ignites a grim warning from the chief executive of the NSW Farmers' Association, John White. 'The risk of hatred from this is immense,' he says. 'Hatred leads to violence . . . people are not going to walk off their land without a fight.'

Appealing for calm, Keating goes to a meeting of the Council of Australian Governments in Melbourne, on 8 June, hoping for national consensus. After ten hours of talks, Tasmanian Premier Ray Groom says the premiers have not even managed to agree on the meaning of 'native title'. The talks collapse in disarray. Several states, following the lead of West Australian Premier Richard Court, declare they will introduce their own laws to validate land titles, extinguish native title and replace it with a lesser title based on 'traditional usage'. In a febrile environment, Victorian Premier Jeff Kennett subsequently says suburban backyards might not be safe from Aboriginal land claims.

At a National Party conference at Wagga Wagga, Tim Fischer warns the Mabo decision has the capacity to 'put a brake on Australian investment, break the economy and break up Australia'. 'Rightly, or wrongly, dispossession of Aboriginal civilisation was always going to happen,' he says. 'Those in the guilt industry have to consider that

developing cultures and peoples will always overtake relatively station-
ary cultures. We have to be honest and acknowledge that Aboriginal
sense of nationhood or even infrastructure was not highly developed.
At no stage did Aboriginal civilisation develop substantial buildings,
roadways, or even a wheeled cart as part of their different priorities
and approach.'

In Seoul, Korea, Keating attacks Fischer's speech as 'crude and
primitive'.

But June ends with miner Hugh Morgan declaring in a speech to
the Victorian RSL that 'guilt industry people have great difficulty
accepting or recognising that Aboriginal culture was so much less
powerful than the culture of Europeans, there was never any possibility of its surviving' and that some cultures will 'wither away'. On
6 July, Northern Territory Chief Minister Marshall Perron tells international journalists that Aboriginal people are 'centuries behind us
in their cultural attitudes and aspirations', lacked hygiene and slept
with dogs. In August, Henry Bosch, former head of the National
Companies and Securities Commission, describes Aboriginal people
as 'a backward Stone Age people'.[18]

Lowitja speaks at many gatherings, national and international, black
and white, attempting to ease fears about what native title might mean,
urging respect and recognition. In Vienna in June she tells a United
Nations' World Conference on Human Rights that native title is facing
powerful opposition. She criticises a rash of 'extravagant and unrealistic
land claims' that have inflamed prejudice, and the politicians who have
sown the seeds of 'fear and hatred'.[19] In Perth, she tells a conference
convened by the West Australian Police Department that in many parts
of Australia 'racist hysteria' over Mabo has elevated tensions between
Aboriginal and non-Aboriginal people to a dangerous level.[20] In Geneva
in July, she tells the UN Working Group on Indigenous Populations
that positive and negative responses to Mabo are precariously balanced.
'The question is, which will dominate?' she wonders.

On 30 June, the Wik peoples of Cape York—the first Indigenous Australians with whom Europeans made contact, when Dutch sailors from Willem Jansz's *Duyfken* clashed with them at Cape Keerweer in 1606—lodge a native title case in the federal court. The case will determine whether native title can coexist alongside Australia's vast pastoral leases, some of them as large as a small European country. As the case begins, lawyer Ron Castan, lead counsel in the Mabo case, and a close adviser to Aboriginal leaders negotiating with the federal government, holds up a thousand-page anthropological report called 'Aak', the Wik word for country, or homeland, which he says will be the foundation for their argument.

———

At the start of August, more than four hundred Aboriginal people attend a bush meeting convened by the Council for Aboriginal Reconciliation at Eva Valley station (Manyallaluk), on Jawoyn land, a hundred kilometres east of Katherine in the Northern Territory. They call for 'legislation to advance Aboriginal rights to land' and for the Commonwealth to exclude the states from involvement in Indigenous issues. Mick Dodson accuses Keating of not negotiating. Keating denies it and says Aboriginal leaders have to accept the responsibility and burden of leadership.

———

On 2 September, Keating releases a detailed outline of the government's proposed legislation. He says it provides 'ungrudging and unambiguous' recognition of native title, but Aboriginal people will not have a right of veto over mining and the government is still committed to a 'technical suspension' of the Racial Discrimination

Act. Hundreds of Aboriginal people meet again, at Boomanulla Oval, Canberra, where the 'Eva Valley working group' vows to lobby black African states to boycott the Sydney Olympics, call on the Queen to stop the governor-general from giving royal assent, and take the legislation to international courts. They march to Parliament House and burn a copy of the draft bill.

Warlpiri artist Michael Nelson Tjakamarra removes a stone from his mosaic in the Parliament's forecourt, saying the government is weakening Aboriginal laws and customs.

In September, Lowitja goes back to Quorn, to open the town show. 'I have so many fond memories of Quorn and our show,' she says. 'As some of you know, Quorn has a very special place in my heart and I know I shall forever be a part of this town, the town I call my home.'[21] A few days later, at the National Library of Australia in Canberra, she opens an exhibition of poignant regalia, the sad and humiliating metal breastplates bestowed by white people, throughout the nineteenth century and into the twentieth, upon the Aboriginal 'kings' and 'queens' and 'last of their tribes' who lived in ragged destitution on the fringes of their towns.

———

Late on the night of 7 October, Robert Tickner sits slumped in his office, his head in his hands, contemplating resignation. Cabinet is edging towards pushing through the Mabo legislation it is drafting with the states, including 'technically' suspending the Racial Discrimination Act and giving the states a greater role in dealing with native title land. Mick Dodson is describing it as a 'contemporary, conscious act of racial discrimination'. Noel Pearson is accusing the government of 'moral scurvy'.

Tickner feels defeated, demoralised, lonely in his views. The swirling debate around native title has felt like one long, continuous assault.

He is also in the throes of trying to make contact with his birth mother. Although he has always known he was adopted, since the birth of his son he has felt an 'irrepressible need' to find his birth family.

As he sits there, surrounded by Aboriginal artefacts, Lowitja appears in the open doorway. She seems happy, absurdly hopeful. It is too much for Tickner. He starts weeping. He tells her Cabinet is focused on a deal with the states.

'I'm so sorry,' he says. 'I just don't know what to do.'

Lowitja stares at him for a moment, and then turns and strides away, angrier than he has ever seen her.

'Lowitja, can we talk?' Tickner calls after her.

'I've got to go,' she replies, not turning.

Separately, the directors of the Northern and Central land councils, Darryl Pearce and David Ross, are told by a government adviser that Keating is preparing to do a deal with West Australian Premier Richard Court at a meeting in Perth. In a phone call around midnight, Pearce is told, 'He's going to fuck you over and do a deal with Court.'

At a press conference the next day, Lowitja sits flanked to her left by Social Justice Commissioner Mick Dodson and Indigenous academic Marcia Langton, who is working for the Cape York Land Council. To Lowitja's right are Cape York lawyer Noel Pearson and Cape York elder Peter Costello. Lowitja accuses Keating of being more concerned with states' rights than the human rights of Aborigines and says his Redfern Park speech will 'come back to haunt him' if the government does not deliver a better deal. Mick Dodson says the government appears to have decided that the states and territories and powerful vested interests can do more damage to it than Aboriginal people. Pearson says he has done his share of cajoling and arguing and 'sleazing around the corridors', but now Keating must decide whether he wants to be reconciled with Aboriginal people, or the states.

In order to emphasise that Keating has no deal with Aboriginal leaders, and to undermine his talks with Court, Pearce and Ross have flown home, to Darwin and Alice Springs.

Keating erupts with a lacerating anger that shakes the Aboriginal negotiators. He again challenges them to summon the authority to negotiate, and to compromise. 'I don't know why such bad faith is being shown by the Aboriginal leaders, but this cannot help the process of getting the Bill to finality,' he says. 'I'm not sure whether indigenous leaders can ever psychologically make the change to decide to come into a process, be part of it and take the burdens of responsibility that go with it. That is, whether they can ever summon the authority of their own community and negotiate for and on their behalf.'

His anger and frustration flows down through the government. At ATSIC, chief executive Peter Shergold receives a phone call from one of Keating's senior advisers that he remembers as 'pretty ugly'. Shergold is left in no doubt that there will be retribution. In the shadow world of the public service, he hears it said of him that he has 'gone feral' and requires a period of rehabilitation.

It is Friday 8 October 1993. They call it Black Friday.

Keating's attack is bitter and chastening. 'He was dead right,' Noel Pearson will recall twenty years later. 'We had this great psychological inability to do a deal because people didn't want to be held to account, in history and back with the mob. It was offensive, but he challenged us to leadership in a very intense psychological way.'[22]

But Keating, stung by the criticism of the Aboriginal leaders, is also convinced that he must not proceed without Aboriginal support. An impediment is overcome when a legal solution is found to validate land titles without suspending the Racial Discrimination Act. The Native Title Act will constitute a 'special measure' under the Racial Discrimination Act for the benefit of Aboriginal and Torres Strait Islander people.

Before and after Black Friday, letters are sent to Keating by key

Aboriginal negotiators setting out their position. They are signed by Darryl Cronin, Noel Pearson, Darryl Pearce, David Ross and Lois O'Donoghue, representing the Aboriginal land councils of northern Australia and Central Australia, where native title will mostly apply, and ATSIC. They call themselves the Combined Aboriginal Organisations Working Group, but it is the nucleus of a group that is quickly dubbed the 'A Team'. When negotiations resume, Lowitja grasps the nettle and advises Keating to negotiate only with them.

From the beginning, the legitimacy of the negotiations with Keating had been questioned within Aboriginal Australia. In the bearpit of Aboriginal politics, the negotiators are abused and maligned, as is Rick Farley and other leaders of the National Farmers Federation, for negotiating on native title rather than demanding extinguishment. Charlie Perkins calls the Aboriginal negotiators 'an unrepresentative elite'. They are called amateurs and traitors and accused of dealing away the future of Aboriginal people. Lowitja, convinced that ATSIC and the land councils are negotiating the best possible deal with a tough but sympathetic prime minister, dismisses the critics. 'I couldn't get any sense out of them,' she says.

Keating is full of admiration.

—————

Just before midnight on Monday 18 October, Cabinet agrees to the legislation. During the final deliberations, the Aboriginal negotiators have convened in an office provided for them close to the prime minister's office, in case there is a need for last-minute negotiation. They stay to celebrate with Keating until 2.30 am. Keating issues a statement: 'As Mabo was an historic judgment this is historic legislation, recognising in law the fiction of terra nullius and the fact of native title. With that alone the foundation of reconciliation is laid—because after 200 years, we will at last be building on the truth.'

On Tuesday 19 October, the Labor caucus gives Keating a standing ovation. He says a historic agreement has been reached 'which will warm the soul of the Labor Party for two generations'. He pays tribute to 'the Aboriginal leadership under Lois O'Donoghue who did the courageous thing, took the step, seized the moment to negotiate rather than to demand, and to sit down and work out where Aboriginal interests truly lie and where they could be offset against the legitimate economic interests of the country'.

The Native Title Act will be 'a new deal' for Aborigines, Keating says. It will provide ungrudging and unambiguous recognition and protection of native title, but will also provide certainty for miners and farmers; the states will continue their role in charge of the economic use of land, if they adhere to the spirit and principles of the Racial Discrimination Act; Aborigines will have 'a genuine right of negotiation' over land use, but no veto; they will have a choice of federal or state tribunals or courts to adjudicate their claims; and where native title is extinguished there will be 'just compensation', which Keating concedes will amount to hundreds of millions of dollars.

The Coalition parties remain opposed and West Australian Premier Richard Court says he has no option but to introduce his own legislation, which will ultimately be challenged in the courts and found to be discriminatory. But there is wide support for the deal and the headline in *The Age* is 'Keating's Mabo Triumph'.

Lowitja tells a press conference that 'with the understanding of the Prime Minister, we have secured a remarkable settlement and a historic agreement'. She says the debate 'brought out the best and the worst' of Australia.

Noel Pearson calls it Ruby Tuesday. But in the national Aboriginal leadership there is tension. Rob Riley, his life in turmoil, calls the deal 'the most serious mass extinguishment of the rights of Aboriginal people since white settlement'.[23] An Aboriginal 'B Team', more radical in disposition, attempts to negotiate eleventh hour concessions with the minor parties, who hold the balance of power in the Senate. Tasmanian radical and lawyer Michael Mansell is prominent. He regards the High Court's Mabo decision as 'something for those who are grateful for small blessings, but nothing in the way of justice'.[24]

In a ten-minute address to the nation on 15 November, Keating appeals to morality, democratic instincts and fair play. He says the High Court's Mabo decision was 'unquestionably just' and presented Australia with an issue it could not ignore, either legally or morally. 'This generation cannot be held responsible for the cruelty of previous generations,' he says. 'But to ignore Mabo would be the final cruelty, and we would be held responsible—by the world and by future generations of Australians.'

The following day, 16 November 1993, with Aboriginal leaders watching from the galleries, Keating rises in the House of Representatives to move the second reading of the Native Title Bill 1993. 'Today is a milestone,' he begins. 'A response to another milestone: the High Court's decision in the Mabo case. The High Court has determined that Australian law should not, as Justice Brennan said, be "frozen in an era of racial discrimination". Its decision in the Mabo case ended the pernicious legal deceit of terra nullius for all of Australia—and for all time. The court described the situation faced by Aboriginal people after European settlement. The court saw a "conflagration of oppression and conflict which was, over the following century, to spread across the continent to dispossess, degrade and devastate the Aboriginal people". They faced "deprivation of the religious, cultural and economic sustenance which the land provides" and were left as "intruders in their own homes".

'To deny these basic facts would be to deny history—and no self-respecting democracy can deny its history.'

Responsibility for navigating the legislation through the Senate falls to Labor's Senate leader, Gareth Evans, a man possessed of a volcanic temper who, as a young lawyer, helped found the Victorian

Aboriginal Legal Service. In 1980, as an Opposition senator, he joined Aboriginal protesters at Noonkanbah. He was also deeply affected by the suicide of a young Aboriginal man in Alice Springs in 1980, Brian Kamara Willis, a law student who had stayed in Evans's home and 'one of the brightest and most engaging of his generation'. When he speaks of it in the parliament, in May 1997, he will weep uncontrollably. 'I think the only time in my public life when I completely lost it,' he will recall.[25]

When two contrarian West Australian Greens senators, Christabel Chamarette and Dee Margetts, who are unconvinced the legislation advances Aboriginal rights, attempt to delay it, Lowitja accuses them of hijacking Aboriginal authority and endangering a fragile consensus. Keating says that those 'trying to turn the screws on the government . . . are playing into the hands of the opponents of justice for Aboriginal people and a sound and workable outcome on Mabo'.

It is midnight, Wednesday 22 December 1993, and, after 116 amendments, the 115-page legislation passes the Senate. Debate has lasted almost fifty-two hours. For almost all of that time, Evans has been on his feet, withstanding the attacks of Opposition senators, who oppose the bill clause by clause, and negotiating in back rooms and corridors. On the second last day of debate, the Opposition takes more than eight hours to deal with a single question. Every member of the Coalition votes against the Native Title Act.

On the floor of the Senate, Evans, exhausted but euphoric, tingles with excitement. It is the proudest, most moving and exhilarating moment of his twenty-one-year parliamentary career. Democrats leader Cheryl Kernot, who will soon begin a five-year affair with Evans and defect to the Labor Party, feels 'utterly exhilarated'.

In the packed public gallery, there is cheering and foot stamping and whistling. Mick Dodson feels satisfied, but not fully. Marcia Langton is euphoric—and relieved—after a 'harrowing' eighteen months of explaining and lobbying, trawling the corridors of power. 'Just an enormous sense of relief,' she says. Darryl Pearce feels as though a long game is just beginning. Later, when he walks past government offices filled with booze and celebration, he thinks 'this is not us' and leaves with David Ross to mull it over.

Frank Brennan—lawyer, Jesuit priest, eldest son of High Court justice Gerard Brennan, whose Mabo judgment has been the catalyst—is elated. 'Deo Gratias,' he thinks to himself. 'Thanks be to God. It's done. You bloody ripper!' But Brennan also sees the anomaly, the weakness in the scene: all the black faces in the gallery, and all the white faces in the parliament.[26]

———

Later in the morning, the native title legislation passes through the House of Representatives. The day is cloudy, wet underfoot from the previous night's rain. Lowitja sits at the back of a half-filled public gallery, watching; she then joins a woman who has been sitting alone in a front seat, to the side—Paul Keating's wife, Annita.

At 9.20 am, on the last sitting day of the Australian Parliament in the United Nations Year of Indigenous People, the legislation passes seventy-eight to sixty-two.

For Lowitja, and the national Aboriginal leadership, these are golden days. But it is an illusion, a trick of the warm light in which they bathe for a moment.

As Mick Dodson will remark, it is the culmination of an era that has offered Indigenous people the hope of a fairer place in the Australian nation. 'Alas!' he says. 'That future was not to be.'

But among those who were there, the regard for Lowitja is great. For academic Marcia Langton, Lowitja was 'the glue' holding the negotiations together. For ATSIC chief executive Peter Shergold, who would go on to be head of Prime Minister and Cabinet under John Howard, she was the difference between success and failure. 'It was ATSIC in general and Lois in particular who were able to hold that group together to achieve those outcomes,' he says. 'It would have fractured, in my view, without her.' For Northern Land Council director Darryl Pearce she was the shepherd: 'She kept the wolves off our backs.'

In 2011, Paul Keating will deliver the Lowitja Oration, named in her honour by the Don Dunstan Foundation in Adelaide, and will pay her lavish tribute, describing her as a remarkable Australian leader who saw with great clarity that the High Court had opened a door of possibility that could quickly close and moved to seize the moment: 'She knew that in the dismal history of Indigenous relations with European Australia, this was an illuminated breakout; a comet of light in an otherwise darkened landscape . . . Only she could do it. She was the chair of ATSIC. This gave her a pulpit to speak from but no overarching authority, much less power. But this is where leadership matters: she decided, alone decided, that the Aboriginal and Torres Strait Islander peoples of Australia would negotiate, and I emphasise negotiate, with the Commonwealth Government of Australia—and that the negotiators would be the leaders of the Indigenous land councils. She decided that. And from that moment, for the first time in the 204-year history of the settled country, its Indigenous people sat in full concert with the government of it all. This is why I am here tonight: to acknowledge that moment of leadership and to celebrate it.'[27]

Noel Pearson will deliver the Lowitja Oration in 2018 and call her the greatest Aboriginal leader of the modern era. During the native title negotiations, he will recall, she was 'the rock who steadied us in the storm. Resolute, scolding, warm and generous—courageous, steely, gracious and fair. She held the hardest leadership brief in the nation and performed it bravely and with distinction'.

Robert Tickner will smile a warm smile when he later speaks of her: 'She changed the course of Australian history,' he will say. 'She literally seized the day.'

XXXIII

Pain sweeps through Lowitja's chest on 19 April 1994, and she is hospitalised after suffering an angina attack at the Aboriginal and Torres Strait Islander Commission (ATSIC) offices in Canberra. She is admitted to intensive care and transferred to coronary care, where her condition is described as serious but stable. Cards and letters and flowers pour in from high and low: from Paul Keating; High Court judge Bill Deane; John Howard, whose political career hovers between being yesterday's man and tomorrow's; and from ATSIC offices and Aboriginal organisations.

The American ambassador Edward J. Perkins sends a message that he is distressed to learn she is in hospital. In Geneva, Erica-Irene Daes, chairperson of the UN Working Group on Indigenous Populations, says she is extremely disturbed by the reports. Academic Bill Jonas, the first Aboriginal person to be awarded a PhD and whose grandfather was a showman who performed at the coronation of King George V, leaves a message saying he knows what she is going through.

She keeps them all. She always does. Every message of concern and admiration, every invitation and thanks, every birthday and Christmas card. Everything.

After the elation of the native title negotiations, Lowitja has spent months defending ATSIC from criticism, including calls for the administration of Aboriginal health to be returned to government departments. In March, she talks about her people, the Yankuny-tjatjara, whose lands extend into the Great Victoria Desert. 'It has always been one of my deepest regrets, and certainly the most painful experience of my life, that my spiritual identity with this area was interrupted when I was taken away from my mother as a small child and placed in the Colebrook Home at Quorn'.[28]

In May, she accuses Charlie Perkins, who has re-emerged from exile to become ATSIC deputy chairman, of plotting to replace her in a boardroom coup. Perkins denies it, but *Koori Mail* cartoonist Danny Eastwood draws him blowtorching Lowitja's name off the chair-person's desk. If John Hewson had won the 1993 election, Perkins had agreed to be part of a 'kitchen cabinet' of prominent Australians. But Hewson loses what had seemed an unlosable election and then loses the Liberal leadership to Alexander Downer.

In the aftermath of Paul Keating's 'sweetest victory', Lowitja is regularly discussed as a contender to replace Governor-General Bill Hayden when he retires in February 1996.

Labor MP Garrie Gibson, chairman of the House of Representatives Standing Committee on Aboriginal and Torres Strait Islander Affairs, writes to Keating suggesting the next governor-general, who is expected to be the last before Australia becomes a republic, should be a woman. He says there would be powerful symbolism in appointing an Aboriginal woman, and there would be strong support for Lowitja to be that Aboriginal woman.[29] South Australian senator Chris Schacht suggests another Aboriginal woman—fiery magistrate Pat O'Shane. Asked for her response, Lowitja says the appointment of an Aboriginal person would signify 'a very substantial shift in the attitude of non-Aboriginal Australians towards Aborigines' and would be 'a very big step towards reconciliation'.[30]

Under the headline 'Mother of the nation', journalist Deborah Stone writes in Melbourne's *Sunday Age* in May 1994 that Lowitja is being widely discussed as Australia's next governor-general, or first president. 'Lois O'Donoghue, elder stateswoman of Aboriginal politics, has learnt to grieve quietly,' she writes. 'To relinquish, to wait, to fight, to reconcile, to move on. The pattern beats through the story of her own life as much as through the unfolding narrative of her people . . . No life, it seems, could be a better preparation for the slow reconciliation of a nation.'

She describes Lowitja as a plain-speaking woman, 'with a comfortable warmth that does not show off the sharpness of her intelligence. But her stories are so spellbinding that she is like the ancient mariner, reducing the listener to an enchanted "three-year child".' Born a 'half-caste' at a time when it was a slur, she has become a bridge between people: 'In the words of the psalmist, "The stone the builders rejected has become the cornerstone".'

Lowitja does nothing in this interview to douse the speculation. 'I don't think about it for a minute and haven't,' she says. 'If I were to think about it I'd only think about it in these terms: How could it be possible to come from a lowly birth like mine in the bush, no birth certificate, and I could rise to be the Governor-General? The mind boggles that it's even a possibility.'[31]

At the end of May, she is in Western Australia, appealing for action to reduce the rates of imprisonment in a state where Aboriginal people are twenty-four times more likely to be jailed than non-Aboriginal people, and make up almost a third of the prison population. 'In Western Australia,' she says, 'if you are an Aboriginal person and employed, you are 13 times more likely to be incarcerated than non-Aboriginal people. If you are Aboriginal and unemployed, you are 259 times more likely to be incarcerated. In Western Australia, if you are an Aboriginal person and you finished school, you are nine times more likely to be incarcerated than non-Aboriginal people.

If you are an Aboriginal person and you did not finish school, you are 127 times more likely to be incarcerated.'[32]

In June, she says ATSIC often feels like an organisation that is 'under constant political and media siege'. But she celebrates the appointment of her closest confidante, Pat Turner, as the commission's chief executive officer. The nation's peak Aboriginal organisation, with a budget of almost $1 billion and responsibility for lifting the nation's poorest people out of poverty, is now led by two Aboriginal women. Turner is the niece of Charlie Perkins. She has known Lowitja, who is twenty years her senior, since Federal Council for the Advancement of Aborigines and Torres Strait Islanders (FCAATSI) conferences in the 1970s, when 'she was well known throughout Aboriginal Australia and I was a young angry woman, I suppose, wanting to right the wrongs that Australia had perpetrated against our people'.

The two women have designed the ATSIC boardroom together, with an enormous oval table as the centrepiece, which allows Lowitja to look over her glasses and see all of the commissioners, including those who will ultimately bring the organisation to its knees.

In July in Geneva, Lowitja tells the United Nations Working Group on Indigenous Populations that the High Court's Mabo decision, while essentially conservative, would be seen as one of the great watersheds in Australia's history: 'I say this because I believe it has unlocked the door which has separated indigenous and non-indigenous Australians for two centuries,' she says. 'The Mabo decision will prove to be a spur to the reappraisal of Australian history and a new basis for the future relationship between indigenous and non-indigenous Australia.'[33]

In September, she speaks at Australian studies conferences at Kent University, England, and at Guangzhou, China. She speaks about change, and possibility. On 27 September, she briefs delegates at a Labor Party national conference on an Aboriginal Land Fund to assist dispossessed Indigenous peoples to acquire and manage land—the second stage of the Keating government's native title package—and a proposed social justice package to address the social, cultural and economic legacy of dispossession.

But in November, when she speaks at the Council for Aboriginal Reconciliation's first report to parliament, she wrestles with how much of her anger she will reveal. In her handwritten notes, she writes that bipartisan support for reconciliation has become a 'sham', given the Opposition's attack on native title. 'In preparing my speech today I agonised over what I might say for there are some serious concerns I believe I should raise,' she says. 'The reconciliation concept is certainly a noble one. It is certainly noble and ambitious to attempt to achieve in one decade an understanding and respect for indigenous Australia on the part of non-indigenous Australia after two centuries of indifference and racism.' With Alexander Downer sitting stony faced, she says Indigenous people have watched with sadness as Opposition parties have attacked native title. She also says there needs to be a treaty between Indigenous and non-Indigenous Australia.[34]

At Christmas, Lowitja surprises ATSIC board members, and disappoints some who had hoped to replace her, by announcing she has been reappointed chairperson for a further two years. In his announcement, Tickner says Lowitja has played 'a significant role in the evolution of ATSIC from a new but untested vehicle for greater indigenous self-determination to a strong and increasingly-effective representative body for Aboriginal and Torres Strait Islander people'.[35]

But in the months that follow, ATSIC loses control of Aboriginal health, and Cabinet decides against major infrastructure spending in Aboriginal communities. Tickner feels sick to his stomach, but is soon embroiled in controversy when he stops construction of a bridge to Hindmarsh Island, South Australia, after some Ngarrindjeri women claim the island is sacred to them as a fertility site.

A report has been prepared on significant Aboriginal sites that might be affected by the bridge's construction and, as part of that, claimed cultural secrets have been written down and sealed in two envelopes marked 'Confidential: to be read by women only' and forwarded to Tickner. Without reading the contents of the envelopes, he accepts there is enough reason to ban construction of the bridge. Litigation and a state royal commission follow.

Boycotted by the Ngarrindjeri women, the royal commission finds the claims were fabricated and 'secret women's business' becomes a disparaging idiom that dogs Tickner for the remainder of his time in politics. At the height of the controversy, Aboriginal Social Justice Commissioner Mick Dodson says, 'It is hard to find the right words to convey the mixture of outrage, distress and shame that I feel about what is happening in South Australia . . . What we have in this royal commission is the abuse of the human rights of Aboriginal people masquerading as a lofty legal procedure.'[36]

The bridge is built and opened in March 2001. Five months later, federal court judge John von Doussa says he is 'not satisfied that the restricted women's knowledge was fabricated or that it was not part of genuine Aboriginal tradition'.

After eight calamitous months, and a decade of infighting, Alexander Downer loses the Liberal leadership to John Howard in January 1995. Howard is—in his own words—Lazarus with a triple bypass.

In March, Lowitja hands Keating a report titled *Recognition, Rights and Reform*, which is ATSIC's proposed social justice package—the undelivered third act of Keating's response to the Mabo decision. Among 113 recommendations, the 177-page report calls for: the negotiation of a treaty; constitutional recognition of Indigenous people as the first Australians; compensation for dispossession; Indigenous representation in parliament; official recognition of Aboriginal and Torres Strait Islander flags; and regional autonomy. 'What we are talking about in this report is the basis of Australia's nationhood, the fulfilment of its federation, and the realisation of its fairmindedness,' she says. In the *Weekend Australian*, she writes, 'Our history since 1788 has been a painful one, dominated for the most part by disease and genocide, dispossession, resistance, attempts to assimilate us, poverty and marginalisation. We do not seek to divide the nation. Rather, we seek special recognition of our status within the nation. We seek to be included, because our past has been one of powerlessness and exclusion.'[37]

In May, the government announces the Human Rights and Equal Opportunity Commission will conduct an inquiry into the Stolen Generations—the removal of fair-skinned children from their Aboriginal families by government agencies and church missions.

Raised by missionaries who taught her to pray for charity and to forget her past, Lowitja continues to be advanced as a contender for governor-general. In an article in the *Sun-Herald* by Deborah McIntosh, headlined 'The rise and rise of Lois O'Donoghue', Lowitja recalls that, when she was made Australian of the Year in 1984, she was called a Judas by some Aboriginal people and says she would not accept any appointment without consulting her people. But she again allows herself to imagine that such a thing is possible: 'I mean, you're the first lady. You're the first! There are those sort of mixed feelings when I think, here I am, born in the bush, no birth certificate, removed when I was two and that I could rise to be the Governor-General or the first president. There are times when I think that it's some sort of fairyland.'[38]

On 3 June, in Townsville, she speaks at celebrations to mark the third anniversary of the Mabo judgment and the unveiling of a tombstone for Eddie Koiki Mabo: 'For Aboriginal and Torres Strait Islander people, he is a hero,' she says. 'The judgment that Eddie Mabo fought for has changed the world in which we live.'[39]

During the night, the grave is desecrated: it is sprayed with red swastikas and the word Abo, and his smiling likeness is prised from the headstone. A wave of anger and dismay rolls through Aboriginal Australia and the Torres Strait Islands. Lowitja calls it a hideous and sickening manifestation of racism, 'an act of violence against a man who fought for the rights of his people'. Political leaders condemn it. In Townsville, Eddie Mabo's widow, Bonita, says, 'Look what they have done to his grave now. I'd like to shoot the bastards—it's like it's starting all over again.'[40]

His body is exhumed and reburied on the island of Mer. On the night of the reinternment, islanders perform a traditional ceremony for the burial of a Meriam king, a ritual not seen on the island for eighty years.

In the final weeks before Keating appoints a new governor-general, support within the Labor Caucus centres on three women: Lowitja; Betty Churcher, director of the Australian National Gallery; and Elizabeth Evatt, former chief judge of the Family Court. In England, the *Guardian* reports, 'An Aboriginal woman seems likely to be made Australia's next head of state, in what could be the last such appointment by the Crown before the country becomes a republic.'[41]

But Keating is circumspect. Asked whether the time is right to appoint a woman, he replies, 'I think the time is right for a person to be appointed who will fulfil the role and responsibility adequately, who understands the sentiment in the country and the fact that the country is now—has been for a decade—in a very large transition. I think they are the requirements, rather than gender requirements.'[42]

In the Aboriginal community, there is support for Lowitja, but also rumblings of discontent. In a feature in the *Sydney Morning Herald*, under the headline 'Sell-out or saviour?', Jodie Brough and Debra Jopson write of Lowitja's journey:

If Lois O'Donoghue gets to preside over State dinners around the long, polished tables of Yarralumla, she will be the first Governor-General who was regularly saved from starvation by charity as a child. Travelling the globe promoting Australia, she would also be the first Governor-General who needed a reference from a church mission to obtain a passport. O'Donoghue, 62, the chairwoman of the Aboriginal and Torres Strait Islander Commission (ATSIC) since 1990 and now an apparent frontrunner to succeed Bill Hayden, has scrambled from the cold, loveless institution she was consigned to as a child to the boardrooms of Canberra and Geneva. From a powerless beginning, she has become arguably the most powerful indigenous woman since the British came to Australia.[43]

In the article, Central Land Council director David Ross, who worked closely with Lowitja during the native title negotiations, describes her as a calm and rational voice, tough and analytical in the furnace of Aboriginal politics. 'Anyone can go out in the street and yell and rant and rave,' he says. 'When you have to sit down around a table and work out a solution, that calls for different skills . . . she never walks away from the hard stuff.' Another native title negotiator, former Northern Land Council director Darryl Pearce, says, 'With Lois, it's presence. It's quiet, ongoing direction. In all the storms over native title she was like an anchor point. She got very sick during that process, yet she still came to Parliament House. We had to check that she was looking after herself. Lois is pragmatic. It's no good people screaming about sovereignty when they can go home and have running water and so on. She tried to ensure Aboriginal people live to fight another day.'[44] But the article also hints at a view within Aboriginal Australia that she is part of a bureaucratic clique.

As the scrutiny continues, activist Gary Foley calls her 'a servant of the system'; Sharon Firebrace, director of the Koorie Research Centre at Monash University, says she has been 'nurtured by the government humidicrib'; New South Wales magistrate Pat O'Shane offers, 'Lois is not a person who is ever going to question the process. She's always going to play it safe; she's a conservative.'[45] In South Australia,

Faith Thomas, who grew up with Lowitja at the Colebrook Home for Half-Caste Children, and was the first Aboriginal woman to represent Australia in sport, wonders whether there might not be better choices. 'Lois never rocked the boat in her life,' she says. 'I suppose that's the sort of person they want.'[46]

In the *Sydney Morning Herald*, political columnist Alan Ramsey writes that it is beyond time to appoint a woman and he believes Keating will do so. 'But not a black woman. Despite all the recent media hype, I don't think Lois O'Donoghue ... was ever really seriously considered, irrespective of her many qualities. Such a contentious appointment—and nobody should kid themselves it wouldn't be contentious—would be extremely high risk electorally for a government struggling as this one is. I just don't see Keating, for all his courage, taking such a risk. The politics of it simply rule it out, at this time under this Government.'[47]

On 21 August, Keating announces that he has appointed as governor-general the High Court judge Sir William Deane—a shy, graceful man by nature; an intellectual leader of the court; principled, socially progressive, and the first Catholic to be so appointed. Deane will take office in February 1996 and agrees to end his appointment on 31 December 2000, two months short of the conventional five-year term, clearing the way for the next head of state, a president, to take office on 1 January 2001—the centenary of the Commonwealth of Australia—if Keating can convince Australians to vote for it. As a former High Court judge, Deane would be well-placed to oversee the constitutional transition to a republic.

The appointment is well received across the parliament. Opposition leader John Howard describes him as 'a very distinguished Australian'. Among those thought to have been contenders, Betty Churcher says she was barracking for Lowitja. Robert Tickner faxes Lowitja a scrawled handwritten note: 'Dear Lois, you will always be my Governor General.'

At ATSIC, Lowitja issues a statement congratulating Deane. 'Sir William's judgment was one of the leading judgments in the High Court's historic Mabo decision which recognised indigenous rights by overturning the legal fiction of *terra nullius*. It is a comfort to know that the person who could be Australia's last Governor-General will have an understanding of and sympathy with the aspirations of indigenous Australians. I am confident that, in his new position, Sir William will continue his commitment to the achievement of social justice for all Australians, making a meaningful contribution to the process of reconciliation between indigenous and non-indigenous Australians.'[48]

In *The Australian*, journalist Michael Gordon writes, 'O'Donoghue was the woman pushed by many in the ALP Caucus, largely because of the symbolism her appointment would represent. She would be a first on two counts: the first woman and the first Aborigine to hold the office. But while O'Donoghue's contribution to public life has been long and impressive, her appointment would have created contro-versy—not because she was black or a woman, but because of her occasionally strong criticism of the Coalition's stance on Aboriginal issues.'[49]

Writer Tom Keneally suggests that Deane has been chosen because a woman is 'being saved up' for the first president of an Australian republic. In Keating's office, speechwriter Don Watson reaches a similar conclusion. Watson was trudging through soft ground on his father's back hill when Keating called to tell him he had appointed Deane. 'He had had Deane in mind for months,' Watson writes. 'He saw him as the "intellectual leader" of the High Court, knew him to be a republican in sympathy, the most ardent of the Mabo judges and a man of compassion and integrity. Keating knew that many people expected him to appoint a woman . . . The Prime Minister knew that Lois O'Donoghue in particular would be disappointed. But he believed that with constitutional debates looming, Deane would be the better person for the job. Better if O'Donoghue were to be the first president of the republic.'[50]

In later years, when asked, Lowitja will say that she would have refused the vice-regal position. 'I'm a republican,' she says.

The moment passes.

Book Eight

'My name is Lowitja'

XXXIV

On 2 March 1996, John Howard storms to victory in a landslide, ending thirteen years of Labor government and ushering in a new conservative era.

Bathed in blue, surrounded by his family, he says he feels a deep sense of humility, and that the things that unite Australians are infinitely more important and enduring than the things that divide Australians. He pays tribute to the vanquished Paul Keating, who has, he says, been 'a great warrior' for his political cause. But he makes it clear that change is coming: 'I want to make it clear that although uniting the Australian people will be the cornerstone of my approach in Government, we have been elected with a mandate, a very powerful mandate. And whilst I will seek at all times unity and a common point of view, we have not been elected to be just a pale imitation of the Government that we have replaced.'

The previous month, on the ABC's *Four Corners* program, he described his vision for Australia as a country: 'I would like to see an Australian nation that feels comfortable and relaxed about three things: I would like to see them comfortable and relaxed about their history; I would like to see them comfortable and relaxed about the present and I'd also like to see them comfortable and relaxed about the future . . . It is very important that we don't as a nation spend our lives apologising for the past.'

Paul Keating's big picture and challenging vision is taken down off the wall and replaced with something much more familiar.

Despite two decades in the parliament, Howard has had little contact with Aboriginal people—but he has strong views about them. When Bob Hawke proposed a treaty in 1988, he said it was 'repugnant to the ideal of one Australia' and he would rip it up. That year, he visited an Aboriginal community for the first time—Ernabella, the former mission in the Musgrave Ranges founded by Charles Duguid. It did not go well; Yami Lester, blind elder of the Yankunytjatjara, criticised the Coalition's 'One People, One Nation' policy and told Howard that, in the ways of the Anangu, he was like a young boy. 'We are willing to talk to you, we are happy to teach you,' he explained to an affronted Howard, who would not enter another Aboriginal community for a decade.

In his policy manifesto, 'Future Directions: It's Time for Plain Thinking', Howard derided the notion of a treaty with Aboriginal people as an 'absurd proposition' and lamented that Australians were being taught to be ashamed of their past by 'professional purveyors of guilt'. He had opposed the creation of the Aboriginal and Torres Strait Islander Commission (ATSIC) and was a constant critic of it. On 4 July 1993, he asserted the Mabo debate had introduced 'cultural McCarthyism' into Australian politics, in which anyone opposing conventional wisdom on matters of race was 'belted over the head with a bit of four-by-two on the basis that they are racist or extremist'.[1]

The 1996 election has also delivered onto the political stage a fiery red-haired fish-and-chip shop owner from Ipswich, Queensland— Pauline Hanson.

After a young black prisoner was found hanging from a length of rope in his cell in Townsville on New Year's Day, Hanson, at that time the endorsed Liberal candidate for the seat of Oxley—the safest Labor seat in Queensland—wrote a letter to the Ipswich newspaper, the *Queensland Times*, arguing that Aborigines should be treated no differently to any other race: 'I would be the first to admit that, not that many years ago the Aborigines were treated wrongly, but in trying to correct this we have gone too far,' she wrote. 'I don't feel responsible for the treatment of Aboriginal people in the past because I had no say but my concern is now and for the future. How can we expect this race to help themselves when governments shower them with money, facilities and opportunities that only these people can obtain no matter how minute the indigenous blood is that flows through their veins, and that is what is causing racism. Until governments wake up to themselves and start looking at equality not colour then we might start to work together as one.'[2]

Disendorsed by the Liberals for her comments, Hanson ran as an unapologetic independent and won Oxley with a twenty-three per cent swing. She arrives in Australian politics like a shock wave.

Six days after the election, Lowitja speaks at an International Women's Day event in Canberra. With the political pendulum swinging so dramatically, she fears there has not only been a change of government, but a backlash that is hostile to Aboriginal interests. She speaks about hopes rather than dreams. 'Australians have just voted overwhelmingly to change their government and also, as is inevitable, some of the direction of national affairs. In this new environment, I can only hope that Aboriginal and Torres Strait Islander issues continue to get the attention that they deserve and demand.' She says it is wrong to suggest that Aboriginal people, impoverished and marginalised and subjected to inhuman policies, are equal, and absurd to say that they are privileged.[3]

On Sunday 31 March 1996, allegations of rorting and mismanagement at the New South Wales and Victorian Aboriginal legal services are aired on Nine's *Sunday* program. Although ATSIC has already referred complaints to the Australian Securities Commission and commissioned an independent audit, it exposes weaknesses in ATSIC's structure, and strengthens John Howard's resolve. Interviewed after his first night at The Lodge, he says his government is committed to reconciliation, but Aboriginal organisations have to be accountable and the government is 'not going to be scared off doing things that are necessary in the interests of Australian taxpayers by some kind of politically correct quarantining of certain activities from any kind of scrutiny'. He says Aboriginal health standards are a 'national disgrace', and Australians are ashamed about it, but Australians are also entitled to question how taxpayer money is spent 'without being accused of prejudice or bigotry'.[4]

Publicly, Lowitja has promoted and defended ATSIC, arguing that it cannot be held responsible for two hundred years of neglect, and that its $1 billion budget is only enough to fill the potholes of Indigenous disadvantage, not the craters. But behind closed doors, she has warned constantly of the dangers of nepotism, mismanagement and corruption and now, with a hostile new government at the gate, she says Indigenous people have not been helped by prominent organisations that over a long period have resisted calls to be more accountable.

In an interview with *The Age*'s political editor, Michelle Grattan, Lowitja proposes sweeping change, with funding decisions taken away from elected commissioners and councillors to eliminate conflicts of interest. She also supports the new government's intention to retain an appointed rather than elected chairperson, to keep the position beyond vested interests: 'We've been preoccupied with trying to keep the elected representatives straight and on the rails in their decision-making processes,' she says. 'Pat [Turner, chief executive] and I have had long discussions about it. It's just been so difficult for the CEO and the Chair—we're killing ourselves.'[5]

On Tuesday 9 April, Lowitja has dinner with the new Aboriginal Affairs minister, Queensland senator John Herron, at Canberra's

Chairman and Yip restaurant. Herron is a former surgeon, deeply affected by his work as a volunteer doctor in Rwanda two years earlier, after the genocide there. Despite a strained relationship with the Coalition, Lowitja hopes to establish a rapport with him. Her call for the reform of ATSIC has enraged some commissioners—western NSW commissioner Steve Gordon, who was raised in an old tin shack on a riverbank at Brewarrina, says he 'could not sit in the same room as her'—but it has ensured some common ground with Herron. Their discussion, over lamb curry and mussels, is congenial.

At 10 am the next morning, Lowitja is on a conference call with angry ATSIC commissioners, staving off calls for her resignation. She reminds them that for six years she has warned them about conflicts of interest and nepotism, but that her warnings have fallen on deaf ears. Her deputy, 'Sugar Ray' Robinson, shouts that they need to have this discussion face to face. Like Steve Gordon, Robinson was raised in a tin shed, outside the Queensland town of Charleville, where he was always hungry; a former boxer, he was convicted of rape and sentenced to six years' jail in 1963 when he was seventeen, in what he calls 'a great injustice', and spent another two years in jail for rape from 1989 to 1991 before a retrial ordered by the High Court found him not guilty.

At 11.30 am that Wednesday, Lowitja and Pat Turner drive from ATSIC's Woden offices for a meeting with Herron at his Parliament House suite. Lowitja wonders whether their dinner was her last supper and if she is about to be sacked. What she does not know— what Herron has not told her—is that at its first meeting in Canberra the previous day, Cabinet has decided to appoint a special auditor to oversee ATSIC grants and loans to Aboriginal organisations—at a cost of $1.4 million, which will be deducted from ATSIC's budget. The government intends to retain an appointed chairperson and to reduce the number of regional councillors. It also seeks the power to appoint an administrator if the minister finds evidence of mismanagement, fraud, or a failure to follow ministerial directions; but this move is ultimately blocked by the Senate.

In his office, Herron outlines the plan to Lowitja and Turner, and then he joins Howard to announce it. Howard refuses to rule out scrapping ATSIC and speaks of 'an apparent haemorrhage of public funds'.

Lowitja's position is shored up on Saturday 13 April at crisis talks attended by seventeen Indigenous leaders in Canberra, including Mick and Pat Dodson. But there is great tension. The following day, the tyres of her car are slashed.

On Monday 15 April, Herron meets with the ATSIC board for more than four hours. He describes the mood as 'fairly heated'. At one point, he turns to Lowitja and says, 'Do you realise you earn more than I do!' Lowitja, whose salary of $170,000 is fixed by the Remuneration Tribunal, replies, 'Perhaps I'm worth more than you are. Are you implying that we ought to accept lower pay because we are black?' Afterwards, she describes their discussions as 'full and frank'.

———————

On 1 May, West Australian Aboriginal leader Rob Riley hangs himself in a Perth motel room. Among the Aboriginal leadership, Riley is admired and loved. Separated from his mother when he was eight months old, he grew up in a children's home known as Sister Kate's— started by Anglican nun Katherine Mary Clutterbuck. He was almost ten years old before he knew his mother was alive and it was another two years before they were reunited. He went to school at Pingelly, a wheatbelt town where in 1967 two justices of the peace asked the West Australian premier for the right to whip Aboriginal people.

At twenty-five, Riley was chief executive of the Aboriginal Legal Service; at thirty, he was chairman of the National Aboriginal Conference. After Bob Hawke's election, he was a policy adviser to

Aboriginal Affairs Minister Gerry Hand. He was head of the Aboriginal Issues unit of the Deaths in Custody royal commission and a key figure during the native title negotiations, when he received death threats. But there was something gnawing at his heart, as Pat Dodson will describe it. In 1994, he revealed that he was raped by other boys at Sister Kate's. Depression, trauma, drugs, grief, all collided in him.

Lowitja is with Pat Turner and senior public servants Mick Gooda and Jackie Oakley at ATSIC when they learn that Riley is dead. Gooda will recall that they were inconsolable. 'The anguish was profound.'[6] In his eulogy, in a crowded Perth cathedral, Pat Dodson says that Riley has been killed by pain and ignorance.

Former Aboriginal Affairs minister Robert Tickner sits at the back, his life falling apart. Voted out at the election, he is unemployed and won't find work for another two years. He was driving across Australia when he heard of Riley's death. He wonders at the gall of West Australian Premier Richard Court, so hostile to native title, but sitting in a pew near the front.

In May, the federal government releases a discussion paper outlining proposed amendments to the Native Title Act, but then withdraws it amid unrest from hardline conservatives, who are demanding the government legislate to extinguish the possibility of native title co-existing on pastoral leases—an issue left unresolved by Keating and that is being tested by the Wik people in the High Court in the cold of a Canberra June. 'So as a nation, we seem once again to be at an impasse on this issue,' Lowitja tells an audience of lawyers that includes former chief justice Sir Anthony Mason. 'It is a disturbing feature of this environment that those opposed to a just and inclusive native title regime are resorting to distortion and scare-mongering. But we are almost used to this.'[7]

With ATSIC facing deep cuts in what looms as a severe Budget, she tells ATSIC commissioners and heads of regional councils: 'Whether we like it or not, the cold fact is that we are in for a period of significant change. We can either seek to influence and manage the processes of change, or let change be imposed on us. It is as stark as that.'[8]

She warns them they are on thin ice. 'What should also be of great concern to us is that our own indigenous constituents are not rushing to the barricades to defend ATSIC in terms of either its principle or its practice,' she says. 'This is perhaps the saddest reflection I have to make. I detect a deep-seated disillusion with the way decisions are being taken. While in part we can explain it in terms of lack of funding, it goes deeper, I am sure, to perceptions of bias in the way decisions are taken.'

In June, as she arrives home in Canberra, at a rented house on a hill not far from the ATSIC offices, she hears what she believes is a gunshot. Without turning, she goes inside and closes the door. The following day she tells her executive officer, Vicki Scott, a former personal assistant to Governor-General Paul Hasluck, that she thinks that someone—and she suspects a powerful Aboriginal rival—is trying to frighten her, but that they will not succeed. Scott is shocked, 'but she seemed so calm and nonchalant about it, I thought maybe it was a car backfiring'. As this comes after the slashing of her car tyres, the Australian Federal Police advise her to use a Commonwealth driver, and to move to more secure premises or improve security at her existing home. She moves to another Canberra suburb; in September, the Australian Electoral Commission removes her address from the electoral rolls and the Australian Securities Commission suppresses her address from public inspection.

On 26 June, Noel Pearson tells the National Press Club he fears for the direction of Aboriginal affairs and that the spirit of Mabo has fallen on a fallow heart. Intending to quit Aboriginal politics and focus on the law, for a while at least, he says: 'I leave this debate with a deal of disquiet about the backward slide we have had in the tone of relations between indigenous and non-indigenous peoples in this country. I am particularly alarmed at the fact that the Minister is at odds with leaders of the indigenous community, particularly with a person of absolutely critical value and importance to the country in this area, Dr Lois O'Donoghue. I fear for the future without her continued leadership.'

Lowitja's first meeting with John Howard as prime minister comes in the late afternoon of Wednesday 3 July, four months after his election. The meeting, seventy-five minutes long, between 4.45 and 6 pm, while the sun is setting, is characterised by the prime minister's office as 'cordial and constructive' and by Lowitja as another 'full and frank discussion'.

But the mood is cold. It is clear to Howard, as he will later recall in his memoir, *Lazarus Rising*, that 'virtually all of the Aboriginal leadership shared the Labor view of Indigenous affairs, which was overwhelmingly about the rights of Indigenous people'. He regards Lowitja as a constant Coalition critic.[9] Howard's head of Prime Minister and Cabinet, Max Moore-Wilton, dubbed 'Max the Axe' by waterside workers, believes the Indigenous leadership is 'in mourning' for the loss of the Labor government and they are not 'willing interlocutors'.[10]

Lowitja, according to her notes of the meeting, tells Howard there is considerable confusion about the government's objectives. She is concerned about the deterioration in the relationship between Indigenous people and the government, and that Howard's references to 'political correctness' and an 'Aboriginal industry' have not enhanced the relationship. She says Aboriginal people have felt under siege since his election and warns him that he risks alienating moderate Aboriginal leaders, like herself. Howard says there is no need for Aboriginal people to feel under siege; he knows that Aboriginal disadvantage has to be addressed, but the Native Title Act has to be made more workable, and ATSIC needs to be more accountable. He says the Hindmarsh Island affair has strained public confidence and that, while most Australians want a remedy to Aboriginal disadvantage, within an undivided nation, they are impatient with the lack of progress and don't like waste. He asserts that they are not interested in the past. Lowitja replies that Aboriginal people 'cannot forget the past'.

They discuss tensions in the Gulf of Carpentaria. Here plans for the world's largest zinc mine, the $1.1 billion Century Zinc project, have combined with a native title claim by the Waanyi people and an Aboriginal firebrand, Murrandoo Yanner, to produce an explosive political cocktail. Lowitja and ATSIC chief executive Pat Turner are attempting to mediate with Yanner, who warns that 'blood will flow' if the mine proceeds.

Lowitja is unhopeful as she leaves the meeting with Howard. 'I'm a moderate and he is alienating me,' she tells reporters.

———

At the end of July, she tells the UN Working Group on Indigenous Populations in Geneva that Australia's Indigenous people are once again at a crossroad, the new government has brought with it 'a changed and hostile attitude', and she fears that damage and bitterness lies ahead.[11]

On 13 August, Herron announces that ATSIC's budget will be cut by more than $400 million over four years, amid severe Budget cuts to repair an $8 billion deficit. Lowitja says the cuts will inevitably lead to more Aboriginal unemployment, more Aboriginal people in jail, less opportunity and more disadvantage.

The following week, 19 August, at the urging of Australian Council of Trade Unions (ACTU) president Jennie George, she speaks at a pre-Budget union rally at Parliament House that unravels into a riot. She has agreed to speak against the advice of those closest to her, including Pat Turner. In the only argument they ever had, Turner tells her she is putting at risk the perception of her impartiality, in the eyes of a government that is looking for any excuse to tear ATSIC down.

Lowitja refuses to listen and she makes an angry, partisan speech:

Let me say, first of all, that I'm not pleased to be here today. I'm not pleased that this sort of action is necessary to attempt to persuade a national government that it has made grave errors of judgement in assessing both what the community needs and what we will tolerate. This is a government that said they would be a government 'For All of Us'. Well, the clear message today is that this is a government for none of us . . . We have been betrayed—there is nothing ambiguous about that. Honest John Howard has shown himself to be untrustworthy. His smug and smiling Treasurer, Peter Costello, has approached this Budget with all the glee of a drunken vandal . . . I call upon all of you here today—union members, community representatives, Aboriginal and Torres Strait Islander peoples—to stand together in solidarity in opposition to this unjust and unworkable Budget. Solidarity forever!

The following day, as the government delivers the Budget, she speaks at the Aboriginal Tent Embassy, and urges protestors to focus their anger on the Howard government.

———

On Tuesday 10 September 1996, Pauline Hanson makes her maiden speech. She calls for cuts to Asian immigration and Indigenous welfare spending:

I come here not as a polished politician but as a woman who has had her fair share of life's knocks. My view on issues is based on common sense and my experience as a mother of four children, as a sole parent, and as a businesswoman running a fish and chip shop. I won the seat of Oxley largely on an issue that has resulted in me being called a racist. That issue related to my comment that Aboriginals received more benefits than non-Aboriginals.

We now have a situation where a type of reverse racism is applied to mainstream Australians by those who promote political correctness and those who control the various taxpayer funded 'industries' that flourish in our society servicing Aboriginals, multiculturalists and a host of other minority groups.

In response to my call for equality for *all* Australians, the most noisy criticism came from the 'fat cats', bureaucrats and the 'do-gooders'. They screamed the loudest because they stand to lose the most—their power, money and position, all funded by ordinary Australian taxpayers.

Present governments are encouraging separatism in Australia by providing opportunities, land, monies and facilities available only to Aboriginals. Along with millions of Australians, I am fed up to the back teeth with the inequalities that are being promoted by the government and paid for by the taxpayer under the assumption that Aboriginals are the most disadvantaged people in Australia.

I do not believe that the colour of one's skin determines whether you are disadvantaged . . .

This nation is being divided into black and white, and the present system encourages this. I am fed up with being told, 'This is our land.' Well, where the hell do I go? I was born here, and so were my parents and children. I will work beside anyone and they will be my equal but I draw the line when told I must pay and continue paying for something that happened over 200 years ago. Like most Australians, I worked for my land; no-one gave it to me.

She calls for ATSIC to be abolished, describing it as 'a failed, hypo-critical and discriminatory organisation that has failed dismally the people it was meant to serve'.

Lowitja receives a copy of Hanson's speech, along with some responses. She marks it, 'Please keep for my record'.

————————

In April 1993, on the same day Keating delivered his H.V. Evatt lecture, in which he spoke of a shameful legacy of injustice, historian Geoffrey Blainey delivered a John Latham Memorial lecture in which he said a patriotic and generally optimistic 'three cheers' view of Australian history had been assailed by a jaundiced 'black armband' view. He said that, while the treatment of Aboriginal people after the British arrived was 'often lamentable', Australia's history as a whole was a story of hard-won success.[12]

In government, Howard embraces this view. In October 1996, he declares: 'I profoundly reject the black armband view of Australian history. I believe the balance sheet of Australian history is a very generous and benign one ... I think we have been too apologetic about our history in the past.'

And then again in November:

I have spoken tonight of the need to guard against the re-writing of Australian political history and, in particular, to ensure that the contribution of Robert Menzies and the Liberal tradition are accorded their proper place in it. There is, of course, a related and broader challenge involved. And that is to ensure that our history as a nation is not written definitively by those who take the view that we should apologise for most of it. This black armband view of our past reflects a belief that most Australian history since 1788 has been little more than a disgraceful story

of imperialism, exploitation, racism, sexism and other forms of
discrimination. I take a very different view. I believe that the
balance sheet of our history is one of heroic achievement and
that we have achieved much more as a nation of which we can be
proud than of which we should be ashamed. In saying that I do
not exclude or ignore specific aspects of our past where we are
rightly held to account. Injustices were done in Australia and
no-one should obscure or minimise them. But in understanding
these realities our priority should not be to apportion blame and
guilt for historic wrongs but to commit to a practical program of
action that will remove the enduring legacies of disadvantage.[13]

It was, said historian Henry Reynolds, an attempt to restore a
'white picket fence view of history that minimises women, Aborigines
and other minority groups'.[14]

It unleashes years of culture wars, vicious and vituperative.

————

At the end of November 1996, exhausted, in ill-health and suffering
a heart condition, Lowitja issues a parting plea as she prepares
to leave ATSIC after six tumultuous years. She calls on the federal
government to take action on several shelved social justice reports, by
ATSIC, the Council for Aboriginal Reconciliation, and the Aboriginal
and Torres Strait Islander Social Justice Commissioner, that might
allow Aboriginal people to 'take their place in the community as
equal partners'. On 25 November, launching a report on black deaths
in custody, 1989–1996, she laments that five years after the Royal
Commission into Aboriginal Deaths in Custody, there are more,
not fewer deaths. 'Five years on, governments continue to regard
indigenous lives as having less value—or less relevance—than others,'
she says. On 27 November, she attacks the government's proposed

changes to the native title laws. She says the number and complexity of its proposed changes is staggering—more than two hundred pages of amendments and explanatory documents—and Aboriginal people have been 'excluded from the negotiating table'.[15] She laments that in Indigenous affairs, there is 'a passing of the buck almost always to the victim'.

At the beginning of December, she retires as head of ATSIC and is replaced by Gatjil Djerrkura, born at Yirrkala of the Yolŋu Wangurri and founding chairman of the Aboriginal and Torres Strait Islander Commercial Development Corporation.

Tributes flow. Labor leader Kim Beazley calls her a great Australian. He says Australians owe her a vote of thanks for her contribution to reconciliation, her selflessness, her dignity and astute judgement. In the parliament, Labor MP Daryl Melham says she guided ATSIC through a tortuous inception and a harrowing change of government. 'It is not easy to hold the position that she has held,' he tells the House of Representatives. 'If you think it is hard politics in this chamber in mainstream Australia, there are no tougher politics than indigenous politics in this country . . . Lois O'Donoghue is someone special. She enriches this country. She enriches all of us. She enriches her people. She is not a bitter person. She has been subjected to some terrible things over the years—and yet she carries herself with distinction and without malice, without ill-feeling.'[16]

Leigh Clifford, managing director of mining company CRA, writes to her: 'Your lifetime of work for your people and particularly the work for ATSIC has been marked by your courage and dignity. You have left a legacy that will endure.'[17] In March the previous year, CRA, after a history of hostile indifference to Aboriginal interests, dramatically changed tack with chief executive Leon Davis declaring the company was satisfied with the central tenet of the Native Title Act, which had laid the basis for cooperation and partnership with Aboriginal people.[18] In August 1996, CRA executive Paul Wand said the company regretted its chequered history in the Kimberley, Pilbara and Cape York.

On 6 December, within the walls of the ATSIC tower, Lowitja makes her farewell speech. She says the months that have passed since the election of the Howard government have been 'a nightmare', but that time is a good healer. She describes the government as mean-spirited. 'I have run the race, I have fought the fight, I have kept the faith and I have finished the course—albeit the worse for wear,' she says. Later, she will say she leaves Canberra feeling 'beaten to a pulp by a new government seemingly hell-bent on removing every advance we had made for Aboriginal and Torres Strait Islanders'.

On 9 December, she is admitted to hospital with bronchitis. Her visitors include John Herron. The former surgeon and the former nurse argue about her diagnosis.

In an editorial, the *Sydney Morning Herald* says that she has guided ATSIC with patience and wisdom: 'Ms O'Donoghue's life is an inspiration to many Australians—not only to Aboriginal Australians—for having overcome the disadvantages of her forcible removal from her mother at an early age and blatant discrimination against her in her attempts to train as a nurse. She has served her people, and her nation, well.'[19]

In Adelaide, her hometown newspaper, *The Advertiser*, editorialises that she has led her people in extraordinary times, which have included the Royal Commission into Aboriginal Deaths in Custody, and the High Court's Mabo decision. 'Through it all she has behaved with dignity and compassion,' it says. 'Her voice of reason in that role will be missed.'

On 18 December, John Howard writes, thanking her for her service:

Dear Miss O'Donoghue,
On behalf of the Government, I would like to thank you for the contribution you have made in your position as Chairman of

ATSIC in representing and furthering the position of Aboriginal and Torres Strait Islander people in Australia.

There were occasions when you had cause to disagree with the government of day [*sic*], but no one could ever doubt your deep commitment to your people, and in particular to improvements in those areas where indigenous Australians sadly continue to suffer profound disadvantage.

I wish you well for the future

Lowitja leaves Canberra, but not the stage. For the next sixteen years—until she is eighty and reluctantly agrees to send the dusty boxes containing the record of her life to libraries and museums, 'the little stock-pile of memories I don't want to let go of'—she continues to speak out as a leader of her people, an Aboriginal matriarch.

And she makes a decision. She will not be called Lois for much longer.

Soon, it will only be Lowitja.

XXXV

Outside Australia's High Court, a Wik woman, Gladys Tybingoompa, is rejoicing: 'I'm the hot woman; I'm the fire. Bushfire is my totem, alright. And I'm a proud woman today of Cape York. It is to me an historic moment as a Wik woman.' She speaks in her language, Wik-Mungkan: 'Ngay thaa'-nganth in. Ngay winynyang ya'am—This is my tongue. I am not afraid of anything.'

And then she dances outside Australia's highest court, with clap-sticks borrowed from an anthropologist.

It is 23 December 1996, and the court has ruled, four to three, that native title rights may coexist with pastoral leases—which are held on more than forty per cent of Australia's land mass. Although the court rules that if there is any inconsistency between the rights of the native title holders and the rights of the pastoralists, the rights of the native title holders must yield, pastoralists and miners attack the decision. The question they ask is fundamental: 'Whose land is it?'

Cape York lawyer Noel Pearson calls it a 'tectonic shift in justice' and in Tybingoompa's isolated community, Aurukun, where the auto-cratic missionary Bill MacKenzie once presided with scripture and chains, Yothu Yindi's song 'Treaty' rings out.

But the headlines are wary—'A decision for chaos,' says the *Sydney Morning Herald*—and National Farmers Federation president Donald McGauchie says the High Court has delivered a body blow to pastoralists. 'Christmas will be grim on farms around the country,' he says.

In early 1997, the National Farmers Federation launches two powerful commercials.

The first shows a weather-hardened pastoralist trying to sink a raw fence post into the ground; he is blindfolded, and his wife and young sons look on helplessly. Voice over: 'Working the land is tough enough. The High Court's Wik decision has made it even tougher. Whose land is it? Who can use it? Farmers want their rights restored and control of their future. The Wik decision. Tell the politicians we need legislation to sort out the mess and get it right. For the sake of black and white.'

The second shows two boys, one black, one white, playing a tangled game of Twister. Voice over: 'Can black and white live in harmony when the High Court's Wik decision on native title has created uncertainty, especially for farmers?'

In May, with Coalition conservatives demanding the extinguishment of native title on pastoral leases, a single legislative act that would breach the Racial Discrimination Act, Howard announces a '10-point plan' to wipe away uncertainty for pastoralists and miners, while showing 'greater respect' for native title than the option of extinguishment. The plan confirms pastoralists' rights; makes it harder to claim native title; and removes the right to negotiate over mining projects on pastoral leases, which the mining industry has portrayed as a 'de-facto veto'. Howard uses the imagery of a pendulum that is out of balance and needs winding back. 'The fact is that the Wik decision pushed the pendulum too far in the Aboriginal direction,' he says. 'The 10-point plan will return the pendulum to the centre.'[20]

Mick Dodson wonders how 'two hundred years of dispossession and horror' has been reduced to the swing of a political pendulum.[21]

On 17 May, Howard goes to the Australian Stockman's Hall of Fame at Longreach, Queensland, to reassure angry graziers that his 10-point plan will provide them with security, while avoiding the instability, expense and years of constitutional challenge that would inevitably result from blanket extinguishment. He begins by saying, 'I have always had an immense affection for the outback and for the bush.' He says no pastoralist will be thrown off his land, nor stopped from building a fence, or sinking a dam. He says the right to negotiate—a 'stupid property right that was given to native title claimants alone'—will be abolished, and the bogus claims that have proliferated and are repugnant and un-Australian will come to an end.

'Look, you have my assurance,' he says. 'You'll love it.'

Deputy Prime Minister and National leader Tim Fischer tells ABC radio there will be 'bucketfuls of extinguishment in the 10-point plan, on a fair basis'.

———

The report of the National Inquiry into the Separation of Aboriginal and Torres Strait Islander Children from Their Families, titled *Bringing Them Home*, is tabled in the federal parliament on 26 May 1997. The inquiry has been conducted by former High Court judge and president of the Human Rights and Equal Opportunity Commission Ronald Wilson and the Aboriginal Social Justice Commissioner Mick Dodson. They conclude that, in the period 1910–1970, between one in three and one in ten Indigenous children were forcibly removed from their families and communities in 'an act of genocide aimed at wiping out indigenous families, communities, and cultures, vital to the precious and inalienable heritage of Australia'.

In Melbourne, John Howard, who opposes a national apology to the Stolen Generations, speaks at a reconciliation convention marking the thirtieth anniversary of the 1967 referendum. He is

introduced by the chairman of the Council for Aboriginal Reconciliation, Pat Dodson, who says 'it is only when we listen that we can hear
what might be beyond the words'.

Howard knows he is not among friends. He will recall in his
memoir: 'I knew this meeting would be hard and though I intended to
recognise symbolic sensitivities I was determined to avoid the abject
apologetic language so often used by members of the Labor Party and
others.'[22] He drinks symbolically from an Aboriginal tamuk of water;
he thanks the Kulin people for the warmth and generosity of their
welcome, and then proceeds to lecture an audience thirsty for a
national apology to the Stolen Generations on 'the overall story of the
great Australian achievement that is there in our history to be told'
and the fairness of his 10-point plan: 'Personally, I feel deep sorrow
for those of my fellow Australians who suffered injustices under the
practices of past generations towards indigenous people,' he says:

> Equally, I am sorry for the hurt and trauma many people here
> today may continue to feel as a consequence of those practices.
> In facing the realities of the past, however, we must not join
> those who would portray Australia's history since 1788 as little
> more than a disgraceful record of imperialism, exploitation and
> racism. Such a portrayal is a gross distortion and deliberately
> neglects the overall story of great Australian achievement that
> is there in our history to be told, and such an approach will be
> repudiated by the overwhelming majority of Australians who
> are proud of what this country has achieved although inevitably
> acknowledging the blemishes in its past history. Australians of
> this generation should not be required to accept guilt and blame
> for past actions and policies over which they had no control.

Howard has made the same comments, almost word for word, six
months earlier, when he delivered the Sir Robert Menzies lecture.

But here, in a room filled with Aboriginal people and their supporters, the word 'blemishes' hangs stalely in the air, even though, when Howard's successor, Kevin Rudd, leads Labor back to government, and apologises to the Stolen Generations eleven years from now, he will use the same expression.

Seated in the audience, Lowitja feels her anger rising.

On the stage, Pat Dodson, who has tried to imagine 'a nation at peace with itself', feels his hopes draining away. 'He's never going to do anything,' he thinks to himself. He gazes into the audience and sees Lowitja stand and turn her back on the prime minister—a symbolic act of contempt. At first, it is a few who do this; and then, in a wave of anger, it is many.

Linda Burney, who will be the first Aboriginal person elected to the New South Wales Parliament, and then the first Aboriginal woman elected to the House of Representatives, also sees Lowitja stand. More than two decades later, in her parliamentary office, it still burns in her memory. 'If there is one woman that you would identify as being someone that inspires you, that terrifies you, that is a symbol of possibility, it would be Lowitja,' Burney says. 'The dignity, I think, is the thing that you remember the most.'[23]

No prime minister has been so publicly shunned.

Howard defends his 10-point plan for native title, which he says is just, fair and workable, and denies it will hand large swathes of land to pastoralists: 'I also need in the name of truth and in the name of a frank discussion of this issue to repudiate the claim that my 10-point plan involves a massive hand-out of freehold title at taxpayer expense. That is an absolute myth, it is absolutely contrary to the fact and I absolutely repudiate it.'

Over boos and jeers, he shouts and pounds on the lectern. It is the worst moment of his prime ministership.

Watching on, Alex Boraine, South African politician, minister of religion, anti-apartheid activist and deputy chairman of South

Africa's Truth and Reconciliation Commission, who reports to Nelson Mandela every night during the convention, is shocked. 'If I wanted to put it very crudely, I would say that your Prime Minister has balls, but he hasn't got a hell of a lot of heart,' he says. Howard storms out in a fury, 'incandescent with rage', according to Dodson.

The day after Howard's speech, 27 May, twenty-six men and women, veterans of the 1967 referendum campaign, are given a standing ovation as they slowly make their way onto the stage at the reconciliation convention. In his speech to the gathering, the Governor-General, Bill Deane—whose Mabo judgment, issued jointly with Mary Gaudron, spoke of a 'conflagration of oppression and conflict' and a 'national legacy of unutterable shame' and 'the darkest aspect of the history of this nation'—says the referendum 'marked the first great turning point in the relationship between Australia's indigenous people and the nation of which they form such an important part'. He says he is personally 'profoundly sorry' that children were taken from their families. He too is given a standing ovation.

Ronald Wilson defends the controversial finding of genocide in the *Bringing Them Home* report, which is causing howls of disapproval: 'Genocide is not the attempt to destroy an individual,' he says. 'Genocide is the attempt to destroy a people, a culture.'

Mick Dodson speaks of theft: 'This nation has stolen. From parents and families and communities, it has stolen children. From children, it has stolen love, and family; language and culture; land and identity.' He describes the agony of the testimony they have heard: 'They told us it was believed they would be better off. Better off without the loving arms of mothers and fathers. Better off enduring harsh physical punishment, sexual abuse, malnutrition, and little or no education. All for their own good. These stolen children recalled being told that their parents were dead or had given them away because their parents did not love them. And they told us what it was like to be taught to hate Aborigines—to hate your own history, your own family and yourself.'

Aboriginal Affairs minister John Herron describes the report as 'very emotive' and 'one-sided' and focused only on 'one view of the separation process'. Later, he will say there was no such thing as 'a stolen generation', because 'there simply were not enough children taken to warrant that word "generation"'.[24]

––––––––

The Howard government introduces the Native Title Amendment Bill 1997 on Thursday 4 September—a 10-point plan that is more than four hundred pages long. Howard then appears on ABC TV, saying again that native title has swung the pendulum too far in the direction of Aboriginal people, and holding up a map of Australia, with three-quarters of it coloured brown, where, he says, Aboriginal people have a 'potential right of veto over further development'.

In a highly charged political environment, Aboriginal leaders trudge back to Canberra. But doors that were open to them in 1993 are closed in 1997. Tempers flare. At the end of October, Noel Pearson, who has described the 10-point plan as a '10-point scam', concocted by small-hearted people, describes the government as 'racist scum'.[25] A month later, speaking to his people at a meeting in Cape York, he calls John Howard 'a miserable moral cockroach' leading a government that 'basically despises black people'.[26]

In November, on the eve of the Senate debate of Howard's native title bill, Lowitja stands arm in arm with Hazel Hawke in front of a 'sea of hands', planted in the lawns of Parliament House and symbolising the desire for reconciliation. But for those who negotiated with Keating, who were invited in from the woodheap, as Noel Pearson described it, these are bad days.

Pat Dodson quits the Council for Aboriginal Reconciliation in despair. 'I fear for the spirit of this country,' he says. At the National Press Club, on Friday 28 November, he describes the spiralling debate in the Senate as a 'lunacy' that is 'bereft of any moral decency' and warns that reconciliation will be finished if Howard's Wik bill is passed. A packed audience gives him a standing ovation when he pleads for an outcome that ensures 'a nation where indigenous peoples are no longer strangers in their own lands'.[27]

On 30 November, in a nine-minute televised address to the nation, Howard says his 10-point plan is 'a fair and decent balance'. He says all Australians would agree that Aboriginal and Torres Strait Islander people 'have been very badly treated' in the past, that more needs to be done to improve their health, housing, employment and education, and that Aboriginal people have 'a very special affinity with the land'. But Australians would also agree on the importance of the rural and mining industries. He says farmers are at the heart of 'the Australia I love'.

He says the High Court has created 'a very big problem' and the time has come to fix it.

At the beginning of February 1998, Lowitja takes her seat at a Constitutional Convention that is called to discuss whether, and in what form, Australia should become a republic. She speaks after National Party leader Tim Fischer, who opposes a republic and has promised bucketfuls of extinguishment of native title. She begins: 'Mr Chairman and fellow delegates, I must begin my speech by acknowledging the Ngunnawal peoples as the traditional owners of this region. In paying my respects to the Ngunnawal people, I must introduce myself and explain why I am on their country. My name is Lowitja and my traditional country is the area around Uluru in Central Australia. I am here as a visitor to this region to attend a meeting that will attempt to define Australia's future. I am a proud republican and I come as an Aboriginal person and a woman. There are too few of us in either category in positions to influence the processes of government in this country.'[28]

She says Australia's system of government has not served Aboriginal people well and that they have suffered the brunt of its faults,

including dispossession, policies of family separation and a hierarchy
of discrimination. 'There might be only a couple of people in this
chamber who can honestly say they understand that experience,' she
says. 'For most of you, you just cannot know or understand the experience of being a second-class citizen in this country. You cannot tell me
how your family would survive living under a bridge while suffering a
range of chronic diseases, while facing limited employment prospects
and while not knowing where to find your mother or your siblings.'

Among other Aboriginal and Torres Strait Islander representatives, magistrate Pat O'Shane begins her address, 'There is an obvious
sweetness to my being here, given that neither women nor Aborigines were allowed to participate in the Constitutional Convention of a
century ago.' She says that Australia after 1788 was 'underwritten with
the values of power, privilege, elitism, oppression and dispossession'
and was 'blatantly exclusionary'.

Speaking first in his Dhangu language, Gatjil Djerrkura says,
'Nhuma ngarra nhama nganapiliny yolŋu bitjuwanginy rrambangi
Australians ga nganapilingu rom malany—I ask you to think about
the place indigenous Australians have in our past and in our future.
Now is the time to right the wrongs of the past.'

But in an impassioned address, former Liberal Party senator
Neville Bonner, the first Aboriginal member of the Australian Parliament, argues against a republic:

> You came to my country. You invaded my land. You took our
> Earth (our everything). You poisoned my waterholes. You
> killed my people. You gave away my land. You imposed your
> law on my people . . . You told my people that your system was
> best. We have come to accept that. We have come to believe that.
> The dispossessed, despised adapted to your system. Now you
> say that you were wrong and that we were wrong to believe you.
> Suddenly you are saying that what brought the country together,

made it independent, ensured its defence, saw it through peace and war, and saw it through depression and prosperity, must all go. I cannot see the need for change.

I cannot see how it will help my people. I cannot see how it will resolve the question of land and access to land that troubles us. I cannot see how it will ensure that indigenous people have access to the same opportunities that other Australians enjoy. Fellow Australians, what is most hurtful is that after all we have learned together, after subjugating us and then freeing us, once again you are telling us that you know better. How dare you? How dare you?'

He ends his speech singing his Jagera sorry chant and then, despite their difference of opinion, embraces Lowitja and ATSIC chairman Gatjil Djerrkura.

At the end of February 1998, in an attempt to engage with John Howard, Djerrkura takes the prime minister to Elcho Island and Yirrkala. Howard is treated with the respect owed to a national elder and is allowed to witness ceremonies. Where his first visit to an Aboriginal community ten years earlier was a scarring encounter, he describes this visit as one of the most moving experiences of his life. 'I have always respected Aboriginal culture, but until today I don't think I had understood the depth of feeling the indigenous people have in relation to their culture,' he says. But it has not changed his view on native title. It was not, he told journalist Ray Martin, his Road to Damascus on Aboriginal land rights.

On 31 March 1998, Gladys Tybingoompa dances again, painted and bare-breasted on the lawns of Parliament House, with Tasmanian senator Brian Harradine, who holds the balance of power in the upper house and fears that if Howard's native title law is not passed, Australia will be thrown into a race-based election that might tear the country apart. Harradine says he is negotiating for an 'honourable compromise'.

But Aboriginal leaders are locked outside the negotiations and when the High Court rules in the Hindmarsh Island case that the federal parliament has the power to partially repeal legislation advantageous to Aborigines, it seems that the 1967 referendum, which gave the parliament the power to make laws for Aboriginal people, had a poisoned double edge. When John Howard offers to fund a test case of his proposed legislation in the High Court, Labor's Senate hero Gareth Evans explodes, 'This bloke never seems to be so happy as when he's bashing blackfellas.'

By Easter, relations between the government and Aboriginal leaders are at breaking point over the right to negotiate with miners over new projects on pastoral leases. ATSIC chairman Gatjil Djerrkura says he is considering resigning. Lowitja declares, 'I've given up on this process. They're just playing Russian roulette with our lives.' She says the Native Title Amendment Bill would be better named 'the Colonial Title Amendment Bill'.[29]

Wik woman Gladys Tybingoompa, whose dances outside the High Court and the parliament have embodied the hopes of her people, walks away from the Senate door distraught. 'This is called the walk away, the last time the message is given to you, the Australians,' she says.

It is Sorry Day, 28 May, and in the absence of a national apology to the Stolen Generations, in a nation deeply divided on the question, many people sign sorry books, deep and heartfelt expressions of sorrow and shame for the pain and damage caused by the removal of Aboriginal children from their families. Lowitja pores over them: 'I'm sorry for all the pain'; 'I would like to express our deep sorry and shame'; 'sorry about everything that happened, I hope you can forgive me as a white person'; 'I'm very sorry'; 'I am deeply sorry for all the suffering'; 'I am so very sorry for all the past injustices'; 'I'm a mother, I can't imagine the grief of losing my daughters'; 'words cannot express how sorry we are for taking you away from your parents'; 'I am sorry and ashamed'; 'I'm so very sorry' . . .

On 31 May, at the site of the last Colebrook Home at Eden Hills, Adelaide, Lowitja unveils a bronze statue, *Fountain of Tears*, in memory of three hundred and fifty Colebrook children. A second statue will follow later—*Grieving Mother*, with her empty arms where a child should be. Seven women, former Colebrook children, sit for the sculptor. In the years that follow, the bronze arms of the *Grieving Mother* are often filled with flowers.

'I was one of the tjitji tjuta—a Colebrook kid—in the thirties and forties,' Lowitja says at the unveiling. 'This memorial is a national symbol, evoking a national tragedy.'

She says the experiences of the Colebrook children were varied, but the consequences for all of them were profound: 'Some people can remember some happy times. Some can remember kindness and acts of love. Some found comfort from being with their brothers and sisters. And for others, their experience was a nightmare—a life of unrelenting fear, loneliness and horrific abuse. For many, the strict regime of religious observance was miserable and oppressive . . . But what all stolen children share is a personal history which has torn them from their roots. Which has denied them their cultural heritage. And which has fractured their identity . . . Many of the missionaries and state officials implicated in the removal and placement of children may have been well-intentioned. But there is no escaping the fact that the policies of the time were based on ignorance and arrogance.'

Bitterly, she recalls the words used to describe Aboriginal children in Violet Turner's Colebrook mission history, *Pearls from the Deep*: 'waste material . . . rescued from the degradation of camp life . . . brought up from the depths of ignorance, superstition and vice . . . to be fashioned as gems to adorn God's crown.'

Lowitja says the nation is diminished by John Howard's refusal to apologise to the Stolen Generations. 'We are at a pivotal time in history,' she says:

It is a time when emotions are being laid bare. When painful experiences are being re-lived and re-told. When injustice is being scrutinised. When a truthful understanding of our history is being revealed, after having been swept under the rug for so long. It is no wonder that our deepest emotions are being exposed. And no wonder that the hidden wounds of the past are so very close to the surface at this time. Yet it has also been noted that, despite the suffering and trauma expressed within the stories of the Stolen Children, the responses of Aboriginal people have been extraordinarily generous. This is a time when we need that spirit of generosity. It is a time to feel the connections of a shared past. It is a time to guard against the things that fragment us. And it is a time to cherish those things which bring us together—those things which have helped us to survive. Those things that will create a better future for us all.

Among the plaques is a poem—'A Loneliness'—by Doris Kartinyeri, who was nursed by Lowitja at Colebrook when she was a baby and Lowitja was a girl.

> We are the stolen children
> who were taken away
> torn from our mothers' breasts
> What can a child do?
> Where can a child turn?
> Where is the guiding hand
> a child is meant to have?

On 27 June 1998, Aboriginal leaders publish an open letter to the prime minister, members of the Commonwealth Parliament and the Australian community. 'Australia is at a crossroads as a nation,' they say. 'We have before us a clear choice to make about our future on the issues of native title and race relations. Indigenous people do not want a race election, but it will be an even greater failure to the nation to pass a law based on discrimination and injustice.'[30]

The first signatory is Eddie Mabo's widow, Bonita. The second is Lowitja.

———

After the longest debate in the Senate's history, surpassing the 1950 Communist Party Dissolution Bill, and Paul Keating's native title legislation, on 7 July the amended laws pass the Senate after 105 hours of acrimonious debate. Harradine has extracted some compromises, including a process to protect Aboriginal cultural sites but not a right to negotiate, the scrapping of an intended six-year sunset clause for native title claims, and a Stolen Generations provision in the tougher new threshold test for native title claims. A race-based double dissolution election has been averted. But unlike the passing of Keating's law, there is no celebration on the floor of the Senate, no applause from the gallery. Aboriginal leaders condemn John Howard.

Reflecting on lost opportunity years later, Noel Pearson will say the changes ripped the heart out of native title and denied Aboriginal people the opportunity to benefit from more than twenty years of 'the greatest minerals boom in the history of the planet', which might have lifted them out of poverty and misery. 'This is how justice gets lost,' he says.[31]

XXXVI

In July 1998, Lowitja contacts South Australia's chief justice, John Doyle, on a personal matter. At the age of sixty-five, she would like a birth certificate.

The chief justice writes to the state's attorney-general, Trevor Griffin, and speaks to the chief magistrate. All are sympathetic.

When she finally has it in her hands, years later, it reflects not everything, but those things that she has decided to include, the things that matter to her. Her name is given not as Lois, but Lowitja O'Donoghue. Born 1 August 1932, at De Rose Hill. The certificate lists only one parent—her mother, Lily, with the surname O'Donoghue. It gives her mother's place of birth as Granite Downs, the date as unknown, and her occupation as 'home duties'. The identity of her father, although she knows it, is 'Not Stated'.

With the stroke of a pen, she embraces her mother and dismisses her father from her life.

Age begins to take its toll. Death comes for loved ones. At her sister Eileen's funeral, Lowitja says in her eulogy, 'Eileen was one of the big girls as I was going through Colebrook. And we loved the big girls and they loved us. We didn't feel particularly loved, except by our big sisters.'[32]

On Australia Day, 26 January 1999, she is invested as a Companion of the Order of Australia, 'for public service through leadership to indigenous and non-indigenous Australians in the areas of human rights and social justice, particularly as chairperson of the Aboriginal and Torres Strait Islander Commission'. She spends the day grief-stricken.

The day before, 25 January 1999, her sister Vi has died. Vi, 'who I dearly loved'. Her sister and protector in the uncertain world of her childhood, 'the most beautiful, gentle woman'.

Lowitja sits in the Broadview Baptist Church, devastated.

The Lord's my shepherd, I'll not want;
He makes me down to lie
In pastures green; he leadeth me
The quiet waters by.

It brings her back to the church. Not the hymns in the desert church of the missionaries, but a strong, quiet faith.

On 12 February, alongside former prime minister Gough Whitlam, she speaks at a memorial service for former South Australian premier Don Dunstan. She remembers Dunstan as a friend and champion of Aboriginal causes. 'Many of our people knew him well and loved him, as I did,' she says. 'He was unstinting in expressing his support for our people.' In 2007, when she delivers the inaugural Lowitja O'Donoghue Oration, supported by the Don Dunstan Foundation, she will say he was distinguished by his courage, determination, wit, dignity and the breadth of his vision.

In March, she attacks a new preamble to the Constitution that has been drafted by John Howard, after consultation with the poet Les Murray. It speaks of a nation 'inhabited' since time immemorial by Aborigines and Torres Strait Islanders who are honoured 'for their ancient and continuing cultures'; but Lowitja calls it gutless and meaningless. 'If ever there was a time to seize the day—a time for brave decision-making and courageous action—it is now. But what have we instead? A gutless preamble to the Constitution which merely acknowledges the indisputable fact that we were here first! This both offends and saddens me. Here was an opportunity for our Prime Minister to craft an aspirational and visionary statement of significance for our nation. Instead, we have meaningless rhetoric about fairness and pride. Rhetoric which deliberately masks the unfairness and shame of our past.'[33]

She is at Uluru on 5 May 1999 for the launch of a Journey of Healing, of which she is a patron. During an inma, a ceremonial dance, members of the Mutitjulu community, at the base of the great rock, invite representatives of the Stolen Generations to dance with them and receive music sticks, painted with symbols of heartache and reconciliation.

'As a Yankunytjatjara woman who was removed from this country as a two-year-old child, I can only think of the pain of my mother who had five children taken from her,' she says. 'Let us all, black and white, hold hands and walk together.'

At the end of May, she speaks to foreign correspondents about the wounds inflicted upon Aboriginal people, for which there is no simple remedy, and attacks Howard for fuelling the fires of division. 'Our way of life was ravaged by white settlement,' she says. 'We were dispossessed of our traditional lands. Our families were ripped apart and our culture was regarded as worthless. All Aboriginal people have been profoundly injured by this legacy. Many of our people have never found their families—and some who have made contact have been devastated at the difficulties of trying to bridge years of separation. Many of our people continually grieve for their lost past. And at the same time they see their own children caught up in problems caused by their marginalisation in the dominant culture.'[34]

It is 26 August and after two years of intransigence, Howard moves a resolution in the parliament expressing 'deep and sincere regret that indigenous Australians suffered injustices under the practices of past generations, and for the hurt and trauma that many indigenous people continue to feel as a consequence of those practices'. Howard's regret is the result of negotiations led by Democrats senator Aden Ridgeway, the lone Aboriginal member of the Australian Parliament and just the second in its history. Howard calls it a historic resolution.

Several Aboriginal leaders support it, including Lowitja, who has been kept informed during the negotiations. 'It's just the beginning,' she says. But several Aboriginal leaders do not support it, including the 'Father of Reconciliation', Pat Dodson, who calls it a 'hasty and disgraceful pretence' and says the word sorry must be used in a national apology.

In October, Lowitja goes to London to visit the Queen, as part of a small delegation comprising some of Australia's most senior and respected Aboriginal leaders: Pat Dodson, Gatjil Djerrkura, Marcia Langton and Peter Yu. Two years earlier, at Mount Anderson station in Western Australia, Yu and Kimberley elders were sitting around a campfire on their swags discussing the approaching centenary of Federation and the Aboriginal relationship with the Crown. 'Their only experience of the Crown was through the police, the jailers and the court system,' Yu tells *The Australian* in London. 'They basically said there is unfinished business with the Crown. If she [the Queen] is top boss, you'd better get over to England and tell her they're taking our land, we never agreed to it and we don't have proper rights.'[35]

It is the first private meeting between Aboriginal people and a British monarch.

At midday on Wednesday 13 October, they arrive at the Grand Entrance of Buckingham Palace, where they are met by the equerry-in-waiting for a 12.20 pm meeting with the Queen. Lowitja has made it clear that she will not curtsy. 'I won't curtsy, I don't curtsy,' she tells officials. Dodson has been told that he will have to remove his trademark Akubra. They have been told the meeting will last twenty minutes. They speak for forty.

Dodson introduces the delegation and shows the Queen photographs of her meeting his grandfather, Paddy Djiagween, in Broome in 1963, when the old man asked her, 'Why can't we have the same rights as the white man?' In a cemetery in Broome, Djiagween, who was thought to be 111 years old when he died in 1991, is buried under the inscription 'The sun rises, wind blows, grass grows, the tide comes and goes. No-one can ever take your land'.

Yu gives the Queen a painting by the Kimberley artist Nyuju Stumpy Brown, who grew up in the Great Sandy Desert and never saw a white person until she was fifteen years old.

The delegation presents the Queen with a statement asking Britain to address 'its historical failure' to recognise Aboriginal people as the first Australians and to support a treaty, constitutional recognition and the protection of Aboriginal rights. They talk about the stuttering process of reconciliation, and the many threats to Aboriginal culture and society.

They find the Queen non-committal, but well informed.

'You've been as busy as ever, Lowitja,' the Queen says.

Lowitja asks her whether she has a view on the looming republic referendum.

'No Lowitja,' she says. 'That is a matter for the Australian people.'

Outside, reporters ask Dodson whether he removed his hat in the company of royalty.

In the evening they go to the theatre to see *'Tis Pity She's a Whore*, a seventeenth century tragedy of star-crossed siblings more often banned than performed.

On 6 November, Australia votes no to a republic. John Howard's constitutional preamble, reflecting his values and irritations, is also overwhelmingly defeated. Malcolm Turnbull says John Howard will be remembered as 'the prime minister who broke this nation's heart'.

On Advent Sunday, 28 November, Lowitja speaks at the induction service of Tim Costello as national president of the Baptist Union. She says she believes that Aboriginal spirituality and Christianity 'can work side by side'. She speaks of the prophet Micah, and his admonition 'What does the Lord require of you but to do justice and to love kindness, and to walk humbly with your God?' And she remembers Vi, whose death has been 'the catalyst which has challenged me about where I stood before the Lord'. She says that since Vi's death 'I have rededicated my life to Christ, to serve him in whatever way he sees fit'.[36]

And her memories fly back to Colebrook: 'I remember well how she carried me around on her back and constantly protected me from what was a strange environment for us. I remember too when in later years she was constantly picked upon and punished for very minor misdemeanours and often because of her generous nature to protect others. It wasn't long before I, as a very tiny tot, started to fight and protect her, often getting between her and the punishment being meted out. I was branded a trouble-maker and was told frequently that I would not succeed in life—I too from an early age decided that when I had the opportunity, I would prove them wrong.'

In January 2000, Lowitja speaks at the Baptist World Congress in Melbourne. As she prepares, she writes down her thoughts in a notebook: 'The Christian message I will leave to other speakers, because my experience of the Christian church and those involved is a mixed experience of good times and bad times, of removal as a child from my mother—my cultural heritage and language, harsh punishment.'

She writes that over the course of her life, she has been called a half-caste and a boong and a coon. Some of her own people have called her a sell-out, a 'coconut'—brown on the outside but white on the inside. People have said, 'Who does she think she is?' She has been called an Aboriginal activist and an 'up-town nigger', a leader and a stooge, a moderate and a conservative. But never an Aboriginal Christian, or just a Christian.

She writes that she misses the old hymns.

On 1 January, she writes, 'I am still anxious and having difficulty in knowing how to pitch my address to such a diverse audience, to take into account the social-political and spiritual.'

When she speaks, she breaks down, for the first time in public.

She arrives home, exhausted. There has been some criticism of her speech, particularly by American Baptists incensed by her criticism of missionaries who took children from their mothers and shocked that Warlpiri women from Central Australia have danced at the opening with ochre-painted bare breasts. There has been talk among the southern Baptists that Satan was at the congress.

Lowitja is angry with herself for letting her guard down and showing her pain. On 7 January, she writes, 'Felt I stuffed it up. Disgraced myself, never before broken down in public. Too many emotions running through me—many raw nerves exposed. Broken in spirit. There was criticism from the overseas visitors, particularly by the Americans, of the Warlpiri welcome—bare breasts. Attitudes disappointed me.'

Worn-out and depressed, she reads her Bible—the book of Luke and 2 Corinthians. She is tormented by childhood memories of separation and rejection, the paternalism and meddling of the missionaries. She frowns at the boxes of papers, hoarded memories, that since her retirement have filled up her apartment; she wonders what to do about them. She also wonders whether she will continue worshipping at her church.

But then an Anglican bishop, George Browning, calls to congratulate her on her speech at the Baptist congress and she begins to think about other matters. She calls her friend and pastor, Malcolm Wilson, first making a note of what she wants to tell him: 'Please continue to pray that I may know God's will for me in this difficult situation and that I will step out in Faith to do his will.'

She delivers the official Australia Day Address in Sydney on Monday 24 January 2000—the first Indigenous person to do so.

'The idea that a woman, and an Aboriginal woman at that, should be speaking to the nation on such an important occasion, would have been undreamt of two hundred years ago,' she says. 'And an improbable scenario even in much more recent times'.

She says that for many Aboriginal people, 26 January signifies invasion, conquest, dispossession and death and calls for a 'neutral' date for Australia Day—'one on which first Australians, older Australians and more recent Australians can come together to tell our stories and share our dreams . . . The past is still with us,' she says.

> To claim that there is no need for apology, on the grounds of no personal responsibility, denies that the price of European prosperity was the near destruction of Indigenous culture. Several months ago, I said that I thought that the Prime Minister had come a long way when he expressed his 'deep and sincere regret' about the stolen generations. I felt that he had opened the door towards reconciliation and that this should be acknowledged. Now I feel as if we're still waiting on that doorstep. I now believe, as do many of my people, that reconciliation will not proceed unless our Prime Minister can bring himself to say that simple 'S word'—Sorry. His refusal to do so on behalf of the government of the day, diminishes him as a person and Australia as a nation.'[37]

An estimated 250,000 people stream across the Sydney Harbour Bridge on Sunday 28 May 2000 in an emotional expression of support for reconciliation. It begins in the bitter cold of the morning and continues for many hours into the early afternoon. Pat Dodson stays away, at his home in Broome. But Faith Bandler, hero of the 1967 referendum, is there; as is Bonita Mabo, who says that 'nobody could be cold on a day like today' and that Eddie would be proud; and Aden Ridgeway, carrying wildflowers; and many people walking with their children, pointing to the Aboriginal flag flying above the bridge.

And Lowitja is there and as she walks she looks up and sees the letter S and then the word 'Sorry' written in enormous letters in the sky. She feels 'a mix of grief and joy and pride and faith'. As she will later recall: 'To be there with so many other Aboriginal and non-Aboriginal Australians, sharing such a wonderful symbolic gesture, was an experience I'll always treasure. That moment—the brief hush of the huge crowd as the first letter of the word Sorry was written on a clear blue sky, and then the cheers for each letter—is certainly etched indelibly on my memory.'[38]

In cities and towns across the nation, many tens of thousands more walked for reconciliation, in the largest, most joyful, most poignant political demonstration in Australian history.

At Corroboree 2000, at the Sydney Opera House the previous day, John Howard, having declared he would not walk, was jeered, while Governor-General Bill Deane was given a standing ovation. 'It's wrong to see those past injustices as belonging, as it were, to another country,' Deane said. 'They have been absorbed into the present and the future of contemporary indigenous Australians and of the nation of which they form such an important part. They reach from the past to shape who and what we are. They and the land that was taken are our country.' He asked Australia's gathered leadership 'to silently mourn for a moment as we reflect upon those past injustices and upon the present disadvantage which flows from them and upon what was taken, what was lost and what might have been.'

Meanwhile, in South Australia, a native title case is taking bitter shape. It involves De Rose Hill; but Lowitja plays no part in it because, although she was born there, her connection to the land and its stories was broken. The state government is attempting to wipe out all land claims by seeking a court ruling that native title was extinguished by the Colonisation Act passed by the British Parliament in 1834—two years before the first white settlers even stepped ashore in South Australia.

At the end of June, Lowitja writes in her diary, 'No-one knows how I feel when I close my door behind me each time I get home with the mountain of paperwork I must get through. Board papers to read, speeches to write, and the many I knock back. Last week, 27 June, was the ninth anniversary of my husband's death and I feel his absence deeply because he was the balance in my life—he would never have allowed me to get into this situation—and I have always been a perfectionist with everything in its place—so am desperate to get things sorted out.' She adds, and underlines, 'It is a difficult time. I need to know God's will for me—then step out in Faith to do his will.' She writes that she is still getting too many letters—'threatening letters, abusive letters, some supportive letters'.

———

As Australia approaches the Sydney Olympics, a constant question is whether Aboriginal people will protest and disrupt, to highlight Aboriginal disadvantage. In April, Charlie Perkins, angry at the federal government's denial of the Stolen Generations, threatens that it will be 'burn baby burn'.

Lowitja, appointed to chair the Sydney Olympic Games National Indigenous Advisory Committee, warns against protest—if only so that Aboriginal runner Cathy Freeman can run freely. 'Basically, because we're a sport-loving people ourselves, we want to be at the Games, we want a successful Games, we want to see Cathy Freeman reach her full potential and get gold,' she says.[39]

On 15 September, the opening ceremony of the Sydney Olympics begins with a lone stockman, and then men and women riding.

But its emotional core is Aboriginal. A girl floats in a deep sea and then is called to an awakening by Djakapurra Munyarryun, a songman. Ngaanyatjarra, Pitjantjatjara and Yankunytjatjara women from Central Australia—Lowitja's people—enter dancing, and are joined by Yolŋu people and the people of the Torres Strait and a giant Wandjina spirit, Namarali, rises from the dust, created by Kimberley artist Donny Woolagoodja, whose father was one of the last lawmen of the Worora people, who were herded away from their country, where there were rivers and mountains and sacred places.

And then Cathy Freeman stands with the Olympic torch in her hand and walks into a shallow pool of water and lights a ring of fire.

Later, she runs the race of her life, winning gold in the 400 metres. As she turns down the back straight, she runs in the twinkling of flash-lights. High up in the stands, an Aboriginal dancer, Reuben Bolt, and his grandmother, Isabelle McLeod, choke back tears, and Llewellyn Williams, who is descended from the Wakka Wakka and Wulli Wulli people and from the Torres Strait Islands, holds a sign above her head that says 'Cos she's free'—echoing the tattoo on Freeman's arm, which proclaims 'Cos I'm Free'.

When it is over, Freeman slumps to the track, exhausted and relieved. Then she partly walks and partly runs a lap of honour, carrying both the Australian and Aboriginal flags.

The Washington Post reports, 'There was no black-gloved salute. She simply ran a race, 400 metres long. And as dramatic as it sounds, she changed a chunk of the world, or at the very least she has set the course. For Australia, a nation that only recently even acknowledged two centuries of uncivil treatment towards its indigenous people, to suddenly have a clear national hero who is black, is a stunning departure from history and was virtually unimaginable before these Olympic Games began.' In London, the *Independent* newspaper reports, 'From start to finish, the Sydney Olympics provided indig-enous Australians with their biggest ever stage and they used it to create lasting, positive images of one of the world's oldest cultures. Ahead of Sydney 2000, there were threats that Aborigines seeking to highlight decades of marginalisation, neglect and abuse would disrupt the Games. Instead, they enriched them.'

In the closing ceremony, Midnight Oil sings 'Beds Are Burning' with the word 'Sorry' printed on their clothes. Yothu Yindi sings its anthem, 'Treaty'.

It is intoxicating—'the euphoria that comes from dreams' as Lowitja will later describe it.[40]

But still only a dream.

On 31 October, Lowitja launches Doris Kartinyeri's memoir, *Kick the Tin*, describing her years at the Colebrook Home and afterwards, about good days when children's hands were stained purple with blackberries, and sad and frightening days.

Lowitja has written the foreword to the book, in which she says it made her smile and weep. She calls it 'a story of courage and survival, powerfully demonstrating how the human spirit can soar despite all the injuries and injustices which threaten to drag it down'. The book is launched at the opening of the Colebrook Memorial Park, on the site of the former Colebrook Home at Eden Hills.

When the sculpture *Grieving Mother* is unveiled, Kartinyeri breaks down: 'The mother I never had,' she says, crying.

XXXVII

On a grey Autumn day, Lowitja O'Donoghue stands at her father's grave for the first time.

She stares down at the polished granite. He is buried under the sign of the Saviour and the Holy Trinity. She feels nothing, she says. 'I make no judgment about him.'

When she returns to the cemetery gates, she is crying. She says she decided early in life that she would never have children 'because I didn't know how to love someone'. She says trust has never come easily.

'I will never accept that my mother willingly gave me up,' she says. 'I will never accept it.'

It is February 2001 and she is at the centre of controversy and filled with pain after a newspaper story, by conservative columnist Andrew Bolt, claims she has 'confessed' and made a tearful 'shock admission' that she was not necessarily 'stolen' from her mother, but was 'removed', or given away, by her white father when she was handed over to missionaries. She said she had no memory of her removal, at the age of two. Sobbing, she said she had never forgiven her father for what was done.[41]

'I wasn't stolen—Lowitja O'Donoghue admission,' the headline says. It runs on the front pages of Rupert Murdoch's newspapers across the nation.

Lowitja is outraged—and hurt. She says the article is 'simplistic, sensationalist, misleading and mischievous'. But John Howard calls her reported comments 'highly significant'. He urges Aboriginal people to stop using the phrase 'stolen generation' and to drop legal claims for compensation. He says the removal of children 'never amounted to genocide, it never amounted to the systematic persecution of a race, as has been alleged'.[42]

In the weeks that follow, she goes back to where it began.

At a roadhouse at Kulgera, near the border of the Northern Territory and South Australia, a group of Yankunytjatjara women greet her with the loving remorse reserved for people who have been removed from their country, stroking her and keening 'Ngana! Ngaltutjara! (Dear one, poor thing, poor bugger!)'

'Did you know my mother? Did you know Lily?' she asks.

'Uwa' (yes), one of the women replies and tells her that her mother was called 'Shilling' because she was a card player and a gambler. She grins and imitates the action of someone dealing cards. Lowitja laughs.

At the Anangu community of Indulkana, young Aboriginal people roam the streets with cans of petrol fixed to their faces. 'Why do you want to do this?' Lowitja asks, hugging a thin girl with a beautiful face, who looks up at her and says, 'You are my nana.'

She asks a group of senior Anangu men why she was taken away. 'Things were rough before,' they reply. 'They say, "That's a walypala kid [whitefella kid]—take her away".' She asks whether her mother would have had any say in whether her children were handed to missionaries. They shake their heads and say her mother would have been 'frightened walypala'—frightened of the white man.

At De Rose Hill, a man with a shotgun says that native title has almost killed him; but then he softens enough to point the way to the remains of an old bough shed where her father is supposed to have lived with her mother by Agnes Creek. It is a place of ghost gum and acacia, saltbush and wild boronia. She stands looking at the shade of the creek bed. 'I like this place,' she says. 'I think it would have been a good place to be a child.'

At Oodnadatta, she passes by the sandhills where her mother is buried. At Quorn, she sits on the veranda of the old Colebrook Home for Half-Caste Children, now Aboriginal-owned, sharing memories with Clara Coulthard, another former 'inmate', as the children were known. Cockatoos screech in the trees. 'At night-time, that was the time when you would hear sobs,' Coulthard says. 'That was the time our thoughts went back to our people back home.' During long hours on the road, Lowitja says she has lived between worlds, neither one nor the other, 'apacatcha, half-caste', she says bitterly and then falls silent.

In Adelaide, Lowitja knocks on a door and an elderly white woman, who is intent on carrying the O'Donoghue family's secrets to the grave, looks straight at her and closes the door, without a word. And then she stands at her Irish grandparents' grave and her father's grave for the first time, and stares down at the polished granite and there are no answers here, only heartache.

In March, Lowitja addresses a tense Stolen Generations conference in Adelaide. 'I have spent my entire life working with and for my people,' she says. 'I am black, and I am proud.'

She says there were many ways for children to be stolen from their Aboriginal families: 'From my own mother's point of view, she would have had no legal recourse. She would have had no moral support, and no understanding that she might never see her children again. And no assurance that her children would all be together. From her point of view, of course we were stolen, and her life destroyed . . .

'I have no memories that pre-date Colebrook. But I can remember as a small child at the Home spending many hours absorbed in my own thoughts. I brooded about questions like: Who is my mother? Who is my father? What am I doing here? Where did I come from? These questions were never answered of course. And I never felt special or loved.'

In Perth, an Aboriginal singer, Fred Penny, writes a song called 'Lowitja Lowitja'.

He says he feels as though someone has hurt his mother. He writes to her saying, 'In the song I have likened you to a warrior fighting battles and I am sure you will agree that it is just that, and I am sure you have fought many over the years.'

———————

She continues to speak out. But the focus shifts from rights and recognition to violence.

On 17 October 2001, she delivers the Hyllus Maris Memorial Lecture on The Future for Aboriginal Women and observes: 'Many children are growing up in communities where violence has become a normal and ordinary part of life. It is not uncommon in some communities for children to suffer regular sexual abuse. And it is not uncommon for young people to see adults in their communities behaving violently towards each other. The result of this, not surprisingly, is horrific.'

On 23 October 2002, she delivers the Mahatma Gandhi Lecture on Non-Violence at McMaster University, in Ontario, Canada. She describes human rights and reconciliation in Australia as an unfinished journey. 'Australia is often described as a young country and a lucky country,' she says. 'Both those perceptions, of course, assume that you are white. From an Indigenous perspective Australia is neither young nor lucky.' She talks about being taken from her mother: 'The grief I have felt, and still feel about this, is profound. And the pain my mother must have felt, having five children removed, is unimaginable.'

LOWITJA

At the National Press Club, June 2003, Mick Dodson speaks about violence in Aboriginal communities. It is searing. 'Violence is undermining our life's very essence, it is destroying us, and there are very few Aboriginal families that are not struggling with the debilitating effects of trauma, despair and damage resulting from their experiences with violence . . . Child violence includes neglect, incest, and assault by adult carers, paedophilia, and rape of infants by youths. Our children are experiencing horrific levels of violence and sexual abuse beyond comprehension.'[43]

In July 2003, John Howard calls a small group of Indigenous leaders, including Lowitja, Mick Dodson and Noel Pearson, to a meeting in Canberra to discuss domestic violence in Aboriginal communities, saying a new approach is needed. 'I have been impressed that an increasing number of indigenous leaders have spoken out about the reasons and appalling consequences of violence and abuse within indigenous communities,' he says. 'I want to hear and understand their views at first hand.'[44]

Of fifteen Indigenous leaders invited, eleven are women. ATSIC chairman Geoff Clark, who is at this time defending a civil damages proceedings for rape, is not invited.

The Aboriginal and Torres Strait Islander Commission (ATSIC), the organisation intended to hand Aboriginal people the power to determine their future, which was led by Lowitja for its first six years, is now in terminal decline.

Geoff Clark is at the centre of constant controversy. After being elected ATSIC chairman in December 1999, ahead of Charles Perkins and Gatjil Djerrkura, seven months later his cousin, Joanne McGuinness, alleges he raped her when she was eighteen. Clark is charged but the case is dismissed. In June 2001, *The Age* newspaper publishes the allegations of four women that Clark raped them in the 1970s and 1980s. The headline says, 'Geoff Clark: Power and Rape'. He denies the allegations. In August 2002, one of his alleged victims, Carol Stingel, files a statement of claim, alleging Clark raped her when she was sixteen.

In December, despite a deepening crisis within the organisation, Clark is re-elected chairman and 'Sugar Ray' Robinson is re-elected deputy chairman. At an angry press conference, Clark lashes out. 'Don't put us on the margins,' he says. 'Don't put us in a situation where Aboriginal people are strapping bombs to themselves.' Only one woman, Alison Anderson, is elected to a seventeen-person board. Clark thanks women for returning 'the traditional role' to men. Lowitja calls his comments 'disgusting' and Anderson says it has 'rubbed salt into the wounds of Aboriginal women hurt by domestic violence'.

After a wide-ranging review into the role and functions of ATSIC, and with both Clark and Robinson facing ruinous allegations, in April 2003 Indigenous Affairs Minister Philip Ruddock announces that a new executive agency, Aboriginal and Torres Strait Islander Services, will be established and ATSIC will be stripped of most of its staff and $1.1 billion budget. ATSIC commissioner Steve Gordon calls it 'the start of the dismantling of the commission'.[45]

In August 2003, after being convicted of obstructing police and behaving in a riotous manner at a Warrnambool hotel, Clark is suspended as ATSIC chairman for misbehaviour. In March 2004, after it becomes known that ATSIC commissioners have voted to allocate $85,000 towards his legal fees, Lowitja says Aboriginal people have lost faith in their elected leaders and Clark should resign. 'Other than when we had fewer rights, this is one of the lowest points I can recall in Indigenous affairs history,' she says.[46] On 30 March 2004, federal Labor leader Mark Latham announces Labor will abolish ATSIC if it wins office at the upcoming general elections. 'ATSIC is no longer capable of addressing endemic problems in Indigenous communities,' he says. 'It has lost the confidence of much of its own constituency and the wider community.'

This is all the encouragement John Howard needs. On 15 April, he announces that when the parliament resumes in May the government will abolish ATSIC; all relevant functions, programs, assets and appropriations will be transferred to mainstream Australian government departments. 'We believe very strongly that the experiment in separate representation, elected representation, for Indigenous people, has been a failure,' he says. 'We will not replace ATSIC with an alternative body. We will appoint a group of distinguished indigenous people to advise the Government on a purely advisory basis.'

Lowitja writes in her notebook on 8 May, 'I am disappointed and angry that our elected leaders have brought us to this serious crisis in Indigenous affairs.'

In June 2004, in the final edition of ATSIC's inhouse magazine, *ATSIC News*, under the headline 'Once was ATSIC', Lowitja reflects on the agency's achievements and failures. Among the achievements, she lists ATSIC's recognition at the United Nations, its role in the establishment of the UN's Permanent Forum on Indigenous Issues, and ATSIC's activism at the UN to draw attention to the living conditions of Australia's Indigenous people. She recalls long nights discussing the recommendations of the Royal Commission into Aboriginal Deaths in Custody with Aboriginal Affairs Minister Robert Tickner, and 'heady and heavy days' leading native title negotiations with Paul Keating. But she says there was 'far too much pork-barrelling' and ATSIC commissioners 'were just a law unto themselves'.

On 25 August, South Australian Premier Mike Rann appoints Lowitja and Baptist minister Tim Costello as special advisers on the troubled Anangu Pitjantjatjara Yankunytjatjara Lands—her mother's country, which is now stricken with petrol sniffing, youth suicides by hanging, and bitter clan and family disputes. They find that, while older people are still powerfully connected to the lands, 'their children are fundamentally disconnected from tradition, culture and lore and the petrol sniffing is simply the terminal expression of this profound dislocation and disconnection'.[47]

They deliver their report and then, in an emotional address to a South Australian parliamentary committee that reduces some members of parliament to tears, Lowitja attacks the state government's commitment to the Anangu Pitjantjatjara Yankunytjatjara lands. 'We are in a state of constant grieving,' she tells the Adelaide *Advertiser*.[48] 'The problems are horrendous. There is family and domestic violence, rape, child abuse and drug dealing as part of daily reality.' A newspaper photograph shows her in a state of despair.

In January 2005, Lowitja is asked by Andrew Sayers, director of the National Portrait Gallery, to sit for a portrait. She agrees, and requests that it be painted by South Australian artist Robert Hannaford. The sittings take place the following year.

She is seventy-four. She has been showered with awards by governments and honorary degrees by universities. After she is awarded the papal honour of Dame of the Order of St Gregory the Great, she becomes Dr Lowitja O'Donoghue AC CBE DSG. She accepts them all, on the basis that they might help her to open a door and make a difference; with every award she remembers Matron Ruby Hyde, who told her she would never amount to anything.

Hannaford is recovering from cancer, most likely caused by a forty-year habit of holding the stems of his paint brushes, covered with lead and cadmium, in his mouth. Paul Keating, another subject of his portraiture, had warned him not to do it. Hannaford had laughed, but in February 2006 he was diagnosed with cancer at the back of his tongue. During months of debilitating treatment, chemotherapy and radiotherapy, he painted himself naked, hooked up to a feeding tube, staring down the disease.

Lowitja arrives at his Adelaide studio wearing a blazing red suit with gold buttons, a black jumper, and Aboriginal jewellery—the red, black and yellow colours of the Aboriginal flag. Hannaford takes her into a studio bathed in the cool reflected south light favoured by artists in the southern hemisphere, and sits her in a chair of English oak. Over days of sittings, they talk about her life and Hannaford perceives 'a vast understanding and sympathy in her face, a sadness'. She calls him Alfie.

He paints her unsmiling, strong but ageing. He fills her eyes with loss. When it is finished, Lowitja says she would have preferred to have been painted smiling; but she also says, 'Deep down, in the person that is Lowitja O'Donoghue, is a lot of hurt, a lot of pain, an experience, I think, that he has managed to convey in that portrait. He really got right under my skin, I thought, and he really understood the life that I have lived.'

At the opening of a Hannaford exhibition in December 2006, she says people may find the portrait discomforting. 'I myself even felt a shock of recognition as I saw an aspect of my personality I don't readily acknowledge or display.'[49]

––––––––––

In May 2006, an Alice Springs Crown prosecutor, Nanette Rogers, releases a horrific dossier of child sexual abuse and neglect in Aboriginal communities in the Northern Territory, including a two-year-old girl who needed 'internal and external' surgery after being sexually abused; a six-year-old girl who was drowned while being raped by an eighteen-year-old man; and a twelve-year-old girl taken from her community by her tribal 'husband', who tied her to a tree for several weeks and raped her repeatedly. She eventually became pregnant and gave birth.[50]

An inquiry is set up to investigate the abuse. The report by former prosecutor Rex Wild and human rights activist Pat Anderson—*Ampe Akelyernemane Meke Mekarle 'Little Children are Sacred'*—concludes that there has been a 'breakdown' in Aboriginal culture and society, leading to neglect and abuse including child abuse. It warns of a looming disaster, and recommends action by the federal and Northern Territory governments 'in genuine consultation with Aboriginal people'.

Instead, on 21 June 2007, Prime Minister John Howard, and Indigenous Affairs Minister Mal Brough announce an intervention in the Northern Territory, a 'national emergency response to protect Aboriginal children' from sexual abuse and family violence. Howard suspends the Racial Discrimination Act and introduces sweeping measures for sixty Aboriginal settlements, including alcohol and pornography bans; the scrapping of permits to enter Aboriginal communities; compulsory medical checks for every Aboriginal child under the age of sixteen; more police; managers with powers of home inspection; and fifty per cent of welfare payments quarantined for food and other essentials. Army troops roll into Aboriginal communities, including Mutitjulu, in the shadow of Uluru.

'We are dealing with children of the tenderest age who have been exposed to the most terrible abuse from the time of their birth and any semblance of maintaining the innocence of childhood is a myth in so many of these communities,' Howard says.[51]

The intervention sharply divides opinion.

'The nation cannot avert its eyes and close its ears to the abuse and violence being suffered every day by children, women and men in our communities,' says West Australian children's court magistrate Sue Gordon, chair of the government-appointed National Indigenous Council, which replaced ATSIC in 2004, and chair of the prime minister's Intervention taskforce. But Aboriginal academic Boni Robertson, author of a report on sexual violence in Queensland Aboriginal communities in 1999, attacks the Intervention, describing it as 'an absolute outrage' that will 'segregate and quarantine a section of the Australian community' and impose laws that do not apply to other Australians.

Lowitja supports the key recommendation of the *Little Children are Sacred* report, that Aboriginal communities should be empowered to 'lead themselves out of the malaise'. She opposes the Intervention, saying that stripping people of control is not the answer.[52] 'You can't just come over the top of people, you've got to talk to them,' she says.

XXXVIII

It is 9 am on 13 February 2008 and Prime Minister Kevin Rudd rises in the House of Representatives to offer a national apology to the Stolen Generations, to say the word sorry. It is the first act of a new parliament and the anticipation is great. Above him, the galleries are filled with Aboriginal people, many of them members of the Stolen Generations, or their children, or grandchildren. Some have travelled a long way. Some are very old. Four of the nation's five living former prime ministers—Gough Whitlam, Malcolm Fraser, Bob Hawke and Paul Keating—are there, and with them former governor-general Sir William Deane. John Howard is not. Keating calls it 'a day of open hearts'.

In the House, seventeen Aboriginal people, representing the thousands of children who were taken from their families, are seated in an area reserved for distinguished guests. They hold one another's hands. Lowitja, a patron of the Stolen Generations Alliance, is among them, thinking about her mother, Lily. Close by is Yankunytjatjara elder Bob Randall, a traditional owner of Uluru whose song 'My Brown Skin Baby', was the first anthem of the Stolen Generations; it was written in 1964 and tells of how he was taken from his mother. In the Great Hall of the parliament, hundreds are watching on giant screens; thousands more are on the lawns outside, and in cities and country towns, far beyond the parliament.

In Melbourne's Federation Square, singer-songwriter Archie Roach, who was taken away from his family at the age of three, dedicates the performance of his song 'Took the Children Away' to the mother he was separated from, and to his children. In the remote town of Lightning Ridge, June Barker, a granddaughter of Aboriginal agitator William Ferguson, watches on TV at the local high school and says it is like watching man step onto the moon.

Within the Labor Party, Rudd has been advised against making the apology the first parliamentary gesture of his prime ministership. Lowitja has been a sounding board for Indigenous Affairs Minister Jenny Macklin, who has led the consultations with Indigenous leaders. Lowitja has advised her, 'Just get on with it, don't wait.'

The day before, 12 February, an Aboriginal 'welcome to country' was performed for a new parliament for the first time, by Ngambri elder Matilda House-Williams. She wore a possum cloak, but came with bare feet, like Jimmy 'King Billy' Clements and John 'Marvellous' Noble, the Wiradjuri men who attended the opening of the Australian Parliament in May 1927, dressed in worn-out clothes, barefoot, dogs at their side and asserting their sovereignty over the Limestone Plains upon which Canberra was founded.

Mr Speaker, Rudd says, as a deep silence descends. *I move that*:

Today we honour the Indigenous peoples of this land, the oldest continuing cultures in human history.

We reflect on their past mistreatment.

We reflect in particular on the mistreatment of those who were stolen generations—this blemished chapter in our nation's history.

The time has now come for the nation to turn a new page

in Australia's history by righting the wrongs of the past and so moving forward with confidence to the future.

We apologise for the laws and policies of successive Parliaments and governments that have inflicted profound grief, suffering and loss on these our fellow Australians.

We apologise especially for the removal of Aboriginal and Torres Strait Islander children from their families, their communities and their country.

For the pain, suffering and hurt of these stolen generations, their descendants and for their families left behind, we say sorry.

To the mothers and the fathers, the brothers and the sisters, for the breaking up of families and communities, we say sorry.

And for the indignity and degradation thus inflicted on a proud people and a proud culture, we say sorry.

We the Parliament of Australia respectfully request that this apology be received in the spirit in which it is offered as part of the healing of the nation.

For the future we take heart; resolving that this new page in the history of our great continent can now be written.

We today take this first step by acknowledging the past and laying claim to a future that embraces all Australians.

A future where this Parliament resolves that the injustices of the past must never, never happen again.

A future where we harness the determination of all Australians, Indigenous and non-Indigenous, to close the gap that lies between us in life expectancy, educational achievement and economic opportunity.

A future where we embrace the possibility of new solutions to enduring problems where old approaches have failed.

A future based on mutual respect, mutual resolve and mutual responsibility.

A future where all Australians, whatever their origins, are truly equal partners, with equal opportunities and with an equal stake in shaping the next chapter in the history of this great country, Australia.

In his speech, Rudd says it is time 'to remove a great stain from the nation's soul'.

He has agonised over the words.

A few days earlier, on a Saturday morning, he has visited a woman by the name of Lorna Nungala Fejo, who was born in the late 1920s in a bush camp outside Tennant Creek in the Northern Territory and who now lives in Canberra. He took her a bag of oranges and listened to her story, which became the centrepiece of his speech.

'She remembers the love and the warmth and the kinship of those days long ago, including the traditional dancing around the campfire at night,' Rudd recounts. 'She loved the dancing . . . But then, sometime around 1932, when she was about four, she remembers the coming of the welfare men. Her family had feared that day and had dug holes in the creek bank where the children could run and hide. What they had not expected was that the white welfare men did not come alone. They brought a truck, two white men and an Aboriginal stockman on horseback cracking his stockwhip. The kids were found; they ran for their mothers, screaming, but they could not get away. They were herded and piled onto the back of the truck. Tears flowing, her mum tried clinging to the sides of the truck as her children were taken away to the Bungalow in Alice, all in the name of protection.'

She did not see her mother again.

In the still and silent parliament, Rudd says the time has come to face a cold, confronting truth.

'To the stolen generations, I say the following: as Prime Minister of Australia, I am sorry. On behalf of the government of Australia, I am sorry. On behalf of the parliament of Australia, I am sorry.

I offer you this apology without qualification. We apologise for the hurt, the pain and suffering that we, the parliament, have caused you by the laws that previous parliaments have enacted. We apologise for the indignity, the degradation and the humiliation these laws embodied. We offer this apology to the mothers, the fathers, the brothers, the sisters, the families and the communities whose lives were ripped apart by the actions of successive governments under successive parliaments.'

———

It is the finest moment of Rudd's prime ministership. Veteran political journalist Paul Kelly calls it 'an essential act of contrition and a uniquely confessional event for Australia's soul'.[53]

Afterwards, in the parliament, Rudd takes Lowitja's hands in his and he says, 'A long time coming, Lowitja. Sorry us whitefellas are so slow. But we finally got there.' And the little girl who was taken away from her mother when she was two years old, and raised by missionaries to be a servant, tells the prime minister that he has done well.

Afterwards, she says her thoughts were with her mother. 'My mother is not here to witness this and neither are my two older sisters and so my thoughts are with them today,' she says. 'And particularly my mother, who . . . said to me when I first met her, "your name Lowitja—they've been taken away, they been taken away".'[54]

At the end of May, Lowitja announces that she is bowing out of public life.

Standing in the pulpit at St Peter's Anglican Cathedral in Adelaide, she speaks about being taken away, the years of hymns and rigid discipline and boiled cabbage at the Colebrook Home, where she was taught to sing that the Blood of the Lamb would wash her 'whiter than snow', and the strained reunion with her mother after more than thirty years apart. 'We could not speak to each other—except through our eyes,' she says. 'And what I saw was a woman who had been undone by her grief. She spent a lot of that visit looking at the floor.'

She says Kevin Rudd's apology was 'magnificent' and has lifted a weight from her shoulders, but that compensation should be paid to those who suffered.

'I am sometimes identified as one of the "success stories" of the policies of removal of Aboriginal children,' she says. 'But for much of my childhood I was deeply unhappy. I felt I had been deprived of love and the ability to love in return. Like Lily, my mother, I felt totally powerless. And I think this was where the seeds of my commitment to human rights and social justice were sown.'

XXXIX

Bonython Hall, Adelaide.

Noel Pearson has delivered the Lowitja O'Donoghue Oration, in which he has called for constitutional reforms and described Lowitja as the greatest Aboriginal leader of the modern era. 'For she gave her all in the service of our people the continent over,' he said. 'In the twilight of a life spent in long, selfless service, I know I speak for all of us whose gratitude flows brimming from our hearts, in telling her we love and honour her so.'

Lowitja walks slowly to the stage, old age upon her, and the night ends with the singing of an old song, 'We Shall Overcome'. A gospel song that became a protest song, a protest song that became an anthem of the civil rights movement:

We shall overcome
We shall overcome
We shall overcome, some day

Oh, deep in my heart
I do believe
We shall overcome, some day

Black and white together
Black and white together
Black and white together, some day
Oh, deep in my heart
I do believe
We shall overcome, some day.

The next day, in morning sunshine, she sits talking, flicking through old photographs.

And there she is—a little girl dressed in second-hand clothes, full of fight and character.

And when she's done, I ask her why she lived the life she lived.

'Because I loved my people,' she says.

Acknowledgements

This biography began long before the first words were written, at a moment of doubt and vulnerability and pain for Lowitja, after a question was raised, of whether a small girl taken from her powerless mother and handed to missionaries by a father she never knew was entitled to call herself 'stolen'.

In a newspaper interview, Lowitja was said to have 'confessed' that in her case it might be more accurate to say she was 'removed' rather than 'stolen', although she had no memory of it, at the age of two. Sobbing during the interview, she said she had never forgiven her father for abandoning her.

'I wasn't stolen—Lowitja O'Donoghue admission', the headline said and it ran on the front pages of Rupert Murdoch's many newspapers. A prime minister called her comments 'highly significant' and said it was time to stop 'navel gazing about the past' and to move on. Lowitja was appalled and hurt and called the article 'simplistic, sensationalist, misleading and mischievous'.

As a journalist, I knew Lowitja well and suggested that we go back to where her life began, to follow its course from the desert and the gibber plains of Central Australia, and to search the archives of the missionaries and the Aboriginal 'protectors' to find what was there to be found. She agreed, and so we journeyed together and more than once she cried and, when she spoke of it later, she called it 'one of the most painful and emotionally powerful experiences of my life'.

'I felt as close to my mother during this journey as I have ever done before,' she said. 'And it has confirmed one thing for me—I will never accept that my mother willingly gave me up.'

From time to time, in the years that followed, we talked about whether this biography should be written, but she was always too busy living. She was more than eighty years old and packing her memories into boxes before she thought it might be something worth doing and then she called me and said 'let's get on with it', and I wrote the title first: *Lowitja*, the name her mother gave her.

I am indebted to many people, for all manner of assistance, beginning with Lowitja, who entrusted me with her story, contributed her memories, and waited impatiently. Thanks also to the publishing team at Allen & Unwin, and in particular Richard Walsh, who encouraged and cajoled and advised; and Rebecca Kaiser and Margaret Bowman; members of the extended O'Donoghue family, and in particular Deborah Edwards and Michael O'Donoghue; Stephen Watkins, who did much of the initial research, and helped safeguard Lowitja's personal papers; the exemplary staff of the National Library of Australia; staff of the South Australian Museum and the State Library of South Australia; Frank Brennan and the Australian Institute of Jesuit Studies, who gave me a bed in Canberra and played the music of Shane Howard; Linda Burney; Fred Chaney; Tim Costello; Darryl Cronin; John Dallwitz at the Ara Irititja project; Mick Dodson; Pat Dodson; Gareth Evans; Gary Foley; Ros Gooden; Bill Gray; Patrick Hamilton; Cheryl Kernot; Paul Lane; Marcia Langton; Jenny Macklin; Ken Manley; Michael Mansell; Denise McFadyen; George Menham; Brendan O'Dwyer; Darryl Pearce; Noel Pearson; Lindsay Rae; Kevin Rudd; Vicki Scott; Peter Shergold; Giuseppe Stramandinoli; Peter

Sutton; Leah Swann; Robert Tickner; Pat Turner; Joan Webster; and in India: Johnson Das; Tanurupa Goswami; Khiren Borgoary; Arjun Basumatary; and Samad Ali.

And at the heart of it all, thanks to Karen, Jack, Jesse and Sean, for their love and understanding.

Notes

Book One   Land of fierce lights

1. Eric Richards, 'Irish life and progress in Colonial South Australia', *Irish Historical Studies*, vol. 27, no. 107, May 1991

2. *Register* (Adelaide), 25 October 1848, p. 2. The previous year, known in Ireland as 'Black '47', Stephen de Vere, son of a baronet poet, wrote hauntingly of his voyage to Canada: 'Hundreds of poor people, men, women and children of all ages from the drivelling idiot of 90 to the babe just born, huddled together, without light, without air, wallowing in filth and breathing a fetid atmosphere, sick in body, dispirited in heart; the fevered patients lying between the sound.' De Vere's report was read aloud in the House of Lords by the Secretary for the Colonies, Earl Grey. See P.J. Meghen, 1967, 'Stephen de Vere's voyage to Canada, 1847', *The Old Limerick Journal*

3. The first Afghans arrived in South Australia in 1838, but the first commercial shipment of camels and their handlers disembarked from the steamer *Blackwell*, to the wonder of a great crowd, at Port Augusta on New Year's Day 1866, imported by pastoralist–entrepreneur Thomas Elder. Known collectively as 'Afghans', these cameleers, who opened up desert areas for commerce and exploration where horses could not travel, came from a range of regions, predominantly Baluchistan, Kashmir, Sind and Punjab in present-day Pakistan, Afghanistan, north-western India and eastern Iran.

4. D.W. Meinig, *On the Margins of the Good Earth*, Adelaide: Rigby, 1970, pp. 78–85

5. Edmund Barton, Immigration Restriction Bill, *Hansard*, Parliament of Australia, 26 September 1901, p. 5233

6. Hugh Mahon, *Austral Light*, 1 March 1902, pp. 198–201

7. *Advertiser* (Adelaide), 27 November 1913

8. Diary of 2nd Lieut. William Cameron, C Squadron, 9th Regiment, 3rd Light Horse Brigade, 1915, Australian War Memorial. In his diary entry for 17 August, Cameron wrote that after severe fighting, thousands of lives had been lost for little gain. 'On that eventful Friday when the advance was ordered, I was placed in charge of the Regtl. Sharp Shooters and took up position on the left at three o'clock in the morning and waited the rush forward of our comrades. The eighth Regt. was the first out. We saw them climb out and move forward about ten yards and lie flat. The second line did likewise; meantime the Turkish fire increased in intensity, and as they rose to charge the Turkish Machine Guns just poured out lead and our fellows went down like corn before a scythe.' Cameron called it heroic—and murder.

9. Annie Lock, *Australian Aborigines Advocate* (AAA), 9 April 1924; Catherine Bishop, 'A woman missionary living amongst naked blacks', MA thesis, Canberra: Australian National University, 1991, pp. 211–12

10. Violet Turner, *Pearls from the Deep*, Adelaide: United Aborigines' Mission, 1936, p. 4

11. Lowitja O'Donoghue, Eulogy for Parker O'Donoghue, 30 January 2003, O'Donoghue papers 1940–2013, Canberra: National Library of Australia

12. Lock, AAA, 30 September 1925, p. 5

13. R.M. Williams with Olaf Ruhen, *Beneath Whose Hand*, South Melbourne: Macmillan, 1984, p. 25

14. Stuart Rintoul, 'Looking for Lowitja', *Weekend Australian Magazine*, 21 April 2001

15. Turner, *Pearls from the Deep*, p. 35

16. Jen Gibson and Bruce Ward, *Oodnadatta Aboriginal Heritage Survey 1985–86*, Adelaide: Dept of Environment and Planning, 1987; also Melanie Hogan, *Stolen Generations Testimonies Project*, Australian Federal Government, Canberra, 2009–2012

17. 'From the country—Quorn', *Chronicle* (Adelaide), 31 December 1927, p. 13

18. 'Colebrook Home', *Mercury* (Quorn), 13 July 1928, p. 3

19. MacDiarmid to McLean, correspondence, 19 July 1932; and subsequently McLean to SA Commissioner of Public Works, correspondence, 27 August 1932

20. Michael Terry, *Untold Miles,* London: Selwyn & Blount, 1933, pp. 160–1

21. Ion Idriess, *Flynn of the Inland,* Sydney: Angus & Robertson, 1932, p. 118

22. Lowitja O'Donoghue, interviewed by Frank Heimans, Film Australia, December 1993

Book Two   Iti (the baby)

1. Sally Goold & Kerrynne Liddle (eds), *In Our Own Right: Black Australian nurses' stories,* Maleny: eContent Management, 2005

2. Lowitja O'Donoghue, Ecumenical Service, Australian Centre for Christianity and Culture, 26 May 2002

3. Turner, *Pearls from the Deep,* p. 40

4. Turner, *Pearls from the Deep,* pp. 41–2

5. Truganini had feared her body would be mutilated and her remains displayed. Her dying wish was to be sewed into a bag weighed down by a stone and thrown into the deepest part of the D'Entrecasteaux Channel, 'because I know that when I die the Tasmanian museum wants my body'. 'Truganini's request in diary', *Mercury* (Hobart), 15 October 1949, p. 12

6. Elkin Archives, 21 May 1937, quoted in Fiona Probyn-Rapsey, *Made to Matter: White fathers, Stolen Generations,* Sydney: Sydney University Press, 2013, p. 30

7. A.J. La Nauze, 'The study of Australian history 1929–1959', *Historical Studies,* vol. 9, no. 33, November 1959, p. 11

8. Clive Turnbull, 'Aborigines petition the King', *Herald* (Melbourne), 7 August 1937, p. 31

9. Kevin Gilbert, 'Pearl Gibbs: Aboriginal patriot', in 'Three tributes to Pearl Gibbs', *Aboriginal History,* 1983, vol. 7, no. 1

10. 'Why Blacks Left', *Argus* (Melbourne), 27 February 1939, p. 2

11. Samuel Rabain Parsonage to Commissioner of Police, correspondence, Aborigines Department records, South Australia, AD no. 21, 8 August 1938

12. South Australia Pastoral Board minutes, secretary K.R. Snell, 21 September 1937, no. 5517

13. Doug Fuller to Cecil Goode, correspondence, 6 March 1940, South Australian Government archives

14. Tom O'Donoghue to Director of Lands, correspondence, 18 June 1940

15. South Australian *Police Gazette,* 20 November 1940, p. 445, C.11242

16. Bradey to Penhall, correspondence, 11 June 1940

17. Penhall to Bradey, correspondence, 4 December 1940, AD 5A/40

18. Bradey to Penhall, correspondence, 10 December 1940

19. South Australian *Police Gazette*, 19 February 1941, C.1469

20. Bernard O'Neil, interview with Doug Fuller, 25 October 2005, Animal and Plant Commission history project, South Australian Government

21. 'Colebrook Home—Children now established at Eden Hills', *Mercury* (Quorn), 28 April 1944, p. 4

22. Rintoul, 'Looking for Lowitja'

23. Jen Gibson et al. with Dunjiba Community Council, *Oodnadatta Genealogies*, Adelaide: Dept of Environment and Planning, 1988, p. 95

24. Dick Monks, 'The aborigines say he's human', *The Mail* (Adelaide), 22 August 1953, p. 9

25. Ronald Berndt, Catherine Berndt & John Stanton, *A World That Was: The Yaraldi of the Murray River and the Lakes, South Australia*, Carlton: Melbourne University Press, 1993, p. 7

26. Robin Hughes, 'Lowitja (Lois) O'Donoghue', *Australian Biography: Extraordinary Australians talk about their lives*, Film Australia, 1993–1994

27. Lowitja O'Donoghue, Eulogy for Miriam Graham, O'Donoghue papers, 1940–2013

28. Lowitja O'Donoghue, interviewed by Frank Heimans

29. Lowitja O'Donoghue, author interview, June 2018

Book Three   An old suitcase and a wedding picture

1. Ramindjeri Heritage Association, 'Kondoli, the whale man', Victor Harbor, South Australia

2. Hughes, 'Lowitja (Lois) O'Donoghue'

3. Lowitja O'Donoghue, author interview, June 2018

4. Lowitja O'Donoghue, 'Standing at the Crossroads', speech for Bicentennial, 26 January 1988, O'Donoghue papers 1940–2013

5. Lowitja O'Donoghue, opening speech, Wooden Boat Festival, 11 March 2007

6. Yvonne Nicholls, *Not Slaves, Not Citizens*, Melbourne: Australian Council for Civil Liberties, 1952

7. Lowitja O'Donoghue, author interview, 2017; see also Stewart Cockburn, *Notable Lives: Profiles of 21 South Australians*, Adelaide: Ferguson Publication, 1997

8. Goold and Liddle, *In Our Own Right*, p. 53
9. Lowitja O'Donoghue, speech to women as Australian of the Year, Port Augusta, 28 November 1985
10. Charles Duguid, *Doctor and the Aborigines*, Adelaide: Rigby, 1972, p. 94
11. Nancy Barnes, *Munyi's Daughter: A spirited brumby*, Henley Beach: Seaview Press, 2000
12. Duguid, *Doctor and the Aborigines*, p. 115
13. *News* (Adelaide), *Children See New Sights*, 21 December 1935, p. 5
14. Barnes, *Munyi's Daughter*, p. 91
15. 'Part-Aboriginal taxpayers tell of colour bar', *News* (Adelaide), 1 September 1953, p. 2
16. Hughes, 'Lowitja (Lois) O'Donoghue'
17. Margot O'Neill, 'Against all odds: The double struggle of black women', *Age*, 18 April 1985, p. 11
18. Lowitja O'Donoghue, author interview, 2017
19. *Royal Tour: The Queen in Adelaide*, British Movietone, 1954
20. Freda Young, 'Dusky bride wore white satin: Aboriginal wedding had a film star touch', *Australian Women's Weekly*, 10 March 1954, p. 13
21. 'Petition launched on Aborigines: Tears over Aborigine film', *Tribune*, 1 May 1957 p. 2
22. Sue Taffe, *Black and White Together*, St Lucia: University of Queensland Press, 2005, p. 5
23. Jack Horner, *Seeking Racial Justice: An insider's memoir of the Movement for Aboriginal Advancement 1938–1978*, Canberra: Aboriginal Studies Press, p. 61–3
24. Hughes, 'Lowitja (Lois) O'Donoghue'
25. Goold and Liddle, *In Our Own Right*, p. 53
26. Goold and Liddle, *In Our Own Right*, p. 52
27. Lowitja O'Donoghue, author interview, June 2018

Book Four   Lily's daughter

1. Furreedpore, East Bengal, India, became Faridpur, Bangladesh, in 1971.
2. Silas Mead, a man of Quakerish appearance, arrived in Adelaide on board the *Parisian* in July 1861. Burning with missionary zeal, when he farewelled the Five Barley Loaves in October 1885, he preached: 'Tonight we are bidding farewell to five women going to the millions of women in what I shall

designate the Australasian District of East Bengal. What are these among so many? Possibly in some degree what the five loaves were to the hungry thousands around Him in Judea. Yes, five Australian sisters . . .' See Tony Cupit, Ros Gooden & Ken Manley (eds), *From Five Barley Loaves: Australian Baptists in global mission 1864–2010*, Northcote: Morning Star Publishing, 2014; and Rosalind Gooden, 'Five Barley Loaves: An Icon for Australasian Baptist Missionary Work', Trans-Tasman Missions History Conference, ANU, Canberra, 2004.

3. 'Crowds stood still in heart of Sydney', *Dawn: a magazine for the Aboriginal people of NSW*, August 1962, vol. 11, issue 8, p. 1
4. 'Crowds stood still in the heart of Sydney', p. 1.
5. Lowitja O'Donoghue, address to India Australia Association, Canberra, 18 August 1985
6. Hughes, 'Lowitja (Lois) O'Donoghue'
7. Jodie Brough & Debra Jopson, 'Sell-out or saviour?', *Sydney Morning Herald (SMH)*, 22 July 1995, *Spectrum* section, p. 3
8. Hughes, 'Lowitja (Lois) O'Donoghue'
9. Lowitja (Lois) O'Donoghue, *Vision*, 13 February 1963
10. 'Evacuee nurse returns', *Advertiser* (Adelaide), 12 December 1962, p. 26
11. Hughes, 'Lowitja (Lois) O'Donoghue'
12. Hughes, 'Lowitja (Lois) O'Donoghue'
13. Margaret Forte, *Flight of an Eagle: The Dreaming of Ruby Hammond*, Adelaide: Wakefield Press, 1995, p. 71
14. Forte, *Flight of an Eagle,* p. 83
15. Charles Perkins, *A Bastard Like Me*, Sydney: Ure Smith, 1975, p. 77
16. Perkins, *A Bastard Like Me*, p. 90
17. Vincent Lingiari in Frank Hardy, *The Unlucky Australians*, Melbourne: Nelson, 1968, p. 72
18. Hardy, *The Unlucky Australians*, p. 26
19. Gary Foley, *Chicka 'The Fox' Dixon: Heroes in the struggle for justice*, Koori History Website
20. Foley, *Chicka 'The Fox' Dixon*
21. Lowitja O'Donoghue, author interview, June 2017
22. Lowitja O'Donoghue, speech to National Congress of Australia's First People, 8 June 2011
23. Hughes, 'Lowitja (Lois) O'Donoghue'

24. Henry Kingsley, 'Eyre's March', in *The Boy in Grey and Other Stories and Sketches*, London: Ward, Lock & Bowden, 1865

25. Hughes, 'Lowitja (Lois) O'Donoghue'

26. Kim Beazley, 'Now action is needed for Aborigines', *Canberra Times*, 1 June 1967, p. 2

27. Pat O'Shane, interviewed by Stuart Rintoul, *The Wailing: A national Black oral history*, 1993, Port Melbourne: William Heinemann Australia, pp. 39–54

28. Goold and Liddle, *In Our Own Right*, p. 54

29. Lowitja O'Donoghue, author interview, June 2018

30. Helen Caterer, *Sunday Mail*, 24 May 1969

31. Lowitja O'Donoghue, interviewed by Frank Heimans

32. Brough and Jopson, 'Sell-out or saviour?'

33. Lowitja O'Donoghue, Ecumenical Service, Australian Centre for Christianity and Culture, 26 May 2002

34. Lowitja O'Donoghue, interviewed by Frank Heimans

35. Lowitja O'Donoghue, speech to United Nations Association of Australia, Canberra, 14 September 1991

36. Hughes, 'Lowitja (Lois) O'Donoghue'

Book Five   The wind across the sandhills

1. Paul Daley, 'Finding Mungo Man: The moment Australia's story suddenly changed', *Guardian*, 14 November 2017

2. Lowitja O'Donoghue, as told to Joan Cunningham and Karen Jennings, *Lowitja*, Kingswood: Working Title Press, 2003, p. 7

3. Goold and Liddle, *In Our Own Right*, p. 55

4. Rohan Rivett, 'A rose and "the brigands" ', *Canberra Times*, 7 March 1968, p. 22

5. W.E.H. Stanner, 'After the Dreaming', Boyer Lectures, 1968; see Stanner, *The Dreaming and Other Essays*, with an introduction by Robert Manne, Collingwood: Black Inc., 2010

6. H.C. Coombs, *The Australian*, 6 January 1969

7. Perkins, *A Bastard Like Me*, p. 109

8. Perkins, *A Bastard Like Me*, p. 158

9. Perkins, *A Bastard Like Me*, pp. 172–3

10. Jack Horner, *Report of the 13th Annual Conference of FCAATSI, 27–29 March 1970*, McGinness papers, AIATSIS, Canberra

11. Duguid, *Doctor and the Aborigines*, p. 193

12. Duguid, *Doctor and the Aborigines*, p. 196

13. Duguid, *Doctor and the Aborigines*, p. 202

14. John Fogarty and Jacinta Dwyer, 'The First Aboriginal Land Rights Case', *More or Less Democracy & New Media*, 2012, p. 186; see also Edward Woodward, *One Brief Interval: A memoir,* Carlton: Miegunyah Press, 2005

15. Perkins, *A Bastard Like Me*, p. 169

16. Gough Whitlam, *The Whitlam Government 1972–1975*, Ringwood: Penguin, 1985, p. 468

17. Hughes, 'Lowitja (Lois) O'Donoghue'

18. Stewart Cockburn, 'The Saga of Lois O'Donoghue: an Aboriginal leader in a white society', *Advertiser* (Adelaide), 13 March 1975

19. Cockburn, *Notable Lives*

20. *Advertiser*, 4 July 1975

21. Hughes, 'Lowitja (Lois) O'Donoghue'

22. Hughes, 'Lowitja (Lois) O'Donoghue'

23. Deborah Stone, 'Mother of the nation', *Sunday Age*, Agenda section, 15 May 1994, p. 5

24. *Advertiser*, 10 February 1976, p. 11

25. Editorial, *Advertiser,* 11 February 1976

26. Ian Viner, address to NACC, Canberra, 5 March 1976

27. Don Dunstan, interviewed by Sue Taffe, 26 November 1997

28. Don Dunstan, *Felicia: The political memoirs of Don Dunstan,* Melbourne: Macmillan, 1981

29. Robert Ball, *Advertiser*, 17 May 1978, p. 5

30. Hughes, 'Lowitja (Lois) O'Donoghue'

31. Hughes, 'Lowitja (Lois) O'Donoghue'

32. *Advertiser*, 31 December 1982, p. 4

33. Clyde Holding, *Hostel News*, August 1983

34. Bob Hawke, Media Release, 11 November 1983

35. *The Transcontinental*, Port Augusta, 7 March 1984, p. 1

36. Fred Chaney, John Button Oration, 23 August 2014

37. Lowitja O'Donoghue, author interview, 2018

38. *Australian Women's Weekly*, April 1985

39. Lowitja O'Donoghue, speech, Women's Health in a Changing Society, Adelaide, 4 September 1985

Book Six 'Pagan' woman rises

1. Lowitja O'Donoghue, 'Standing at the Crossroads'
2. Peter Read, *Charles Perkins: A biography*, Ringwood: Penguin, 2001, p. 275
3. Jack Davis, *John Pat and Other Poems*, Melbourne: Dent, 1988
4. Paul Kelly, 'Bicentennial', Sony/ATV Music Publishing, September 1987
5. Gerry Hand, *Hansard*, Parliament of Australia, 10 December 1987, p. 3152
6. Lenore Taylor, 'ADC rebels throw in towel over reorganisation', *Canberra Times*, 24 May 1988
7. Bob Hawke, ALP conference, Hobart, 6 June 1988
8. Bob Hawke, *The Hawke Memoirs*, Port Melbourne: William Heinemann Australia, 1994, p. 435
9. Bob Hawke, *Hansard*, Parliament of Australia, 23 August 1988, p. 137
10. John Howard, *Hansard*, Parliament of Australia, 11 April 1989, p. 1328
11. Gerry Hand, Minister for Aboriginal Affairs, Media Release, 13 December 1989
12. Mark Metherell, 'Giving more power to the people as traces of assimilation vanish', *Age*, 16 December 1989
13. Lenore Taylor, '"Pagan" woman rises from the turbulence', *Australian*, 15 December 1989
14. Lowitja O'Donoghue, speech to Royal Australian Institute of Public Administration, 13 June 1990
15. Lowitja O'Donoghue, 'Review of developments', speech to UN Working Group on Indigenous Populations, Geneva, Switzerland, 30 July 1990, in *Lois O'Donoghue Speeches 1990–1996*, ATSIC, vol. 1, 1997, pp. 32–4
16. Lowitja O'Donoghue, speech at Apiwentye, Northern Territory, 18 October 1990, in *Lois O'Donoghue Speeches*, vol. 1, pp. 50–1
17. Karen Harbutt, 'Low turnout for ATSIC vote', *Australian*, 5 November 1990, p. 3
18. Lowitja O'Donoghue, *ATSIC Annual Report 1990–1991*; see also Lowitja O'Donoghue, 'New developments in Indigenous affairs in Australia', speech to a forum at the University of Auckland, New Zealand, May 1991, in *Lois O'Donoghue Speeches*, vol. 1, pp. 74–81
19. Lowitja O'Donoghue, 'Towards a new understanding of Indigenous Australia', A.W. Jones Lecture, University of Adelaide, 4 October 1995, in *Lois O'Donoghue Speeches*, vol. 3, pp. 97–106
20. Robert Tickner, *Taking a Stand: Land rights to reconciliation*, Crows Nest: Allen & Unwin, 2001, p. 54

21. Robert Tickner, *Taking a Stand*, p. 28

22. Janet Hawley, 'The Strehlow Collection: preserved in vitriol', *Good Weekend*, *SMH*, 28–29 August 1987, pp. 28–32

23. Lowitja O'Donoghue, 26 June 1991, in *Lois O'Donoghue Speeches*, vol. 1, pp. 91–2

24. Lowitja O'Donoghue, Sir Robert Garran Oration, Royal Institute of Public Administration National Conference, Darwin, NT, 11 September 1991, in *Lois O'Donoghue Speeches*, vol. 1, pp. 107–18

25. Sigrid Kirk, 'Mr Mowaljarlai's gift is for the white man too', *SMH*, 3 September 1991, p. 4

26. Lowitja O'Donoghue, 'The window of opportunity', speech to Drug and Alcohol Services National Congress, Adelaide, 3 December 1991, in *Lois O'Donoghue Speeches*, vol. 1, pp. 130–6

27. Lowitja O'Donoghue, 'One nation: promise or paradox?', speech to National Press Club, Canberra, 20 May 1992, in *Lois O'Donoghue Speeches*, vol. 1, pp. 183–90

Book Seven   Only she

1. Marcia Langton, 'Foreword' in Noel Loos and Koiki Mabo, *Edward Koiki Mabo: His life and struggle for land rights*, St Lucia: University of Queensland Press, 1996

2. *First Australians: We are no longer shadows*, Ep 7, Blackfella Films, SBS and Screen Australia, 2008; see also Henry Reynolds, *The Law of the Land*, 2nd ed., Ringwood: Penguin, 1992, pp. 185–6

3. Loos and Mabo, *Eddie Koiki Mabo*, p. 199

4. Paul Keating, *Hansard*, Parliament of Australia, 4 June 1992, p. 3586

5. Keating, Adelaide Festival of Arts, 6 March 1992

6. Neville Bonner to Lowitja O'Donoghue, correspondence, 1 August 1992, O'Donoghue papers 1940–2013

7. A Mabo Ministerial Committee was established in October 1992, chaired by Keating. After the March 1993 election, it comprised Paul Keating (Prime Minister), Michael Lavarch (Attorney-General), Frank Walker (Special Minister of State), Duncan Kerr (Justice), Michael Lee (Resources), Simon Crean (Primary Industries & Energy), Alan Griffiths (Industry), John Dawkins (Treasurer) and Ralph Willis (Finance). Keating chaired the committee and immersed himself deeply and personally in the negotiations.

Behind the scenes, the government's chief advisers were Sandy Hollway, Bob Hawke's chief of staff 1988–1990, who was brought in by Keating to negotiate with the states and who was regarded by the Aboriginal leadership as the key bureaucrat 'in charge of the brake van on the train'; Robert Orr, from the Attorney-General's department; Mike Dillon from Aboriginal Affairs; lawyer Phillip Toyne, who negotiated the Pitjantjatjara Land Rights Act in 1976 and represented the traditional owners of Uluru in 1983; and former journalist Simon Balderstone.

8. Don Watson, *Recollections of a Bleeding Heart: A portrait of Paul Keating PM*, Milsons Point: Knopf, 2002, p. 405

9. The twenty-one Aboriginal representatives who met with Keating and Cabinet ministers on 27 April 1993 were Galarrwuy Yunupingu and John Ah Kit, from the Northern Land Council; Bruce Breaden and David Ross (Central Land Council); John Watson and Peter Yu (Kimberley Land Council); Jean George and Noel Pearson (Cape York Land Council); Manuel Ritchie and Danny Chapman (NSW Land Council); Pat Dodson and Wenten Rubuntja (Council for Aboriginal Reconciliation); Rob Riley and Ted Wilkes (West Australian Aboriginal Legal Service); Tauto Sansbury and Esther Williams (South Australian Aboriginal Legal Rights Movement); Getano Lui Jr (Torres Strait Regional Council and the Island Co-ordinating Council); Mick Dodson, the first Aboriginal and Torres Strait Islander Social Justice Commissioner; and Lowitja, Gerhardt Pearson and George Mye, from ATSIC. Lowitja sat directly opposite Keating, who regarded her as the natural leader of the Indigenous negotiators.

10. Noel Pearson, 'White guilt, victimhood and the quest for a radical centre', *Griffith Review*, Winter 2007, no. 16

11. Drafted as the Red Centre Statement in Alice Springs and then honed down to eight key principles, the Aboriginal 'peace plan' sought the recognition and protection of Indigenous rights; no extinguishment of Indigenous title but co-existence and revival; no extinguishment or impairment without Indigenous consent; a declaration of Indigenous title in reserves and other defined lands; a tribunal to recognise Indigenous land title; a long-term settlement process for Indigenous benefit; security for sacred sites and heritage areas; and negotiation with Indigenous people for constitutional recognition. In exchange, they would accept validation of titles between 1975 and 1992 that might otherwise be invalid by virtue of the Racial

Discrimination Act. See Tim Rowse, 1993, 'How we got a Native Title Act', *Australian Quarterly*, vol. 65, no. 4, The Politics of Mabo, p. 197; see also Darryl Cronin, 'Dialogue and Indigenous policy in Australia', PhD thesis, Sydney, UNSW, 2015, p. 270

12. Letter from O'Donoghue to Keating, 1 February 1993, O'Donoghue papers 1940–2013

13. Kerry O'Brien, *Keating*, Crows Nest: Allen & Unwin, 2015, p. 543

14. Interview with author, Canberra, 22 July 2019

15. Paul Keating, 'New Visions for Australia', H.V. Evatt Lecture, Sydney, 28 April 1993

16. Lowitja O'Donoghue, Memorial service for Mr Marika, MBE, Yirrkala, Northern Territory, 22 January 1993, in *Lois O'Donoghue Speeches*, vol. 2, pp. 4–5

17. Interview with author, Canberra, 22 January 2019

18. Paul Chamberlin, 'Bosch faces sack for "Stone Age" jibe', *SMH*, 27 July 1993, p. 5; see also Robert Manne, 'The hidden face of freedom of speech', *SMH*, 9 August 1993, p. 17

19. Lowitja O'Donoghue, speech at UN World Conference on Human Rights, Vienna, Australia, 14–25 June 1993, in *Lois O'Donoghue Speeches*, vol. 2, pp. 74–7

20. Lowitja O'Donoghue, speech to Police, Aboriginal and Torres Strait Islander Peoples' National Conference, Perth, Western Australia, 22 June 1993, in *Lois O'Donoghue Speeches*, vol. 2, pp. 78–83

21. Lowitja O'Donoghue, speech, opening Quorn Show, Quorn, South Australia, 11 September 1993, in *Lois O'Donoghue Speeches*, vol. 2, pp. 112–13

22. Richard Guilliatt, 'Noel Pearson, land rights leader', *Weekend Australian Magazine*, 21 September 2013

23. Quentin Beresford, *Rob Riley: An Aboriginal leader's quest for justice*, Canberra: Aboriginal Studies Press, 2006, p. 299; *West Australian*, 20 October 1993

24. Michael Mansell, 'The Court gives an inch but takes another mile', *Aboriginal Law Bulletin*, August 1992, vol. 2 no. 57

25. Gareth Evans, *Incorrigible Optimist: A political memoir*, Carlton: Melbourne University Press, 2017, pp. 35–6

26. Rebecca Lang, 'Call for Law to look at history', *Herald Sun*, 1 August 1995

27. Paul Keating, Lowitja O'Donoghue Oration, Don Dunstan Foundation, Adelaide, 31 May 2011

28. Lowitja O'Donoghue, speech to Australian Association of National Parks Support Groups, Adelaide, 23 March 1994, in *Lois O'Donoghue Speeches*, vol. 2, pp. 214–17

29. Garrie Gibson to Paul Keating, correspondence, 20 April 1993, O'Donoghue papers 1940–2013

30. *Advertiser*, 14 April 1993

31. Deborah Stone, 'Mother of the nation'

32. Lowitja O'Donoghue, speech at Aboriginal Justice Advisory Committees' National Conference, Perth, WA, 24 May 1994, in *Lois O'Donoghue Speeches*, vol. 2, pp. 228–32

33. Lowitja O'Donoghue, 'Review of developments', statement to Twelfth Session of the UN Working Group on Indigenous Populations, Geneva, Switzerland, 20–29 July 1994, in *Lois O'Donoghue Speeches*, vol 2, pp. 268–74. Among key developments, at the end of 1993 ATSIC regional council chairmen and commissioners were made full-time and paid positions, but the number of regional councils was sharply reduced from sixty to thirty-five, and the number of elected regional councillors was reduced from 788 to 573. Lowitja supported those reforms, as she regarded the initial ATSIC structure as being unwieldy. Nationally, just over thirty per cent of adult Aboriginal and Torres Strait Islander people voted in ATSIC elections on 4 December 1993, while ATSIC's budget was $956 million.

34. Lowitja O'Donoghue, speech at presentation of Council for Aboriginal Reconciliation's first report to the federal parliament, Canberra, 17 November 1994, in *Lois O'Donoghue Speeches*, vol. 2, pp. 321–2

35. Robert Tickner, Aboriginal Affairs Minister, Media Release, 21 December 1994

36. Mick Dodson, Aboriginal social justice commissioner statement, August 26, 1995; see Tickner, *Taking a Stand*, pp. 282–3

37. *Weekend Australian*, 8–9 April, 1995; see also Lowitja O'Donoghue, speech presenting ATSIC report *Recognition, Rights and Reform* to Keating, Parliament House, Canberra, 27 March 1995, in *Lois O'Donoghue Speeches*, vol. 3, pp. 21–3

38. Deborah McIntosh, 'Mission: Possible—The rise and rise of Lois O'Donoghue', *Sun-Herald* (Sydney), Tempo section profile, 28 May 1995, p. 143

39. Lowitja O'Donoghue, speech at celebrations to mark third anniversary of Mabo judgment and tombstone unveiling of Eddie Koiki Mabo, Townsville, Queensland, 3 June 1995, in *Lois O'Donoghue Speeches*, vol. 3, pp. 40–1

40. Ian Henderson, 'Outrage at desecration—vandalism of Mabo's grave "a racist act"', *Canberra Times*, 5 June 1995, p. 1

41. Christopher Zinn, 'Aboriginal woman tipped to become Head of State', *Guardian*, 27 July 1995, p. 10

42. Michelle Grattan, 'Keating's final thoughts on a Governor-General', *Age*, 6 July 1995, p. 3

43. Brough and Jopson, 'Sell-out or saviour?'

44. Brough and Jopson, 'Sell-out or saviour?'

45. Bill Birnbauer, 'An inside chance', *Age*, 7 August 1995, p. 9

46. Bill Birnbauer, '"Little people" left behind in bid for Yarralumla', *Age*, 7 August 1995, p. 3. Answering criticism that she had cut ties with her Colebrook origins, Lowitja replied that she regarded the children she grew up with as her brothers and sisters. 'The real problem with it is that they live in the little world of Quorn,' she told Birnbauer. 'I come home just for a little bit of rest; they don't understand the world that I operate in. I love them all, but I have moved on.'

47. Alan Ramsey, 'Yarralumla needs a woman's touch', *SMH*, 9 August 1995, p. 15

48. Lowitja O'Donoghue, Media Release, ATSIC, Monday 21 August 1995

49. Michael Gordon, 'Risk-free Deane will ease PM's path to a republic', *Australian*, 22 August 1995

50. Don Watson, *Recollections of a Bleeding Heart*, pp. 596–7

Book Eight 'My name is Lowitja'

1. John Howard, *Meet the Press*, 10 Network, 4 July 1993

2. Pauline Hanson, letters, *Queensland Times*, 6 January 1996

3. Lowitja O'Donoghue, speech to mark International Women's Day, Canberra, 8 March 1996, in *Lois O'Donoghue Speeches, 1990–96*, vol. 3, pp. 141–3

4. John Howard, interviewed by Fran Kelly, *AM* program, ABC radio, 2 April 1996

5. Michelle Grattan, 'Black funds: call for action', *Age*, 8 April 1996, p. 1

6. Mick Gooda, 'Rob Riley Memorial Lecture', 8 May 2015

7. Lowitja O'Donoghue, 'Mabo: 10 years and beyond', speech to Macquarie University Law Society Dinner, Sydney, 15 May 1996, in *Lois O'Donoghue Speeches, 1990–96*, vol. 3, pp. 163–7

8. Lowitja O'Donoghue, speech opening meeting of ATSIC Commissioners and Regional Council Chairpersons, Canberra, 28 May 1996, in *Lois O'Donoghue Speeches, 1990–96*, vol. 3, pp. 174–6

9. John Howard, *Lazarus Rising: A personal and political autobiography*, Pymble: HarperCollins, 2010, p. 273

10. Paul Kelly, *The March of Patriots: The struggle for modern Australia*, Carlton: Melbourne University Press, 2009, p. 342

11. Lowitja O'Donoghue, 'Review of developments', Fourteenth Session of the UN Working Group on Indigenous Populations, Geneva, Switzerland, 29 July– 2 August 1996, in *Lois O'Donoghue Speeches, 1990–96*, vol. 3, pp. 200–1

12. Geoffrey Blainey, Sir John Latham Memorial Lecture, Sydney, 28 April 1993; edited versions appeared as 'Goodbye to all that?' *Weekend Australian*, 1–2 May 1993, p. 16; and as 'Drawing up a balance sheet of our history', *Quadrant*, July–Aug 1993, vol. 37, nos 7–8, pp. 10–15

13. John Howard, 'The Liberal tradition—The beliefs and values which guide the Federal Government', Sir Robert Menzies Lecture, Monash University, Caulfield, 18 November 1996

14. 'PM distorting our history; experts', *SMH*, 20 November 1996, p. 11

15. Debra Jopson, 'O'Donoghue in call for justice as she retires', *SMH*, 30 November 1996, p. 9

16. Daryl Melham, *Hansard*, Parliament of Australia, 5 December 1996, p. 7897

17. Leigh Clifford to Lowitja O'Donoghue, correspondence, 6 December 1996, O'Donoghue papers, 1940–2013

18. Leon Davis, 'New directions for CRA', speech to Securities Institute Australia, Melbourne, 20 March 1995. Breaking ranks with hardline mining companies, Davis said: 'Let me say this bluntly. CRA is satisfied with the central tenet of the Native Title Act. In CRA we believe that there are major opportunities for growth in outback Australia which will only be realised with the full co-operation of all interested parties. This government initiative has laid the basis for better exploration access and thus increased the probability that the next decade will see a series of CRA operations developed in active partnership with Aboriginal people.'

19. 'ATSIC hot seat', editorial, *SMH*, 10 December 1996, p. 14

20. Howard released his 'Wik 10-point plan' on 1 May 1997. Following historian Geoffrey Blainey's metaphor of a pendulum swing to a 'black armband' view of history in his 1993 John Latham Memorial Lecture, Howard frequently said the land rights pendulum after Wik had swung too far towards Aboriginal interests. On 8 May, he said: 'My aim has always been to strike a fair balance between respect for native title and security for pastoralists, farmers and

miners. That is one reason why I staunchly oppose blanket extinguishment of native title on pastoral leaseholds. The fact is that the Wik decision pushed the pendulum too far in the Aboriginal direction. The 10-point plan will return the pendulum to the centre.'

21. Mick Dodson, author interview, Canberra, 16 January 2019
22. John Howard, *Lazarus Rising*, 2010, pp. 276–7
23. Linda Burney, author interview, Canberra, 25 July 2019
24. In a government submission to a Senate inquiry, Herron denied the existence of a stolen 'generation' and argued the proportion of separated children was no more than ten per cent, based on an Australian Bureau of Statistics' survey of 5000 people in 1994. In the furious Aboriginal reaction that followed, Lowitja said she was 'distraught' about the government submission. See: Herron, *Federal Government Submission, Senate Legal and Constitutional References Committee, Inquiry into the Stolen Generations*, March 2000; *Hansard*, Parliament of Australia, 3 April 2000, p. 13116; *The World Today*, ABC; *7.30 Report*, ABC; and Kathy Marks, 'Australia denies "Lost Generation" of Aboriginals', *Independent*, UK, 3 April 2000; and Debra Jopson, 'Disgust at "Brutal" denial of suffering', *SMH*, 3 April 2000, p. 4
25. Noel Pearson, 31 October 1997; see also 'Racist scum', *Koori Mail*, 5 November 1997, p. 1
26. *Cape York Unity News*, 30 November 1997; *Courier Mail*, 1 December 1997
27. Tony Wright, 'Dodson pleads for senators to hold fire', *SMH*, 29 November 1997, p. 10
28. Lowitja (Lois) O'Donoghue, Constitutional Convention, *Parliament of Australia, Transcript of Proceedings*, 4 February 1998, pp. 250–2
29. Margo Kingston, 'Harradine shelters as Aborigines miss the Wik bus', *SMH*, 9 April 1998, p. 2
30. *Weekend Australian*, 27–28 June 1998
31. Noel Pearson, in *Wik vs Queensland*, Dean Gibson, writer and director, Bacon Factory Films
32. Lowitja O'Donoghue, Eulogy for Eileen O'Donoghue, O'Donoghue papers, 1940–2013
33. Lowitja O'Donoghue, Committee for Economic Development of Australia—Minter Ellison Nation Builders Awards, Melbourne, 25 March 1999; see Janine MacDonald, 'PM a wrecker says Aboriginal leader', *Age*, 26 May 1999, p. 4

34. Lowitja O'Donoghue, address to foreign correspondents, Canberra, 25 May 1999, O'Donoghue papers, 1940–2013; see also Lowitja O'Donoghue, 'Going past the PM to the people for healing', *Age*, 27 May 1999, p. 17

35. Trudy Harris, 'From the campfire to the Queen', *Weekend Australian*, October 16–17, 1999, p. 8

36. Lowitja O'Donoghue, Collins Street Baptist Church, Melbourne, 28 November 1999, O'Donoghue papers, 1940–2013

37. Lowitja O'Donoghue, 'Australia Day Address', Sydney, 24 January 2000

38. Lowitja O'Donoghue, 'Reconciliation in Australia', address to the Australian Jesuit Alumni Association, 26 June 2000

39. 'ATSIC summit decides not to disrupt Olympics', *Koori Mail*, 22 September 1999, p. 4

40. Lowitja O'Donoghue, address to heads of Christian Churches Committee, Adelaide, 27 August 2001

41. Andrew Bolt, 'I wasn't stolen: Lowitja O'Donoghue's admission', *Herald Sun*, Melbourne, 23 February 2001, p. 1

42. Rebecca Barrett, 'Stolen generation debate re-ignited', *The World Today*, ABC, 23 February 2001

43. Mick Dodson, National Press Club, Canberra, 11 June 2003

44. John Howard, Media Release, 7 July 2003

45. Debra Jopson, 'ATSIC's disappearing act', *SMH*, 25 April 2003, p. 3

46. 'Resign!' *Koori Mail*, 24 March 2004, p. 1

47. Lowitja O'Donoghue & Tim Costello, *Anangu Pitjantjatjara and Yankunytjatjara Lands Report for South Australian Government*, 23 March 2005

48. *Advertiser*, 16 July 2005

49. Opening of Robert Hannaford exhibition, Adelaide, 6 December 2006

50. 'Paper reveals sexual abuse, violence in NT Indigenous communities', *Lateline*, ABC, 15 May 2006

51. Misha Schubert, Katharine Murphy & Lindsay Murdoch, 'A national emergency: Howard acts', *Age*, 22 June 2007

52. Stuart Rintoul and Stephen Lunn, '"Knee-jerk" laws break the law', *Australian*, 22 June 2007, p. 4

53. Paul Kelly, 'We are sorry', *Australian*, 14 February 2008, p. 1

54. Lowitja O'Donoghue, interviewed by Eleanor Hall, *The World Today*, ABC radio, 13 February 2008

Bibliography

Archival sources

Lowitja O'Donoghue, private papers 1940–2013, National Library of Australia
Records of the United Aborigines Mission
Ships' passenger lists 1876–1877, State Records, Government of South Australia
South Australian Aboriginal Affairs Advisory Board annual reports
South Australian Aborigines Department annual reports
South Australian Aborigines Protection Board annual reports
South Australian Protector of Aborigines annual reports
South Australian State Archives

Books

Anderson, C. (ed.), *Politics of the Secret*, Sydney: University of Sydney, 1995
Angie, V. (ed.), *Women's Voices,* Port Augusta: Kungka Tjutaku Ngura, 1991
Arthure, S., Breen, F., James, S., Lonergan, D., *Irish South Australia: New histories and insights*, Mile End: Wakefield Press, 2019
Attwood, B. & Markus, A., *The 1967 Referendum: Race, power and the Australian Constitution*, Canberra: Aboriginal Studies Press, 2007
Baldwin, S., *Unsung Heroes and Heroines of Australia*, Elwood: Greenhouse, 1988
Bandler, F., *Turning the Tide: A personal history of the Federal Council for the Advancement of Aborigines and Torres Strait Islanders*, Canberra: Aboriginal Studies Press, 1989

Barnes, N., *Munyi's Daughter: A spirited brumby*, Henley Beach: Seaview Press, 2000

Bennett, M.M., *The Australian Aboriginal as a human being*, London: Alston Rivers, 1930

Beresford, Q., *Rob Riley: An Aboriginal leader's quest for justice*, Canberra: Aboriginal Studies Press, 2006

Berndt, R.M., Berndt, C.H., with Stanton, J.E., *A World That Was: The Yaraldi of the Murray River and the Lakes, South Australia*, Carlton: Melbourne University Press, 1993

Bickford, J., *An Autobiography of Christian Labour in the West Indies, Demerara, Victoria, New South Wales, and South Australia, 1838–1888*, London: Charles H. Kelly, 1890

Bleakley, J.W., *The Aborigines of Australia*, Brisbane: Jacaranda Press, 1961

Blieschke, L. (ed.), *Plain of Contrast: A history of Willowie, Amyton, and Booleroo Whim*, Adelaide: District Centenary Book Committee, 1975

Bramston, T., *Paul Keating: The big-picture leader*, Melbourne: Scribe, 2016

Brennan, F., *The Wik Debate: Its impact on Aborigines, pastoralists and miners*, Sydney: UNSW Press, 1998

Brett, H., *White Wings: Fifty years of sail in the New Zealand trade, 1850 to 1900*, Auckland: Brett Printing Company, 1924

Brock, P. & Gara, T., *Colonialism and its Aftermath: A history of Aboriginal South Australia*, Mile End: Wakefield Press, 2017

Broome, R., *Aboriginal Australians*, Sydney: Allen & Unwin, 1982

Carlyon, L., *Gallipoli*, Sydney: Pan Macmillan Australia, 2001

Carlyon, L., *The Master: A personal portrait of Bart Cummings*, Sydney: Pan Macmillan Australia, 2011

Chettle, M., *Jim Robb*, Henley Beach: Seaview Press, 1996

Clark, C.M.H., *A History of Australia*, 6 vols, Carlton: Melbourne University Press, 1962–1987

Cockburn, S., *Notable Lives: Profiles of 21 South Australians*, Adelaide: Ferguson Publications, 1997

Craven, P. (ed.), *Best Australian Essays*, Melbourne: Black Inc., 2001

Cummings, J.B., *Bart: My life*, Sydney: Pan Macmillan Australia, 2009

Cupit, T., Gooden, R. & Manley, K. (eds), *From Five Barley Loaves: Australian Baptists in global mission 1864–2010*, Northcote: Morning Star Publishing, 2014

Curthoys, A., *Freedom Ride: A freedom rider remembers*, Sydney: Allen & Unwin, 2002

Davis, J., *John Pat and Other Poems*, Melbourne: Dent, 1988

Davis, J., *No Sugar*, Sydney: Currency Press, 1986

Davis, J., *The First-Born and Other Poems*, Sydney: Angus & Robertson, 1970

Duguid, C., *Doctor and the Aborigines*, Adelaide: Rigby, 1972

Dunstan, D., *Felicia: The political memoirs of Don Dunstan*, Melbourne: Macmillan, 1981

Egan, T., *Justice All Their Own: The Caledon Bay and Woodah Island killings 1932–1933*, Carlton: Melbourne University Press, 1996

Elkin, A.P., *The Australian Aborigines: How to understand them*, Sydney: Angus & Robertson, 1938

Elkin, A.P., *Citizenship for the Aborigines: A national Aboriginal policy*, Sydney: Australasian Publishing Co., 1944

Evans, G., *Incorrigible Optimist: A political memoir*, Carlton: Melbourne University Press, 2017

Forte, M., *Flight of an Eagle: The Dreaming of Ruby Hammond*, Adelaide: Wakefield Press, 1995

Gerard, A.E., *History of the UAM*, Adelaide: Hunkin Ellis & King, 1945

Gilbert, K., *Living Black: Blacks talk to Kevin Gilbert*, Melbourne: Allen Lane, The Penguin Press, 1977

Grattan, M. (ed.), *Reconciliation: Essays on Australian reconciliation*, Melbourne: Bookman Press, 2000

Haebich, A., *Broken Circles: Fragmenting Indigenous families 1800–2000*, Fremantle: Fremantle Arts Centre Press, 2000

Hale, M.B., *The Aborigines of Australia: Being the account of the institution for their education at Poonindie in South Australia*, London: Society for Promoting Christian Knowledge, 1889

Hardy, B., *Lament for the Barkindji: The vanished tribes of the Darling River Region*, Adelaide: Rigby, 1976

Hardy, F., *The Unlucky Australians*, Melbourne: Nelson, 1968

Harris, J., *One Blood: 200 years of Aboriginal encounter with Christianity—A story of hope*, Sutherland: Albatross, 1990

Hawke, R.J.L., *The Hawke Memoirs*, Port Melbourne: William Heinemann Australia, 1994

Hawke, S. & Gallagher, M., *Noonkanbah, Whose Land, Whose Law*, Fremantle: Fremantle Arts Centre Press, 1989

Hill, B., *Broken Song: T.G.H. Strehlow and Aboriginal possession*, Milsons Point: Knopf, 2002

Hill, E., *The Great Australian Loneliness*, Melbourne: Robertson & Mullins, 1940, prev. London: Jarrolds, 1937

Horner, J., *Seeking Racial Justice: An insider's memoir of the Movement for Aboriginal Advancement 1938–1978*, Canberra: Aboriginal Studies Press, 2004

Horner, J., *Vote Ferguson for Aboriginal Freedom: A biography*, Sydney: Australia and New Zealand Book Co., 1974

Hoskins, P.M., *The Immigrants*, Bloomington: Xlibris, 2013

Howard, J., *Lazarus Rising: A personal and political autobiography*, Pymble: HarperCollins, 2010

Idriess, I., *Flynn of the Inland*, Sydney: Angus & Robertson, 1932

Kartinyeri, D., *Kick the Tin*, North Melbourne: Spinifex Press, 2000

Keefe, K., *Paddy's Road: Life stories of Patrick Dodson*, Canberra: Aboriginal Studies Press, 2003

Kelly, P., *How to Make Gravy*, Camberwell: Penguin Group Australia, 2010

Kelly, P., *The End of Certainty: Power, politics and business in Australia*, St Leonards: Allen & Unwin, 1992

Kelly, P., *The Hawke Ascendancy*, North Ryde: Angus & Robertson, 1984

Kelly, P., *The March of Patriots: The struggle for modern Australia*, Carlton: Melbourne University Press, 2009

Keon-Cohen, B., *A Mabo Memoir: Islan kustom to native title*, Malvern: Zemvic Press, 2013

Kildea, J., *Hugh Mahon: Patriot, pressman, politician*, Melbourne: Anchor Books Australia, 2017

Kingsley, H., *The Boy in Grey and Other Stories and Sketches*, London: Ward, Lock & Bowden, 1895

Lester, Y., *Yami: The Autobiography of Yami Lester*, Alice Springs: Jukurrpa Books, 1993

Loos, N. & Mabo, E.K., *Eddie Koiki Mabo: His life and struggle for land rights*, St Lucia: University of Queensland Press, 1996

Macintyre, S. and Clark, A., *The History Wars*, Carlton: Melbourne University Press, 2003

Manley, K.R., *From Woolloomooloo to 'Eternity': A history of Australian Baptists*, Milton Keynes: Paternoster, 2 vols, 2006

Manne, R., *Left, Right, Left: Political essays 1977–2005*, Melbourne: Black Inc., 2005

Markus, A., *Blood from a Stone: William Cooper and the Australian Aborigines' League*, Sydney: Allen & Unwin, 1988

Markus, A., *Governing Savages*, Sydney: Allen & Unwin, 1990

Martin, R., *Ray Martin's Favourites: The stories behind the legends*, Carlton: Melbourne University Press, 2012

Mattingley, C. & Hampton, K., *Survival In Our Own Land: 'Aboriginal' experiences in 'South Australia' since 1836*, Sydney: Hodder & Stoughton, 1992

Maynard, J., *Fight for Liberty and Freedom: The origins of Australian Aboriginal activism*, Canberra: Aboriginal Studies Press, 2007

McGinness, J., *Son of Alyandabu: My fight for Aboriginal rights*, St Lucia: University of Queensland Press, 1991

McKenzie, R. *Molly Lennon's Story: 'That's how it was'*, as told to Jen Gibson, Adelaide: Department of Environment and Planning, Aboriginal Heritage Branch, 1989

Meinig, D.W., *On the Margins of the Good Earth: The South Australian wheat frontier 1869–1884*, Adelaide: Rigby, 1970

Neill, R., *White Out: How politics is killing Black Australia*, Sydney: Allen & Unwin, 2002

Neville, A.O., *Australia's Coloured Minority: Its place in the community*, Sydney: Currawong Publishing, 1948

O'Brien, K., *Keating*, Sydney: Allen & Unwin, 2015

O'Donoghue, L., *Lowitja*, as told to Joan Cunningham and Karen Jennings, booklet, 30p., Kingswood: Working Title Press, 2003

Oodgeroo, *My People*, orig. *My People: A Kath Walker collection*, Milton: Jacaranda, 1970

Pearson, N., *Our Right to Take Responsibility*, Cairns: Noel Pearson and Associates, 2000

Perkins, C., *A Bastard Like Me*, Sydney: Ure Smith, 1975

Plowman, R.B., *The Man from Oodnadatta*, Sydney: Angus & Robertson, 1933

Pring, A. (ed.), *Women of the Centre*, Apollo Bay: Pascoe Publishing, 1995

Probyn-Rapsey, F., *Made to Matter: White fathers, Stolen Generations*, Sydney: Sydney University Press, 2013

Pybus, C., *Truganini: Journey through the apocalypse*, Crows Nest: Allen & Unwin, 2020

Raynes, C., *The Last Protector: The illegal removal of Aboriginal children from their parents in south Australia*, Mile End: Wakefield Press, 2009

Read, P., *A Rape of the Soul So Profound: The return of the Stolen Generations*, St Leonards: Allen & Unwin, 1999

Read, P., *Charles Perkins: A biography*, Ringwood: Penguin, 2001

Read, P. & Read, J. (eds), *Long Time, Olden Time: Aboriginal accounts of Northern Territory history*, Alice Springs: Institute for Aboriginal Development, 1993

Reynolds, H., *This Whispering in Our Hearts*, St Leonards: Allen & Unwin, 1998

Rintoul, S., *The Wailing: A national Black oral history*, Port Melbourne: William Heinemann Australia, 1993

Roach, A., *Tell Me Why: The story of my life and my music*, Cammeray: Simon & Schuster Australia, 2019

Rubuntja, W. with Green, J. & Rowse, T., *The Town Grew Up Dancing: The life and art of Wenten Rubuntja*, Alice Springs: Jukurrpa Books, 2002

Russell, P.H., *Recognising Aboriginal Title: the Mabo Case and Indigenous resistance to English-settler colonialism*, Sydney: UNSW Press, 2006

Shaw, B., *Our Heart is the Land: Aboriginal reminiscences from the Western Lake Eyre Basin*, Canberra: Aboriginal Studies Press, 1995

Simpson, H. & Dallwitz, J. (eds), *Horrie Simpson's Oodnadatta*, Oodnadatta: Oodnadatta Progress Association, 1990

Spencer, W.B., *The Aboriginal Photographs of Baldwin Spencer*, introduced by John Mulvaney, selected and annotated by Geoffrey Walker, for National Museum of Victoria Council, South Yarra: J. Currey O'Neil, 1982

Spencer, W.B. & Gillen, F.J., *The Native Tribes of Central Australia*, London: Macmillan, 1899

Stanner, W.E.H., *The Dreaming and Other Essays*, with an introduction by Robert Manne, Collingwood: Black Inc., 2010

Strehlow, T.G.H., *Aranda Traditions*, Carlton: Melbourne University Press, 1947

Strehlow, T.G.H., *Journey to Horseshoe Bend*, Sydney: Angus & Robertson, 1969

Strehlow, T.G.H., *Songs of Central Australia*, Sydney: Angus & Robertson, 1971

Sutton, P., *The Politics of Suffering: Indigenous Australia and the end of the Liberal consensus*, Carlton: Melbourne University Press, 2009

Taffe, S., *A White Hot Flame: Mary Montgomerie Bennett—author, educator, activist for Indigenous justice*, Clayton: Monash University Publishing, 2018

Taffe, S., *Black and White Together: FCAATSI – The Federal Council for the Advancement of Aborigines and Torres Strait Islanders 1958–1973*, St Lucia: University of Queensland Press, 2005

Terry, M., *Untold Miles—Three gold-hunting expeditions amongst the picturesque borderland of Central Australia*, London: Selwyn & Blount, 1933

Terry, M., *The Last Explorer: The autobiography of Michael Terry*, compiled by Charlotte Barnard, Rushcutters Bay, Darwin: ANU Press in association with North Australia Research Unit, 1987

Tickner, R., *Taking a Stand: Land rights to reconciliation*, Crows Nest: Allen & Unwin, 2001

Tucker, M., *If Everyone Cared: Autobiography of Margaret Tucker*, Sydney: Ure Smith, 1977

Turner, V., *Pearls from the Deep: The story of the Colebrook Home for Aboriginal children, Quorn, South Australia*, Adelaide: United Aborigines' Mission, 1936

Watson, D., *Recollections of a Bleeding Heart: A portrait of Paul Keating PM*, Milsons Point: Knopf, 2002

Webb, R.A.F., *Brothers in the Sun: A History of the bush brotherhood movement in the Outback of Australia*, Adelaide: Rigby, 1978

Webster, J.V. & Cheney, D.N., *Assam: Not by chance*, Hawthorn: Australian Baptist Missionary Society, 2000

Whitlam, G., *The Whitlam Government 1972–1975*, Ringwood: Penguin, 1985

Williams, R.M., *A Song in the Desert*, Pymble: Angus & Robertson, 1998

Williams, R.M. with Ruhen, O., *Beneath Whose Hand: The autobiography of R.M. Williams*, South Melbourne: Macmillan, 1984

Woodward, E., *One Brief Interval: A memoir*, Carlton: Miegunyah Press, 2005

Speeches

Keating, P. 'Lowitja O'Donoghue and native title: leadership pointing the way to identity, inclusion and justice', Lowitja O'Donoghue Oration, Adelaide, 2011

O'Donoghue, L. *Speeches 1990–1996*, 3 vols, Canberra: Aboriginal and Torres Strait Islander Commission, 1997

O'Donoghue, L. 'Black and white together, we shall overcome, some day', Inaugural Lowitja O'Donoghue Oration, Adelaide: Don Dunstan Foundation, 2007

Pearson, N. 'The Uluru Statement from the Heart: one year on', Lowitja O'Donoghue Oration, Adelaide, 2018

Newspapers, magazines and journals

Aboriginal History Journal

Advertiser (Adelaide)

Age

Argus (Melbourne)

ATSIC News

Austral Light

Australian

Australian Abo Call

Australian Aborigines' Advocate

Australian Geographic

Australian Historical Studies

Australian Journal of Politics and History

Australian Quarterly

Australian Women's Weekly

Bulletin

Canberra Times

Centralian Advocate

Chronicle (Adelaide)

Courier Mail (Brisbane)

Dawn and *New Dawn—A Magazine for the Aboriginal people of NSW*

Guardian Australia

Herald (Melbourne)

Irish Historical Studies

Koori Mail

Mail (Adelaide)

Maritime Workers' Journal

Meanjin

Mercury (Quorn)

Monthly

National Indigenous Times

News (Adelaide)

Oceania

Quadrant

Queensland Times

Register (Adelaide)

Sun-Herald (Sydney)
Sunday Mail (Adelaide)
Sunday Times (Perth)
Sydney Morning Herald
Telegraph (Sydney)
Transcontinental (Port Augusta)
Tribune
United Aborigines' Messenger (prev. *Australian Aborigines' Advocate*)
Vision (magazine of the Australian Baptist Missionary Society)
West Australian

Reports

Bleakley, J., *The Aboriginals and Half-Castes of Central Australia and Northern Australia*, Canberra: Government Printer, 1929

Boothby, J., *Statistical Sketch of South Australia*, London: Sampson Low, Marston, Searle, and Rivington, 1876

Commonwealth Government, *Aboriginal Welfare: Initial Conference of Commonwealth and State Aboriginal Authorities,* 21–23 April, Canberra: Government Printer, 1937

Dodson, M., *Indigenous Deaths in Custody 1989–1996*, Office of the Aboriginal and Torres Strait Islander Social Justice Commissioner, Sydney: Australian Human Rights and Equal Opportunity Commission, 1996

Dodson, M., *Aboriginal and Torres Strait Islander Social Justice Commissioner* reports, Sydney: Australian Human Rights and Equal Opportunity Commission, 1993–98

Gibson, J. & Dunjiba Community Council, *Oodnadatta Genealogies*, Adelaide: Department of Environment and Planning, 1988

Gibson, J. & Shaw, B., *Oodnadatta Aboriginal Heritage Survey 1985–1986*, Adelaide: Department of Environment and Planning, 1987

Horner, J., *Report of the 13th Annual Conference of FCAATSI*, 27–29 March, McGinness papers, Canberra: Australian Institute of Aboriginal and Torres Strait Islander Studies, 1970

Johnston, E. with Dodson, P., O'Dea, D.J., Wootten, H. & Wyvill, L.F., *Royal Commission into Aboriginal Deaths in Custody*, Canberra: Australian Government Publishing Service, 1991

Nicholls, Y., *Not Slaves, Not Citizens: Condition of the Australian Aborigines in the Northern Territory*, Melbourne: Australian Council for Civil Liberties, 1952

O'Kelly, A.H., *Finding of Board of Enquiry Concerning the Killing of Natives in Central Australia by Police Parties and Others and Concerning Other Matters*, Government publication, 1929

South Australian Government, *Report of the Royal Commission on the Aborigines*, Adelaide: Parliamentary Papers of South Australia, 1916

Tindale, N., *Survey of the Half-Caste Problem in South Australia*, Proceedings of the Royal Geographical Society, South Australia, Vol. XLII, 1940–41

Wild, R. & Anderson, P., *Ampe Akelyernemane Meke Mekarle 'Little Children are Sacred'*, Report of the Northern Territory Board of Inquiry into the Protection of Aboriginal Children from Sexual Abuse, 2007

Wilson, R. with Dodson M., *Bringing them Home*, National Inquiry into the Separation of Aboriginal and Torres Strait Islander Children from Their Families, Sydney: Human Rights and Equal Opportunities Commission, 1997

Articles, documentaries and interviews

Austin, T., 'Cecil Cook, scientific thought and "half-castes" in the Northern Territory 1927–1939', *Aboriginal History*, 1990, vol. 14, no. 1

Bishop, C.E., 'A woman missionary living amongst naked blacks: Annie Lock, 1876–1943', MA thesis, Canberra: Australian National University, 1991

Blainey, G., 'Drawing up a balance sheet of our history', *Quadrant*, 1993, vol. 37, nos 7 & 8, July & August

Cronin, D., 'Dialogue and Indigenous Policy in Australia', PhD thesis, Sydney, University of New South Wales, 2015

Foley, G., 'Chicka "The Fox" Dixon: Heroes in the struggle for justice', Koori History Website, 8 April 2010

Gibson, D., *Wik vs Queensland*, Bacon Factory Films, 2018

Gilbert, K., Horner, J. and Goodall, H., 'Three tributes to Pearl Gibbs (1901–1983)', *Aboriginal History*, 1983, vol. 7

Gooden, R., 'Five Barley Loaves: An Icon for Australasian Baptist Missionary Work', Trans-Tasman Missions History Conference, Canberra, Australian National University, 2004.

Goold, S. & Liddle, K. (eds), *In Our Own Right: Black Australian nurses' stories*, Maleny, eContent Management, 2005

Grayden, W., *Their Darkest Hour*, also broadcast as *Manslaughter*, 1957

Hosking, S., 'Homeless at home, stolen and saved: three Colebrook autobiographies', *Westerly Magazine*, August 2001

Hughes, R., 'Charles Perkins', *Australian Biography: Extraordinary Australians talk about their lives*, Film Australia, 1998

Hughes, R., 'Faith Bandler', *Australian Biography: Extraordinary Australians talk about their lives*, producer Frank Heimans, Film Australia, 1993

Hughes, R., 'Lois O'Donoghue, *Australian Biography: Extraordinary Australians talk about their lives*, with prior interview by producer Frank Heimans, Film Australia, 1993–1994

Jackson, L., 'Judgement Day', *Four Corners*, ABC, 3 May 2012

La Nauze, A.J., 'The study of Australian history 1929–1959', *Historical Studies Australia and New Zealand*, November 1959, vol. 9, no. 33

Manne, R., 'The Stolen Generations', *Quadrant*, January–February 1998

Nairn, B., Serle, G., & Ward, R. (eds), 'George Woodroffe Goyder', *Australian Dictionary of Biography*, Carlton: Melbourne University Press, 1979

Pearson, N., 'White guilt, victimhood and the quest for a radical centre', *Griffith Review*, no. 16, Winter 2007

Read, P., '"Cheeky, insolent and anti-white": The split in the Federal Council for the Advancement of Aboriginal and Torres Strait Islanders, Easter 1970', *Australian Journal of Politics and History*, 1990, vol. 36, no. 1

Read, P., *The Stolen Generations: The Removal of Aboriginal Children in New South Wales 1833–1969*, Sydney: Government Printer, 1981

Richards, E., 'Irish life and progress in colonial South Australia', *Irish Historical Studies* vol. 27, no. 107, May 1991

Rintoul, S., 'Looking for Lowitja: stolen or removed? Lowitja O'Donoghue's extraordinary search for the truth', *The Australian Magazine*, 21–22 April; reprinted in Craven, P. (ed.), *Best Australian Essays*, Melbourne: Black Inc., 2001

Rowse, T., 'How we got a Native Title Act', *Australian Quarterly*, vol. 65, no. 4, The Politics of Mabo, Summer 1993

Stevens, Christine, 'Australia's Afghan cameleers', *Australian Geographic*, 27 July 2011

Wilson, B. & O'Brien, J., '"To infuse an universal terror": A reappraisal of the Coniston Killings, *Aboriginal History*, 2003, vol. 27

Windschuttle, K., 'Myths of frontier massacres', *Quadrant*, October–December 2000

Yunupingu, G., 'Tradition, truth and tomorrow', *Monthly*, December 2008

Permissions

Thanks to Robert Hannaford and National Portrait Gallery for permission to reproduce the portrait *Lowitja O'Donoghue*; Paul Kelly and Sony/ATV Music Publishing Australia for permission to use extracts from the song 'Bicentennial'; Paul Kelly, Sony/ATV Music Publishing and Mushroom Records for permission to use extracts from the song 'Treaty' (songwriters: Paul Kelly, Mandawuy Yunupingu, Stuart Kellaway, Cal Williams, Gurrumul Yunupingu, Witiyana Marika, Milkayngu Mununggurr, Peter Garrett); the Ramindjeri Heritage Association for permission to include the story of Kondoli, the whale man; John Wiley and Sons for permission to include Oodgeroo Noonuccal's poem 'Assimilation—No!'; Curtis Brown, for permission to include Jack Davis' poem 'John Pat'; and Spinifex Press for permission to include Doris Kartinyeri's poem 'A Loneliness' from *Kick the Tin*.

Index